Gu Mu: Revolutionary Thinker, Organiser and Technocrat

Liu Huiyuan

Published by
ACA Publishing Ltd.
University House
11-13 Lower Grosvenor Place,
London SW1W 0EX, UK
Tel: +44 (0)20 7834 7676
Fax: +44 (0)20 7973 0076
E-mail: info@alaincharlesasia.com
Web:www.alaincharlesasia.com
Beijing Office
Tel: +86(0)10 8472 1250
Fax: +86(0)10 5885 0639

Author: Liu Huiyuan
Editors: David Lammie and Martin Savery
Translator: Robert A. Kapp
Cover art: Daniel Li

Published by ACA Publishing Ltd in association
with the People's Publishing House

© 2014, by People's Publishing House, Beijing, China
ALL RIGHTS RESERVED. NO PART OF THIS
PUBLICATION MAY BE REPRODUCED IN MATERIAL FORM,
BY ANY MEANS, WHETHER GRAPHIC,
ELECTRONIC, MECHANICAL OR OTHER, INCLUDING
PHOTOCOPYING OR INFORMATION STORAGE, IN WHOLE OR IN PART, AND
MAY NOT BE USED TO PREPARE
OTHER PUBLICATIONS WITHOUT WRITTEN
PERMISSION FROM THE PUBLISHER.

The greatest care has been taken to ensure accuracy but the
publisher can accept no responsibility for errors or omissions, or
for any liability occasioned by relying on its content.

ISBN 978-1-910760-06-2

A catalogue record for *Gu Mu: Revolutionary Thinker, Organiser and Technocrat*
is available from the National Bibliographic Service of the British Library.

Glossary of Terms

CMC	Central Military Commission
CPC	Communist Party of China
CPG	central people's government
CPPCC	Chinese people's political consultative conference
KMT	Kuomintang (Nationalist Party)
NGO	non-government organisation
NPC	national people's congress
PLA	People's Liberation Army
PRC	People's Republic of China
SEZ	special economic zone
SOE	state-owned enterprise
SDPC	state development planning commission
SPC	state planning commission
TCM	traditional Chinese medicine

Democratic figures/personages refer to people of note who are 'members of non-CPC political parties'

Preface

The reform and opening up of China ushered in the socialist road with Chinese characteristics and sparked the dawn of a new era. The immortal and meritorious services of Deng Xiaoping, the initiator, chief designer and commander-in-chief of that road, will be eternally engraved on the minds of the Chinese people. He accomplished these outstanding feats with his selfless comrades-in-arms and senior army generals blazing a trail, and going through fire and water with him. The founding fathers and commanders-in-chief of the reform and opening up prompted hundreds of millions of Chinese people to embark together on the new journey that we are still following today. Their eminent contributions deserve to be documented and their deeds should be remembered and admired. They are the role models and examples for the broad masses of party members and cadres to follow on the new journey of reform and opening up.

To cherish the memory of these founding fathers of reform and opening up and to enable readers, especially party members and cadres, to know them better and to learn from them as role models, we decided to publish the *Pictorial Biographies of the Founding Fathers of China's Reform and Opening Up* series. To present these books to readers at the earliest opportunity, we will publish this series volume by volume as each book is completed.

China has entered a new era of reform and opening up. The party central committee with comrade Xi Jinping as general secretary has declared the epoch-making new manifesto of reform and opening up. The implementation of the manifesto requires the devotion and joint efforts of brave generals keeping pace with the times, losing no time moving ahead, fearing no upheavals, abolishing outdated laws and regulations, and defying the negative statements of others; it requires innumerable cadres hurling themselves into the reform and opening-up process; and it requires the collective efforts of hundreds of millions of people. Only in this way can our great cause keep on advancing!

People's Publishing House, August 2014

Alain Charles Asia (ACA) Publishing Ltd is delighted to be associated with the People's Publishing House to bring this book to an English-speaking readership.

ACA, formerly known as ACP (Alain Charles Publishing) Ltd Beijing, was founded in October 1989 and was the first foreign-owned publishing company to be allowed to open an office in China.

In 2007, ACP Beijing was renamed ACA Publishing Ltd to better reflect its focus on China and the Asia-Pacific region. The company specialises in publishing books about China for international readers and has offices in Beijing and London.

ACA Publishing Ltd, October 2016

Contents

Chapter 1 Star Private School Pupil and Among Top Three in Higher Primary School..............1

Chapter 2 Party Branch Secretary of the 'Seventh Red Army'.........8

Chapter 3 Immersed in the Left-wing Culture Movement in Beijing.....14

Chapter 4 Calm Response to Imprisonment..............18

Chapter 5 Important Documents Retrieved from Battle of Shanghai...21

Chapter 6 First Meeting with Vice-Chairman Zhou Enlai..............25

Chapter 7 Regimental Commander Wan Yi Joins the Party..............28

Chapter 8 Changed Aspect of the 667th Regiment..............31

Chapter 9 Open and Honourable Withdrawal of a Friendly Army.........35

Chapter 10 Independent Brigade 'Divorced' But 'Remaining in the Household'..............41

Chapter 11 New Life of the 111th Division..............47

Chapter 12 Bloodshed on Daqing Mountain..............55

Chapter 13 Witnessing Liu Shaoqi's Thorough Supervision of Work in Shandong..............63

Chapter 14 In the Midst of Battle, Welcoming Victory in the War Against Japan..............71

Chapter 15 Face to Face Alone with Hao Pengju..............75

Chapter 16 Suppressing Chaotic Struggle, Beating and Killing During Land Reform..............80

Chapter 17 Chen Yi Assigns Top Talent to Support the Battle Front........83

Chapter 18 The Story Behind a Rare 66-year-old Portrait of Chairman Mao..89

Chapter 19 Three Successive Reports Receive High Marks from Chairman Mao..........98

Chapter 20 Calmly Reining in a Deviation to the 'Left'..........108

Chapter 21 Mao Zedong Takes Gu Mu with him on his Special Train..........112

Chapter 22 Chen Yi Deploys his Commanders to Assist with the 'Five Antis' Campaign in Shanghai..........115

Chapter 23 Learning from Premier Zhou..........119

Chapter 24 Deputy Secretary of the Third Department at the State Council...122

Chapter 25 Deeply Respecting Zhou Enlai's Opposition to Impetuous and Rash Advance..........125

Chapter 26 Rethinking the Campaign to Make Iron and Steel, in a Specialised and Professional Way..........129

Chapter 27 A 'Small Group of 10' Works to Reverse the Nation's Economic Travails..........133

Chapter 28 Daqing Experience Helps Create Industrial and Transport Political Units..........137

Chapter 29 A Visit to Peng Dehuai amid 'Third Line of Construction' Upsurge..........139

Chapter 30 Showing his Originality in Revolutionising the Design Field....144

Chapter 31 Organising Military Units to Carry Out Capital Construction..148

Chapter 32 Early in the 'Cultural Revolution', with Liu Shaoqi at the Grassroots..........154

Chapter 33 A Talk with his Son, a Red Guard..........156

Chapter 34 A Contest For Power at a Forum on Industry And Transportation..159

Chapter 35 Becoming a Junior Partner in the 'February Countercurrent'...164

Chapter 36 Struggled Against by Day, Working at Night..........171

Chapter 37 The Premier Issues Orders for Harbour Construction..........174

Chapter 38 Working with Deng Xiaoping to Redirect Industry and Transportation..179

Chapter 39 Gu Mu Becomes a Top Target for 'Gang of Four' Attack.......183

Chapter 40 'If I Don't Enter the Bitter Sea, Who Else Will?'...................186

Chapter 41 Acquiring Important Information from the Den of the 'Gang of Four'..191

Chapter 42 Heading a Chinese Government Delegation to Western Europe..195

Chapter 43 Study Tour Emancipates the Minds of Central Leaders.......202

Chapter 44 State Leadership Borrows Foreign Brains to Promote Opening Up...209

Chapter 45 Focusing on Absorbing Funds Without Fear of Debt..........213

Chapter 46 Encouraging Foreign Investment...218

Chapter 47 Carrying Out Major Reform of the Foreign Trade System....221

Chapter 48 Hong Kong China Merchants Group Starts to Build an Industrial Zone..225

Chapter 49 Guangdong Committee Proposes Setting up Provincewide EPZs...228

Chapter 50 Deng Xiaoping Says 'Special Zone' Sounds Better................230

Chapter 51 Gu Mu Decides to Change 'Special Export Zone' to 'Special Economic Zone'..233

Chapter 52 The NPC Approves 'Provisions for Guangdong SEZs'..........237

Chapter 53 Four Economic Zones Emerge from their Cocoons.............239

Chapter 54 Ten Guiding Opinions on the Development of Special Zones...243

Chapter 55 Special Zones Face the Biggest Ideological Upheaval...........246

VII

Chapter 56 Helping to Promulgate 'New Document No. 50'.....................249

Chapter 57 Setting up SEZs Calls not for Tightening, but for Loosening..255

Chapter 58 'Opening to the Outside World' Requires People Who Get the Picture..258

Chapter 59 Linking Key Points to Build a Continuous Belt of Opening To the Outside World...265

Chapter 60 Timely Discovery Leads to Solving New Problems with the SEZs...274

Chapter 61 The Conference at which Gu Mu was Most Critical of the SEZs..277

Chapter 62 SEZ Development Embarks on a New Course......................281

Chapter 63 Twenty-two Detailed Regulations to Improve the Investment Environment...283

Chapter 64 Intentionally Not Raising the Theme 'Hainan Can Catch Taiwan in 20 Years'..290

Chapter 65 First Ask Shen Nong, then Ask Edison...................................292

Chapter 66 For Coastal China and the Linked Chain of Open Areas, a Second Step Forward..295

Chapter 67 Leading the Work of the Confucius Fund............................303

Epilogue..316

Notes..323

Chronology of Gu Mu's Life Events...324

Chapter 1

Star Private School Pupil and Among Top Three in Higher Primary School

Gu Mu was born on 28 September 1914 in Shandong province. He often claimed to be a native of Dongdun in Ningjin village (now known as Ningjin town in Rongcheng city), Weihaiwei. This regional division is based on China's ancient garrison station system. Gu Mu's original surname was Liu, and his given name was Jia in accordance with his family genealogy. His grandfather, a rural scholar, named him Liu Jiayu from the *Family Sayings of Confucius*.

This is the fire beacon (*yandun*, with smoke released from burning wolf's dung) dating back to the Ming dynasty coastal defence system of garrison stations, which Dongdun village was named after. As a child, Gu Mu used to play here with his little friends

Gu Mu and his wife Mou Feng in front of the ancestral home, summer 1978

Gu Mu, who left home at a young age and did not return for many years, sits on a boulder near the old house and reminisces about the past

Gu Mu was born in this farmhouse with a seaweed roof

Gu Mu's forebears lived a comfortable life, but their situation had been on the wane since his grandfather's generation. The family were forced to sell land to raise money to alleviate poverty. In addition to being financially weaker, the family had few descendants. The two preceding generations dating back to his grandfather both produced only one boy. Gu Mu's father was the only child of that generation, and Gu Mu himself was again the only boy, with four younger sisters.

When Gu Mu reached the nominal age of eight, his father died from tuberculosis, adding to the travails of this unfortunate family.

In 1922, Gu Mu followed his grandfather to Moye island and went to private school. Each day before going to school, he would bow to the Confucius memorial tablet to pay his respects to his ancestors, salute his grandfather, who was his teacher, and then sit down to start reading. Beginning with the *Three Character Classic* and the *Hundred Family Surnames*, he went on to read the *Analects of Confucius*, *The Great Learning*, *Doctrine of the Mean*, *Mencius* and the *Book of Songs*. He also read Chinese classics and poetry from the Tang dynasty, such as the *Book of History*, *Guwen Guanzhi* and *Guwen Cileizuan*.

His grandfather adopted a traditional teaching approach, tackling literacy first and then asking students to read and memorise the text. His grandfather only moved on to interpretation once Gu Mu had been reading and memorising for three years. He adopted Zhu Xi's[1] system of interpretation, emphasising moral and ethical guidance. As Gu Mu recalled afterwards, his grandfather was open to new ways of thinking despite being a traditional scholar, so he also taught Gu Mu modern subjects such as simplified Chinese and mathematics.

Of all the students, Gu Mu was among the most diligent and his grades were the best. His grandfather was proud to take Gu Mu to gatherings of intellectuals in the countryside. At the age of 13, Gu Mu travelled to the famous Chaoyang cave in his hometown, and wrote travel notes after returning home. At his grandfather's suggestion, he added a few verses of Sao-style poetry.[2]

The former site of the private school founded by Gu Mu's grandfather, Wang Dongtang. It was a typical building of the Jiaodong countryside, built with stone and with a seaweed-thatched roof

The former site of Rongcheng No. 1 higher primary school

"Glancing at famous mountains while visiting a famous scenic resort; sunset is approaching but I am reluctant to go home; what am I looking for? When I get home, I will use my beloved pen to write travel notes that show respect to all the famous people in history." His literary talents were highly praised by local intellectuals.

When Gu Mu turned 15, his grandfather told him: "I have taught you almost everything I know. If your paternal grandfather wants you to keep studying, you may go to schools in town for further education."

Longing to go to Weihai middle school, but without a diploma, he was instead left with no choice but to join the fifth grade of higher primary school. Being the only other family member, his grandfather had no one to turn to and no option but to sell some 1,300 square metres of land to fund Gu Mu's two years of study in Rongcheng No.1 higher primary school.

Lessons at the school were far from challenging to Gu Mu, as he had already been given a profound and solid foundation in the Chinese classics over a period of seven years. Hard working and sophisticated in his studies, Gu Mu had sufficient time to extensively read works of literature and history, ranging from the *Romance of the Three Kingdoms* and poetry by Guo Moruo, to the novels and essays of Lu Xun, and even social science works. He was astonishingly well read.

Gu Mu used to express his views on society and politics in his compositions, which was much appreciated by his teachers. Gu Mu's classmate, Li Yaowen, who would later become a political commissar in the navy, recalled that nearly all of Gu Mu's essays were marked for special attention, and were put on public display as a model for other students. His work caught the attention of Sun Jizhou, an underground Communist Party member. Around the summer of 1931, Sun Jizhou approached Gu Mu. They had an in-depth discussion and became close friends, regretting that they had not met earlier. At Sun Jizhou's house, Gu Mu noticed confidential documents of the Communist Party's north China department (predecessor of the ministry of public security), and came into contact with much information about the Red Army and the central revolutionary base. Two or three months later, Gu Mu and another of his classmates, Cao Manzhi, joined the Communist Youth League on the recommendation of Sun Jizhou. They were among the first league members in Rongcheng, and actively carried out league activities. Cao Manzhi, who was in the year above Gu Mu, specialised in drawing (and later stayed at the school to become an art teacher). He often illustrated Gu Mu's progressive articles with drawings. Their joint efforts were a combination of talent and wisdom, and they brought out the best in each other.

Gu Mu visits Tang Shuyao, the former head of Rongcheng No.1 higher primary school, 27 August 1978

Sun Jizhou (centre) returns to his hometown in old age, standing in front of the remains of the Qin bridge

    Gu Mu still maintained his academic prowess after joining the league. He was always among the top three in county examinations, including those of Wendeng and Rongcheng combined, and Wendeng, Rongcheng and Weihai combined.

Chapter 2

Party Branch Secretary of the 'Seventh Red Army'

In 1932, Gu Mu graduated from higher primary school. As the family could not afford his further education, his grandfather wanted him to earn the family's living by becoming a teacher at the village higher primary school. But Gu Mu had his heart set on continuing with his studies. At that time, the No. 7 village normal school (Wendeng normal school) of Shandong in neighbouring Wendeng village happened to be established. Not only did the school charge no fees, but each student was actually given a subsidy of Rmb5 per month. Taking into account the Rmb4 cost of meals, there would still be some money left over for incidental expenses. Gu Mu sat the entrance examination and came first.

Sun Jizhou told Gu Mu that Yu Yunting, the principal of Wendeng normal school, was a Communist Party of China (CPC) member from Jinan. He wanted to connect with Gu Mu and had high expectations of him. Through arrangements made by the CPC, Gu Mu became a party member.

The No. 7 village normal school (Wendeng normal school) in Shandong

Party Branch Secretary of the 'Seventh Red Army'

Soon after it was established in 1932, Wendeng normal school's newly elected party branch secretary Liu Jiayu (Gu Mu) held a meeting with party branch committee members Cong Lieguang and Xing Liwen in the house of Yu Yunting (second from left). Pictured writing on the left is Tang Chengjiu, a teacher at the school, and the wife of principal Yu. She was also a party member. This picture was drawn in 2010 by Guo Jinping, a current teacher at the school

The No. 7 village normal school played a significant role in the Jiaodong area because of its party organisation, and it cultivated a significant number of people for the revolution. Thus it later acquired the honorary title of the 'Seventh Red Army'. There were more than 10 party members at the founding of the secret party branch, half of them teachers and half students. Members planned to elect Principal Yu Yunting as secretary of the party branch, but Yu thought he might be exposed easily since he was an obvious target, and recommended electing Gu Mu to the position instead. Moreover, with the excuse that Gu Mu had severe arthritis, the principal arranged a small house for Gu Mu to live in, which became the location for secret party branch gatherings.

By 1933, the party branch of Wendeng normal school had grown to more than 40 members. The future deputy secretary of Shanghai municipal party committee, Wang Yiping, the future minister of the general political department of the People's Liberation Army (PLA) and a major general, Liu Qiren, and the future deputy director and party committee secretary of the institute of mechanics in the Chinese academy of sciences, Zhang Congzhou (who was later associated with famous scientist Qian Xuesen) were, respectively, Gu Mu's classmate, party comrade and close comrade-in-arms.

At the beginning of 1934, an unexpected problem arose within the party branch. Underground party member Zhang Tonghua was chasing after a girl in school. He was utterly shameless, and kept badgering her despite already having been rejected. Principal Yu and Gu Mu criticised him, but Zhang Tonghua became furious and even verbally threatened Gu Mu: I'm not going to inform on you for being red [a revolutionary], I'll use a pistol on you.

Gu Mu stands in front of the old gate of Wendeng normal school in 1978. Unfortunately, the gate was later demolished due to a road-widening project in the city

Under these circumstances, the party organisation arranged for Gu Mu's prompt evacuation from the normal school. Zhang Tonghua had betrayed the party as expected. Anti-communist members of the Kuomintang (KMT) in Shandong province and county policemen jointly captured Principal Yu and transferred him to a provincial prison. The party branch organised a large-scale petition comprising teachers and students. The authorities could not find any evidence against him, so they released him from prison.

Party Branch Secretary of the 'Seventh Red Army'

Gu Mu visits the former principal of Wendeng normal school, Yu Yunting

Dedications to Wendeng normal school, written by Gu Mu (left) and former principal Yu Yunting (right)

Gu Mu, under the pseudonym Liu Mansheng, claimed that he was a student from Beijing and was teaching in a primary school in Jiamagou village, Haiyang county. During that period, he acted as secretary of Jiaodong's CPC special committee and organised a secret liaison station. Six months later, during the summer holiday of 1934, Gu Mu's real identity was exposed once again due to a former Wendeng normal school student returning to Jiamagou village. At that time, because the party organisation in Jiaodong had lost contact with its higher-level organ, a special committee of Jiaodong decided to send Gu Mu to make contact with the party organisation in Beijing.

Before Gu Mu left, his mother Wang Zhu took out Rmb10 that she had been saving for him. She saw him off at the village, though she was reluctant to let him go. Afterwards, Gu Mu engaged in underground work. For the sake of his family's safety, he resisted the temptation to write letters to his beloved mother even though it caused him to shed tears. Time and again he stopped himself from making contact, until his hometown turned into an anti-Japanese base area.

Gu Mu's mother, Wang Zhu

Gu Mu could never forget parting from his mother. Mothers always worry about their sons who are far away. Always thinking of her son, Wang Zhu often stood at the village entrance, standing on tiptoe in the hope that she would see him return. She even took to the streets at night and called out Gu Mu's nickname: "Come back home! Come back home!" Hearing of this, Gu Mu felt forlorn and miserable. Writing poems helped him to bear the agony: 'Deterred by neither chill wind nor cold rain, nightly she roamed the streets crying out for her son's return…'

Chapter 3

Immersed in the Left-wing Culture Movement in Beijing

Between the end of July and the beginning of August 1934, Gu Mu managed to reach Beijing after an arduous journey. Through the introduction of an uncle, he found shelter in the Shandong assembly hall in the Xuanwumen area in southern Beijing, and went to the Shandong high school established by an association of townspeople from the province, temporarily holding a valid identity as cover.

At that moment, the third regiment of the Republic of China's military police commanded by Jiang Xiaoxian (Chiang Kai-shek's nephew) sabotaged the party organisation in Beijing and severed all connections with the party. In those solitary days, Gu Mu was struggling to make a living as a writer. He submitted novels and essays to publishing houses, earning just Rmb3-4 for each published piece. He also gained permission to study at the department of literature in Peking University, attending classes on the history of Chinese literature and history of western literature. While studying, he was trying to find a way to make contact with the party.

Gu Mu in Beijing, 1935

Once, on his way to a publishing house to get paid, he met Wang Yunhe, an author who had read his articles. They got along very well. Wang introduced Gu Mu to Lü Kuilong and the three youngsters became firm friends.

In the summer of 1935, after the He-Umezu agreement was signed between Japan and the Republic of China, the central army retreated south. The political situation in the Beijing-Tianjin area was presided over by Song Zheyuan of the Northwest Army. Severely damaged underground party members and various left-wing groups in Beijing got the chance to recover. At this point, Lü Kuilong and Wang Yunhe introduced Gu Mu to a new 'friend' – Gu Jingsheng.

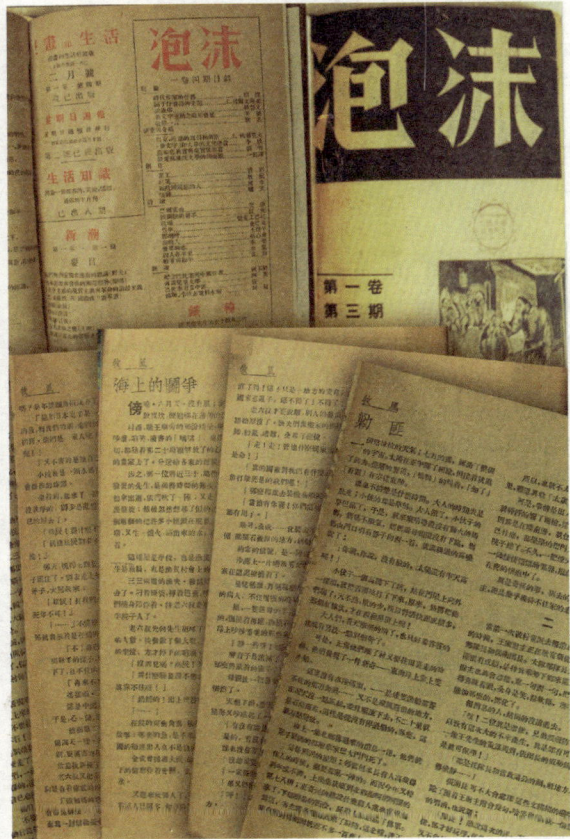

Gu Mu published *Maritime Struggle* and *Eradicate Bandits* under the pseudonym Mu Feng

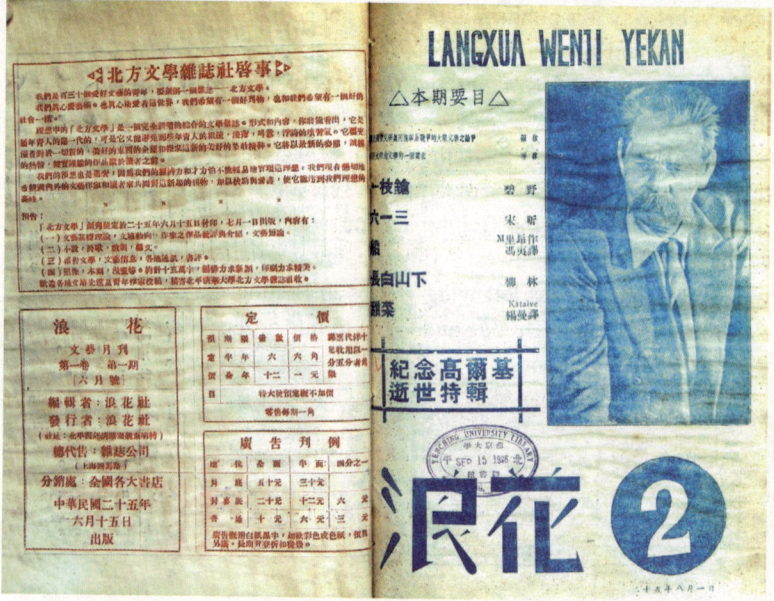

Langhua (Spray) magazine

Gu Jingsheng was then secretary of the underground youth league committee. He met Gu Mu for the first time in Zhongshan Park, and scheduled a couple of meetings afterwards. Gu Mu felt that this man had really profound political insight and was destined to become influential. Having met a few times, he tentatively mentioned that he was looking to make contact with the party organisation. Finally, one day, Gu Jingsheng asked Gu Mu to write down his circumstances, including situations prior to and after joining the party, and his job at Wendeng normal school and the reason he left Jiaodong for Beijing.

In autumn, Gu Mu eventually managed to make contact with the party organisation after he had been in Beijing for more than a year. On behalf of the party organisation, Gu Jingsheng instructed Gu Mu to first of all establish a literary journal, regroup forces and restore the league of left-wing writers. As a result, Gu Mu joined the magazine *Bubble* established by Wang Yunhe and Lü Kuilong, and turned it into a publication of the league. *Bubble* became the spiritual home of young left-wing literati and all lovers of literature.

In November 1935, the league of left-wing writers was restored, with Gu Jingsheng serving as secretary, Gu Mu as commissar in charge of organisation and Yang Cai as commissar in charge of publicity. When the December 9 Movement to Resist Japan and Save the Nation erupted, the party organisation directed Gu Mu and other backbone members of the league not to participate openly in the movement.

Suppressed by the authorities, the situation took a sudden turn for the worse. In February 1936, Gu Jingsheng was arrested and *Bubble* magazine was banned. Gu Mu took over the responsibilities of the league of left-wing writers, and restarted *Langhua* (*Spray*) magazine. By this time, Gu Mu had already changed his strategy of resistance. Instead of appearing publicly, he served as the organiser of *Langhua's* hot-blooded youths.

Chapter 4

Calm Response to Imprisonment

After Gu Jingsheng was arrested, Gu Mu was sent on a mission to Yuncheng in Shanxi province.

On returning to Beijing, Gu Mu set up a secret meeting point in an apartment on Picai Lane, and discussed and handled work of the league of left-wing writers along with Yang Cai, Wei Dongming and Zhang Suping.

On 30 April 1936, Gu Mu's old classmate Wang Yiping, who had come to Beijing after failing to organise an uprising in Jiaodong at the end of 1935, visited him during the night. At 2am, a spy who had long been watching Gu Mu from a neighbouring room suddenly broke into Gu Mu's room along with several military guards. They copied some of Gu Mu's manuscripts, and took the two of them under guard to the police supervision department of Beijing military guards.

The southwestern corner of the compound on 22 Xi'anmen Street where Gu Mu and Wang Yiping were put behind bars is now an auditorium

Gu Mu (second left), Mou Feng (far right), Wang Yiping (second right) and his wife Zhang Meixiu (far left) at the Gezhouba dam, 1981

The next morning, another prisoner was thrown into Gu Mu's cell. He started swearing at the KMT on entering the cell, referred to Gu Mu as "younger comrade" and "younger brother", and asked: "What are you here for?" Gu Mu noticed that his behaviour was unnatural, and thought his captors were trying to infiltrate the group by imprisoning their own man. Consequently, Gu Mu completely ignored him. In the afternoon, the man was removed from the cell. In the evening, when Gu Mu was brought in for questioning, the inquisitor turned out to be the very same person in the cell. He forced Gu Mu to confess to being a communist, and said: "Yang Cai is your leader, and it doesn't really matter if you confess or not." He didn't expect Gu Mu to have discovered the deception. Gu Mu emphatically stated that he was a student, and insisted that they had arrested the wrong person.

The next man to interrogate Gu Mu was a judge with a Jiaodong accent. He believed what Gu Mu had said: "Wang Yiping is a fellow-townsman, and we were mistakenly arrested when he dropped by to see me." Wang Yiping was also a seasoned underground operative, and both he and Gu Mu were careful not to reveal any incriminating evidence during the interrogation.

More than 10 days later, the Shandong judge decided to release them on bail. Wang Yiping was set free first, and he managed to contact the doorkeeper of Shandong assembly hall, a Mr Wang. After he got the warrant for his release stamped with the hall's seal, Gu Mu was finally set free.

After his release, Gu Mu immediately changed his place of residence and the organisation asked him to keep out of sight as much as possible.

But he did take part in some activities of the league of left-wing writers that required his physical presence, such as a meeting held in Peking University to discuss literary trends. In the meeting, a fierce discussion broke out as to whether the slogan should be 'national defence literature' or 'popular literature of national revolutionary war'. "From the bottom of my heart, I preferred 'national defence literature'," said Gu Mu. "It was concise and clear, and capable of mobilising and uniting on a broad scale... But 'popular literature of national revolutionary war' was proposed by the standard-bearer of left-wing writers, and I couldn't disagree with him in public." Thus, he kept his counsel.

In early August, Gu Mu, along with a number of already exposed underground party members and progressive young people, was sent to Xi'an to join an apprentice military unit of the Northeast Army. From this time on, the trajectory of Gu Mu's life, this 'major general' of Beijing's left-wing literary world, would change radically. He arrived at an old army to engage in 'military activities' and started his life as a 'soldier'.

Chapter 5

Important Documents Retrieved from Battle of Shanghai

At the beginning of August 1936, Gu Mu joined the Northeast Army in Xi'an.

Gu Mu, along with more than 100 others, became an apprentice soldier in the Northeast Army when they arrived in Xi'an, and they were stationed at the east city gate. During registration, Gu Mu followed the instructions of the party organisation by claiming to come from Lüshun district in Liaoning province. This is because the local accent resembled that of Jiaodong, and coming from the northeast was helpful in consolidating his position in the Northeast Army. In Gu Mu's memoirs, referring to the high proportion of leaders and cadres from apprentice solider teams, he wrote: "Apprentices in the apprentice soldier teams were not only cultivated in politics and the military, but had also experienced the fierce and frightening storm of the 'Xi'an incident'. All these factors gave these relatively highly educated young soldiers, filled with revolutionary enthusiasm, a rare chance to improve themselves by being involved in a key stage of history and dealing with complicated situations."

In May 1937, the Northeast Army apprentice solider team (first renamed as the youth training class, and then as the second brigade) was dismissed following Chiang Kai-shek's handwritten instruction because of its important role in the 'Xi'an incident'. The party organisation dispersed Gu Mu and a few comrades in the Northeast Army to carry on with military rebellion mobilisation. In June 1937, Gu Mu was appointed to join the 107th division of the 67th Army garrisoned in Xinyang, and became the official clerk. His main responsibilities covered drafting documents, assisting the secretary in protecting the division's official seal, and distributing and maintaining military credentials for officers above regiment level. His direct superior, the secretary, was more than 50 years old and lacked energy. After Gu Mu took office, he assumed the duty of drafting documents, and the secretary did not change a single word. All the secretary did was stamp the documents and send them to the division commander for approval.

The top of Xi'an's broad east city gate, which was the training ground for apprentice soldiers in the Northeast Army

The 'July 7 incident' happened about one month after Gu Mu joined the army. It marked the outbreak of the war of resistance against Japan. The war situation in the north was particularly tense. The 67th Army was engaged in a fierce battle with Japanese divisions led by Lieutenant General Kesago Nakajima and General Kenji Doihara along the Jinpu railway that connected Tianjin with Pukou, outside Nanjing, and the northern section of the Beijing-Hankou railway line.

After the outbreak of the battle of Shanghai on 13 August 1937, the 67th Army received orders to rush to the rescue of Songjiang, support the remnants of the 40th Army and security forces, and defend Songjiang county to the death for a period of three days. After suffering considerable losses, they managed to defend the county. At midnight on 8 November, they successfully accomplished the mission of stopping the Japanese army.

At that time, there was no fixed divisional headquarters. Everyone was tired beyond endurance after three days' battle without respite. In Qingpu county, which was the temporary divisional headquarters, Gu Mu fell asleep on a threshing floor in a small village. On the morning of 9 November, a huge bomb blast woke him, and he discovered that all other division headquarters

Important Documents Retrieved from Battle of Shanghai

members had left. Gu Mu hastily packed up the official seal and important documents of the division headquarters left behind by the secretary during the retreat, and ran all the way to the village entrance to check the situation. All he could see were retreating soldiers, and they told him that the division headquarters had evacuated in a southwesterly direction.

Gu Mu ran in the same direction. Soldiers were scattered along the road, and they walked together for 3-4 km in great haste, until they came across a wide river and a bridge crossing. Gu Mu and his colleagues ran up to the bridge, but were spotted by several Japanese cavalrymen, who dismounted and ran towards them with guns aloft. Gu Mu's most important task was to prevent the official seal of the division headquarters from falling into enemy hands. At such a crucial moment, an excellent idea occurred to him. He threw away his backpack, took off his coat, and jumped into the river carrying only a small bag that contained a pistol and the official seal of the division headquarters, the seal of the division commander and certificates of regiment commanders. He swam downstream, evading detection by the enemy searching the riverbanks. After swimming for more than 1km in the ice-cold river, he went ashore at a point where no one could be seen on either side of the river.

Gu Mu inquired about the division headquarters along the road. When he arrived in Suzhou, the streets were full of defeated and dispersed soldiers, and he couldn't find any food or drink as all the shops were closed. He realised that they couldn't follow the direction of the enemy's march, which was heading westwards. So he led a group of his fellow soldiers from the 107th division, in a southwesterly direction via Taihu lake, and managed the arduous journey to Fuliang in Jiangxi province. Along the way, he gathered about 100 people. They crossed the Yangtze river at its confluence with the Jiujiang river, and arrived in Xinyang in late December.

When he finally met with the division headquarters, the division commander was distressed because the army was running out of soldiers, the official seal had been lost and the army command was in danger of breaking up. The division commander was pleasantly surprised to see Gu Mu still in possession of the official seal of the division headquarters and having assembled some 100 fellow brothers. He commended Gu Mu, apologised for not having informed him about the retreat of the division headquarters, and promised him guaranteed admission to the central military academy and told him he would be entrusted with an important position after graduation.

Gu Mu believed that there was little prospect of restoring the organisational system of the 107th division based on his personal experience of the battle of Shanghai. He realised that he should write a report and hand it over to his own army, the Eighth Route Army. He therefore found a pretext to resign. Being particularly loyal to friends and comrades, the division commander agreed to let Gu Mu go, and gave him an extra 80 silver dollars as travelling expenses.

On 21 July 1982, the CPC held a historical party data collection forum for apprentice soldiers of the Northeast Army in Beijing. This photo shows senior comrades and members of the party historical data group of the Northeast Army. It was taken by comrade Huang Junjie, a member of the party history research centre of the CPC central committee.
Front row (from left to right): Zhang Huadong, Wan Yi, Chen Dazhang, Liao Gailong (deputy director of the party history research centre of the CPC central committee), Xie Xiaonai (deputy director of the CPC for historical party data collection), Song Li, Kang Boying, Gu Mu, Yu Weizhe, Wei Zhi, Wei Guoyun and Gao Jinming
Middle row (from left to right): Wang Shuwen, Yi Hong, Qin Zhongfang, Wang Lei, Wang Tiezheng, Tang Dingguang, Leng Zhuo, Yang Tian, Gao Shanglin, Zhu Ming and Li Wei
Back row (from left to right): Sun Guangchun, Lu Jun, Sun Dasheng, Xu Ruilin, Gu Xiaobo, Sun Shufeng, Ji Yeli, Wang Lin, Liang Yan, Cao Lixin, Wang Qin (researcher from the institute of modern history at the Chinese Academy of Social Sciences (CASS), and granddaughter of Zhang Xueliang's eldest sister)

Chapter 6

First Meeting with Vice-Chairman Zhou Enlai

Gu Mu arrived in Shanghai just after new year's day in 1938. By then, Shanghai and Nanjing had already fallen into enemy hands, and hotels were filled with fleeing high officials and rich merchants. Gu Mu bought a student's uniform with the silver dollars given to him by the division commander, steeled himself to live in an expensive French hotel within the French concession of Hankou, and started at once to write reports to the representative office in Wuhan of the Eighth Route Army.

The reports elaborated on his thoughts about the battle of Shanghai, pointing out that the Chinese army, which had long been engaged in a civil war, was now confronted with a modernised invading army and that the army under our party's command should carefully learn lessons and experiences from the battle of Shanghai.

Gu Mu's report captured the attention of the Wuhan representative office of the Eighth Route Army. It was not long before he was called to a meeting. At the office of the Eighth Route Army, he was first received by Liu Tao and, while reporting to him, Zhou Enlai walked in. Seeing him, Gu Mu stood to attention right away and saluted him respectfully.

"So, you are Gu Mu!" Zhou Enlai shook Gu Mu's hands and said affectionately: "Comrade Li Tao might have told you already. Your report is of great reference value. I was told that you are living in a hotel. Since that's not convenient, I'll let comrade Li Tao arrange a suitable place for you to stay and get you some books and documents first. After that, we shall talk about assigning you a job."

These words made Gu Mu very excited. His life as a drifter had come to an end, and he felt like a traveller returning home.

Gu Mu expressed to Vice Chairman Zhou his strong desire to study in Yan'an, and briefed him about his previous situation in the league of left-wing writers in Beijing. He also mentioned that there was a group of young Beijing writers from the league who were apprentice soldiers in the Northeast Army.

Zhou Enlai measured him up with his sophisticated and wise eyes, paused for a while, and said: "Right now, there are many literary youths spread across areas ranging from KMT-controlled areas to Yan'an. In my opinion, you are most needed to work in the enemy's rear area." He invited Gu Mu to take a seat, and left for other business, leaving Gu Mu and Li Tao to carry on talking.

The Wuhan representative office of the Eighth Route Army

Gu Mu handed over the remaining 50 silver dollars to the party organisation.

On the same day, Li Tao arranged for Gu Mu to stay in the northeast national salvation society in Wuchang. Realising that time was of the essence, Gu Mu earnestly read a batch of party documents. One month later, he was entrusted with another important mission. The bureau of the Yangtze river assigned him and its inspector, Zhang Wenhai, to carry out ideological work on Wan Yi, who was the regimental commander of the 667th regiment, 334th brigade, 112th division, 57th corps of the Northeast Army.

First Meeting with Vice-Chairman Zhou Enlai

Before departure, Li Tao took out the 50 silver dollars and said to him: "This is the money that you handed over to the organisation. Having discussed the matter, the leaders decided to return the money as expenses for this mission."

Chapter 7

Regimental Commander Wan Yi Joins the Party

During the lantern festival of 1938, Gu Mu and Zhang Haiwen arrived in Xinpu, Lianyungang, and lived in the Longhai apartments. They tried to inform Wan Yi, who came from the same town, of their arrival. Wan Yi came soon after, but as he did not know Gu Mu or Zhang Wenhai, the first meeting was rather abrupt. Sensing Wan Yi's wariness, Gu Mu hurriedly went to him and said: "I heard your speech when I was in the apprentice soldier team of Xi'an. Liu Lanbo is our good friend, and he often mentioned you." Hearing this, Wan Yi felt at ease. "Liu Lanbo is my old friend," he said.

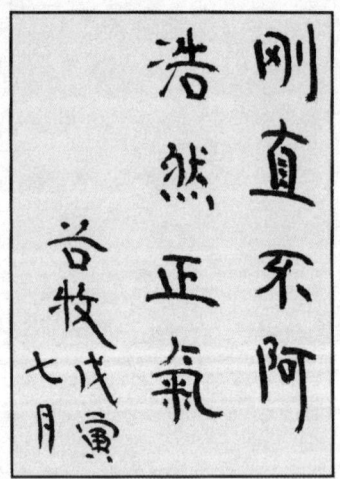

Gu Mu's inscription for *Memoirs of General Wan Yi*: Upright and plainspoken; awe-inspiring righteousness

Wan Yi's graduation photo from the Northeast Army academy

Gu Mu revisits the Longhai apartments

Seeing that Wan Yi's doubts had been dispelled, Gu Mu went on to enlighten him about their identities: "Comrade Zhou sent us here to see how you've been doing." Then they talked about how Zhou Enlai and the Yangtze river bureau cared about his fate during his time in custody. Gu Mu then came straight to the point: "What do you think about joining the Communist Party?"

After thinking about it for a while, Wan Yi replied: "As for fighting against the Japanese and saving our nation, I put my whole heart into it. The Communist Party can rest assured on that point. But theory is my weak point. I have never learned much about it." Seeing him undecided, Gu Mu and Zhang Haiwen did not want to impose on him, and only talked about some facts and reasons.

Wan Yi, a Manchurian born in Jin county, Liaoning province, was a brilliant student of the ninth class of the Northeast Army academy, and was highly regarded by Zhang Xueliang. He came first in a graduation examination among 1,980 students. Zhang Xueliang came to the school in person to present awards to him, which were an officer's sword and a pocket watch. He was righteous and free of the vices of prostitution, gambling, corruption and nepotism. He was a strict disciplinarian and kept the army ranks in good order, which was quite unusual for the Northeast Army.

In January 1936, Wan Yi was appointed as regimental commander of the 627th regiment of the 57th corps. He established contact with an underground Communist Party organisation through Liu Lanbo, and worked as the honorary regimental commander of the anti-Japanese youth league, which was a supportive organisation of the party. During the 'Xi'an incident', he firmly supported Zhang and Yang's policy of resistance against Japan allied with the Communist Party. On 2 February, the Northeast Army experienced internal conflicts, and Wan Yi was arrested and kept in custody by the corps commander, Liao Chengliu. After the 'July 7 incident', Wan Yi was released under the pressure of public opinion, and was appointed as regimental commander of the 672nd regiment. After participating in the battle of Nanjing, he was reappointed as regiment commander of the 667th regiment.

The following day, Wan Yi went to Gu Mu's quarters and solemnly stated: "I have thought it through. If the organisation believes that I'm qualified, I volunteer to join the Communist Party." Afterwards, Wan Yi told Gu Mu that he hadn't been able to sleep following their sincere conversation. After thinking things through, he figured out that only the Communist Party could be relied upon to defeat the Japanese, and that the KMT was unreliable and hopeless.

Chapter 8

Changed Aspect of the 667th Regiment

With Wan Yi joining the party, the underground work committee of the CPC's 112th division began to take root in the 667th regiment. The committee comprised Wu Zhigang, Gu Mu and Li Xi, with Wu Zhigang being the first appointed secretary. Gu Mu and Wu Zhigang were comrades-in-arms in the apprentice soldier team in Xi'an, and also members of the league of left-wing writers in Beijing, having the natural charisma of patriotic educated youth. They followed the example of the Northeast Army's apprentice soldier team and established three classes of new recruits in the 667th regiment. In total, more than 250 progressive and educated young people were trained. Furthermore, they got in touch with Lü Zhi in the 668th regiment, who had been hiding his true identity for a long period of time. In May 1938, the battalion commander of the 1st battalion, Liu Jie, was officially enlisted as a secret party member, which marked another important base for the expansion of the 1st battalion of the 668th regiment. Through the work of the underground working committee of the CPC's 112th division, the backbone structure of the 667th regiment and the 1st battalion of the 668th regiment were changed, and a large number of cadres were fostered for the party.

Comrade Lü Zhi in the 668th regiment of the 112th division in the Northeast Army

During his time as commander of the 627th regiment, Wan Yi composed a song for the regiment to the tune of *La Marseillaise*. A publicity team composed of new recruits of progressive, educated youth soon taught the whole regiment this song. Gu Mu really liked *Under Fire* by the French writer Henri Barbusse. In the 667th regiment, Gu Mu established a tabloid newspaper by the same name, just as he had done in Wendeng normal school.

Influenced by *Under Fire*, the division headquarters and the three other regiments also started to establish tabloids: *Firebrand, Torch, Firelight* and *Flame*. All this activity undermined the basis of the KMT's political training institutions.

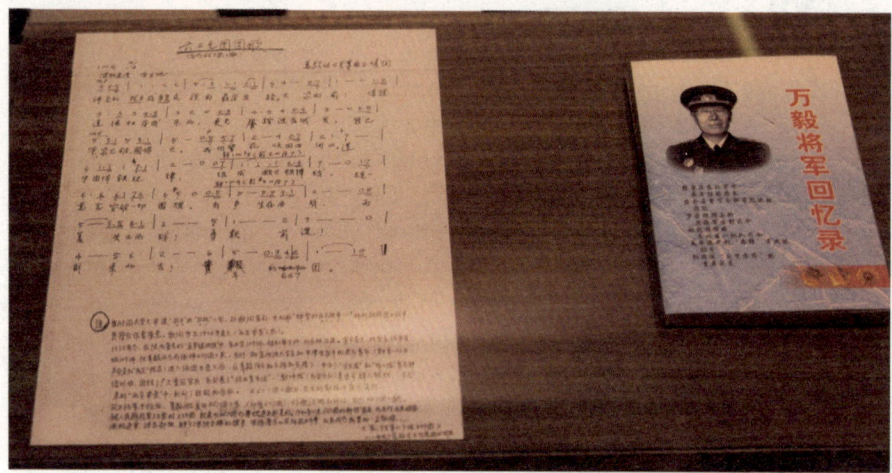

The song of the 627th regiment (and also later used by the 667th regiment) with lyrics composed by Wan Yi, and the *Memoirs of General Wan Yi*

With the work committee of the 112th division expanding their work, more educated youths kept enlisting in the army. With a positive mental attitude and high morale, the fighting capacity of the 667th division improved. The army won the battles of Tai'erzhuang and Lianyungang in quick succession. Moreover, they managed a successful assault on Hefei airport and blew up four planes, sabotaged railways to the south of Teng county, and captured the leader of the 'Japanese economic investigation team of north China', Yoshio Toyama, and his assistant, Shinichi Saruhashi.

Changed Aspect of the 667th Regiment

The youthful spirit and fierce fighting capacity of the 667th regiment attracted wide attention, and many people asked Wan Yi for soldiers. His regiment belonged to the 334th brigade. The commander of the 334th brigade not only received the third class of new recruits of the 667th regiment, but also requested Gu Mu to engage in anti-Japanese publicity and cultural education among the brigade. Later on, a battlefield working group at brigade level was established, and Gu Mu was appointed as director and sub-lieutenant of the brigade. Making the best use of this position, Gu Mu started to develop a backbone force in political training institutions in other regiments, and established publicity teams in all regiments. The battlefield working group was extremely active. It not only performed for its own brigade and regiments, but also for other forces under the same division and for local people. In addition, it taught anti-Japanese songs. For a time, *Flowers in May, Attacking the Enemy from the Rear, Roar of the Yellow River* and other progressive anti-Japanese songs resonated across the military district. Anti-Japanese morale surged among patriotic officers and soldiers, and a healthy atmosphere took hold.

Comrades of the former work committee of the 112th division of the 57th corps and the 111th division and comrades (then in Beijing) from the new recruits team of the first, second and third classes of the 667th regiment. Front row (from left to right): Mao Guohua, Zhang Yi, Li Xin, Wan Yi, Gu Mu, Lü Zhixian, Yi Hong and Tang Qi; Back row (from left to right): Xu Ang, Lan Xiaoyong, Zhao Xin, Mou Feng, Chen Xian, Qin Jiping, Li Hou, Xu Xin, Wang Bing and Qin Dun

During the initial stage of its establishment, the 112th division underground work committee was under the command of the Yangtze river bureau. After the 115th division of the Eighth Route Army entered Shandong Yimeng mountain area, direct command of the work committee was transferred to Luo Ronghuan. This took effect from August 1938. Gu Mu was praised when he reported the work to Luo Ronghuan. Luo recognised the achievements of the work committee, including attracting and fostering progressive educated youth and reforming the existing troops. "Compared with political work in some divisions and regiments of the Eighth Route Army, you are doing very well," he said. "You can't find so many intellectuals even in a regiment of the Eighth Route Army."

Chapter 9

Open and Honourable Withdrawal of a Friendly Army

On the night of 16 September 1939, the battlefield working group of the 333rd brigade was performing for Qibaoshan local townsfolk when the Japanese army launched a surprise attack against the brigade headquarters. In trying to break out of the encirclement, the work committee secretary, Wu Zhigang, was hit by artillery fire, and sacrificed himself.

Gu Mu succeeded Wu Zhigang as the work committee secretary of the 112th division. After the battle of Qibaoshan, many comrades fell into depression, and the work of the publicity team of the 667th regiment was almost in paralysis. Gu Mu came to the division from the brigade headquarters to have a frank talk with comrades, to mobilise and encourage them, and to help readjust the inner party administrative structure's leadership organs. A liaison branch that connected all company branches with the regiment was established, with the result that daily activities of *Under Fire*, such as publishing, rehearsals and learning songs, were revived.

In November 1939, after the sixth plenary session of the KMT's fifth central executive committee, diehard factions kept generating friction with the Eighth Route Army and the New Fourth Army, and the work of military rebellion mobilisation became more difficult.

Wu Zhigang, the first appointed underground work committee secretary of the CPC in the 112th division

Wan Yi at the start of 1940 when he was transferred from 112th division of the Northeast Army to 333rd brigade of 111th division to work as acting brigade commander. He gave this photo to Gu Mu. After the Lushan conference in 1959, Wan Yi was labelled as an 'important member of Peng Dehuai's anti-party clique'. Gu Mu asked his wife Mou Feng to see off Wan Yi and his wife Zheng Yi in Beijing, and showed them this photo as a way of encouraging them to just regard being banished to Shaanxi as opening up a new front. During the Cultural Revolution, the rebels dug out this photo. Gu Mu's family suffered a lot because they couldn't 'clearly explain' why Wan Yi was wearing a KMT badge on the cap and a (captured) Japanese military coat. Towards the end of the Cultural Revolution, which was about investigating truth and facts, materials that had been taken away by rebels were returned, and Gu Mu was gratified that this photo was still there. After Wan Yi was released, they offered to return this photo to him, which surprised him since he could never imagine that it still existed. The white horse was a favourite of Wan Yi's, and the photo depicts the sincere bond between these two comrades

At the beginning of 1940, Wan Yi was transferred to command the 333rd brigade of the 111th division, and Liu Jie was promoted as commander of the 672nd regiment in the 336th brigade. It was at the crest of the first wave of anti-communism, when Wan Yi and Liu Jie were promoted, that Gu Mu came to a clear understanding: they fully deserved their promotions as they had played important roles in illustrious battle victories during two years of the anti-Japanese war. But their promotions had a similar effect to luring a tiger out of the mountains (drawing an enemy out into the open). They had progressive thoughts. The troops they had trained were effective in combat, and were loyal and devoted. Their 'promotions' from the original division only served to weaken progressive power.

Predictably, the successor, Jin Kecai, who was previously in the 667th regiment, obstructed all the initiatives of the work committee. The 667th regiment used to be the major camp base of the work committee in the 112th division, but now it became a difficult place to tread.

At the beginning of 1940, Wang Wuxiu, who was sent by the work committee to join the division's political department, was incited to betray the party. Although his betrayal was discovered in time, and dealt with resolutely and with no disastrous consequences, Gu Mu's true identity was exposed.

Late one night in early February 1940, Gu Mu went to Budaiyu in Fei county to report to Luo Ronghuan, and he received the order for a planned withdrawal. Straight afterwards, Gu Mu held a work committee conference to make detailed plans. After receiving a telegram saying 'Mother sick; come back soon', Gu Mu 'asked for leave' and moved to live in Dalu village where the Yimeng mountain base area rear-service department of the 115th division was located. Given the title of advisor, he maintained the operations of the work committee by delivering oral messages via messenger.

In late July, various signs indicated that the enemy was going to massacre progressive forces in the 57th corps. Confronted with this situation, Luo Ronghuan contacted Gu Mu to discuss and confirm withdrawal plans, which would leave behind only Northeast Army party members who were 'locally born and bred'. Luo Ronghuan emphasised that the withdrawal must be well organised to demonstrate the party's principles and attitudes of being open and honourable while taking into account the overall interests of the group.

Gu Mu joined the Shandong branch in September 1940

Gu Mu led comrades of the 112th division to make careful and meticulous arrangements for the withdrawal plan. They requested withdrawn personnel not to take a single pistol or bullet from the Northeast Army. They were also asked to keep a record of money and items they were in charge of, and to complete an inventory of all returned items. Furthermore, they made detailed plans for the withdrawal, including meeting places, withdrawal routes and contact details. After several days drawing up the plan, the withdrawal started on the evening of 21 September. Gu Mu went to the meeting place to assist in the withdrawal in the company of the Eighth Route Army.

As the morning glow lit up the eastern sky, Gu Mu led hundreds of withdrawing comrades toward where the Shandong contingent were stationed. As the sun was rising, all the withdrawing personnel entered the base area. A female fighter who had twisted her ankle (Shu Xing, who later became comrade Jiang Chao's wife) travelled on horseback. Only with the help of the morning light did she realise that the person who had sent her on horseback was Gu Mu, the supreme leader of the underground work committee.

Former comrades from the 57th corps at Gu Mu's family party in March 1997. Front row, from left to right: Gu Mu and Wan Yi;. Middle row: Lü Zhixian's wife, Mou Feng, Li Hou's wife, Liu Zhun's wife, Zhang Yi's wife and Zhang Qi (Li Xin's wife and Mou Feng's comrade-in-arms in the women's opera troupe). Back row, from left to right: Li Hou, Lü Zhixian, Li Xin, Zhang Yi and Liu Zhun

Liu Huiyuan visits Shu Xing, the widow of General Jiang Chao, former vice principal of the Nanjing advanced infantry school, 3 June 2010. She was also a veteran soldier of the former 112th division of the Northeast Army

On the morning of 22 September, different troops of the 112th division discovered many missing people, but a letter to officers and soldiers of the Northeast Army was placed under the pillows of every missing soldier. Along with each letter were a bill and an inventory, to show that they were free from corruption, bribery, selfishness and cheating.

Officers and soldiers of the 112th division sighed with regret at this turn of events while reactionary officers were alarmed and despondent about the fact that there had been such a large-scale covert CPC organisation in their midst and that it had made good its withdrawal safe and sound without a trace.

Chapter 10

Independent Brigade 'Divorced' But 'Remaining in the Household'

On 14 September 1940, the commander of the 57th corps, Miao Chengliu, sent Yu Wenqing and Dong Hanqing to negotiate conditions for defecting with Li Yapan, who had already deserted to the enemy. Yu Wenqing originally intended to avoid going on this mission, but Wan Yi asked him to take part in the negotiation, and in this way they gathered irrefutable evidence that Miao Chengliu was colluding with the Japanese. The division commander of the 111th division, Chang Enduo, along with Wan Yi, decided to capture Miao Chengliu and his henchman on 22 September.

Chang Enduo, lieutenant general and commander of the 111th division of the 57th corps in the National Revolutionary Army, also leader of the 'August 3' uprising

However, someone divulged the secret, and Miao Chengliu and the director of the political department of the 57th corps ran off. Later that day, Chang Enduo took the lead in sending a telegram around the country, and additional ones to both Chiang Kai-shek in the KMT central government and Yu Xuezhong at the headquarters of the Lusu (Shandong-Jiangsu) guerrilla zone.

Since the elimination of traitors and the retreat of party members and progressive elements of the 112th division occurred on the same day, the division commander, Huo Shouyi, and the brigade commander, Rong Ziheng, were both overcome with fear and felt they were in grave danger. Two months later, Huo Shouyi and Rong Ziheng suddenly ordered the detention of regiment commander Liu Jie, who they believed to be suspicious. But later, Liu found a chance to escape. On 26 November, secret party member Jiang Chao, who was the leader of the 1st company 1st battalion 667th regiment, realised that the battalion commander, Han Zijia, intended to inflict harm on him, and decided on the spur of the moment to run away along with most of the company soldiers. At the same time, deputy platoon commander Wang Lin and squad commander Song Shuren in the 3rd company 1st battalion 667th regiment noticed that company commander Li Baoshu intended to defect to the enemy with the entire team. Therefore, they secretly united six squads and went over to Wan Yi in the 111th division. After requesting permission from the division commander,

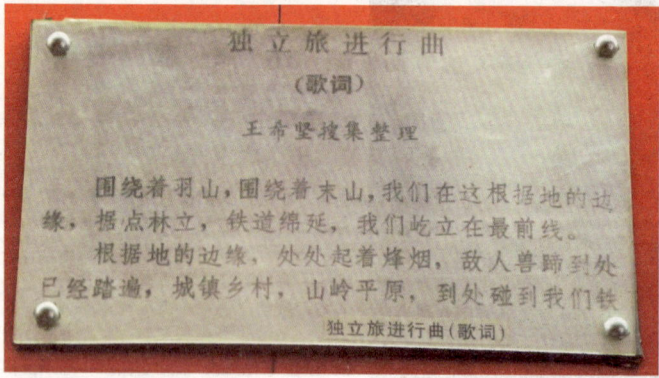

Lyrics of the march of the 57th independent brigade. Information source: An Feng Mountain Martyrs Memorial Park (An Feng Mountain Revolution Museum) of Donghai county

Independent Brigade 'Divorced' But 'Remaining in the Household'

Chang Enduo, Wan Yi commanded Liu Jie and Jiang Chao to take these two companies and deploy them in Mount Yu and Mount Mo in Donghai county. They engaged in guerrilla war in the name of a supplementary regiment of the 57th corps, of which Liu Jie was the regiment leader, and reported the situation to the Shandong branch.

At that moment, Gu Mu affirmed this kind of 'separated (divorced)' yet 'not separated (remaining in the household)' behaviour. He was already the principal secretary of the subcommittee of the Shandong branch army, minister of the united front work department and still secretary of the work committee of the 112th division. He immediately summoned already evacuated Zhang Yi, Wang Chong, Ding Yijiu, Xu Wei, Wang Xijian and other comrades and sent them to the supplementary regiment to set up a party branch.

The first 200 key personnel of the 57th corps supplementary regiment had come from the 667th regiment. As they had been nurtured under the work committee, their anti-Japanese enthusiasm was really strong. Moreover, well equipped with machine guns and other weaponry, they had strong

During his journey to Zhenbao island in August 1976 to visit his frontier-guard son, Liu Jie naturally shows the dignity of a veteran

combat effectiveness. Liu Jie, Jiang Chao and other comrades led the army to storm and occupy the Zhuzi channel. Later on, they captured a fortified site occupied by the Wang Peng-led puppet army and other fortified sites occupied by the puppet army and bandits. They also incorporated local armed forces into their own forces, and established Hailing anti-Japanese base area that covered more than 1,000 square kilometres, thereby connecting the eastern Binhai and Subei (northern Jiangsu) base areas located on either side of Longhai Road.

The Shandong branch attached particular importance to the development and growth of this army. In April 1941, during an inspection by Gu Mu, the minister of the united front work, he declared that this army could keep their unit designation of the 57th corps, and that it would be expanded to form an independent brigade. Moreover, he cited this independent brigade as an example of "an army of friendly forces; the essence of the party army".

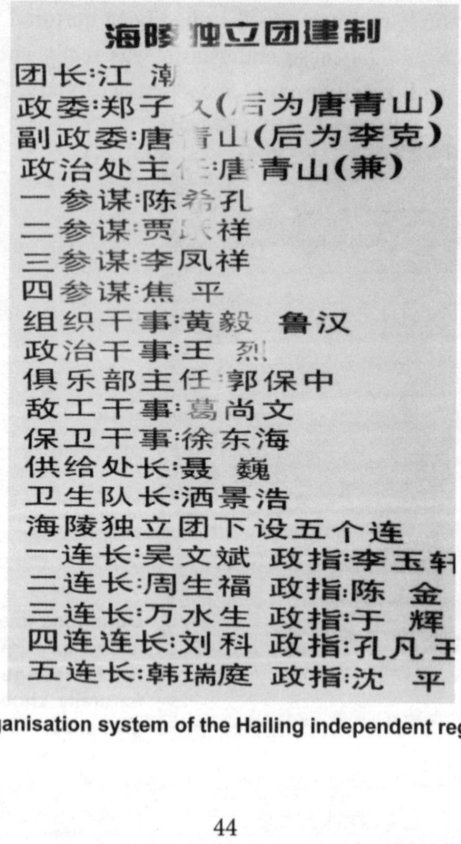

海陵独立团建制
团长:江潮
政委:郑子久(后为唐青山)
副政委:唐青山(后为李克)
政治处主任:唐青山(兼)
一参谋:陈希孔
二参谋:贾凤祥
三参谋:李凤祥
四参谋:焦平
组织干事:黄毅 鲁汉
政治干事:王烈
俱乐部主任:郭保中
敌工干事:葛尚文
保卫干事:徐东海
供给处长:聂巍
卫生队长:洒景浩
海陵独立团下设五个连
一连长:吴文斌 政指:李玉轩
二连长:周生福 政指:陈金
三连长:万水生 政指:于辉
四连连长:刘科 政指:孔凡王
五连长:韩瑞庭 政指:沈平

The organisation system of the Hailing independent regiment

Independent Brigade 'Divorced' But 'Remaining in the Household'

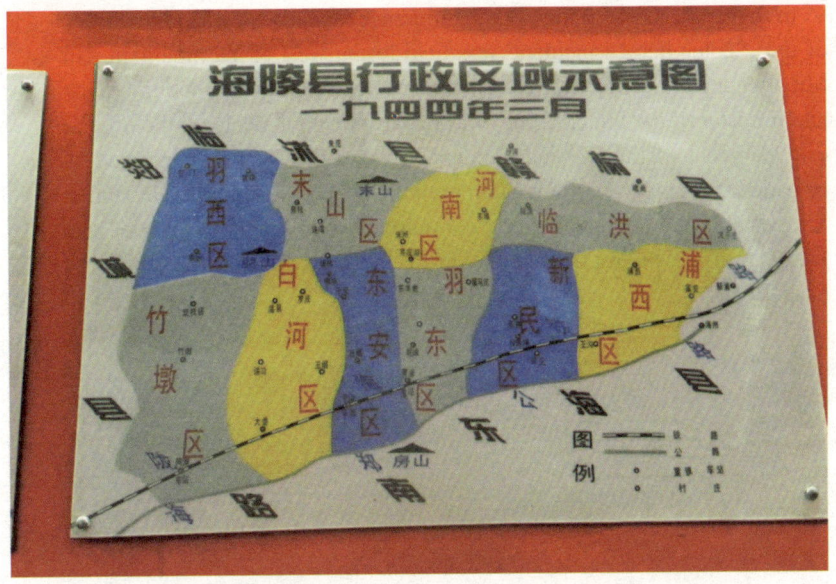

Sketch map of Hailing county administrative region, March 1944

Gu Mu and Zheng Zijiu, who was a former secretary of Hailing county party committee, early 1990s

In September 1941, a memorial conference to mark the 10th anniversary of the 'September 18 incident' was held to the west of Yu mountain. Gu Mu attended the conference as principal secretary of the Shandong branch and minister of the united front work department, and declared the official establishment of the 57th independent brigade. Liu Jie was appointed as brigade commander. In the meantime, the CPC party committee in Binhai area established Donghai work committee, and officially founded the Donghai office, laying the foundation for the construction of Hailing area base.

Chapter 11

New Life of the 111th Division

In October 1940, the unit designation of the 57th Army was cancelled, the 111th and 112th divisions were incorporated into the headquarters of Sulu war zone commanded by Yu Xuezhong, and were under its direct command. At the beginning of 1941, the KMT set off the first wave of anti-communism, contributing to reactionary diehard elements in the 111th and 112th divisions becoming more arrogant and rampant. On 17 February, a diehard faction of the 111th division killed the lieutenant adjutant of the 661st regiment, Song Mucheng, Wan Yi's security officer Li Fuhai, and Hu Tienan, who had been sent by the work committee of the 667th regiment. In addition, they detained Wan Yi and transferred him to Yu Xuezhong.

Guo Weicheng (back left), his third younger brother Guo Jincheng (back right) and family members pictured shortly before the 'August 3 uprising'. Guo Weicheng helped plan the uprising

The Shandong branch immediately sent First Secretary Gu Mu to approach the place where the 111th division was stationed, along with a company of troops. They tried every possible way to rescue Wan Yi, but failed.

Guan Jinghuan, deputy commander and chief of staff of Jilin province military region

Wan Yi thus was held for more than a year. In the early summer of 1942, Chiang Kai-shek sent Yu Xuezhong a telegram with the order to secretly execute Wan Yi. Yu was reluctant to take this extreme measure, so instead he organised an 'open trial' and a 'joint court martial' on 2 August. During the trial, Wan Yi was righteously indignant and stated facts to refute all the criminal allegations made against him. The judge was unable to contradict any of his statements

Guo Weicheng, the head of the government affairs office of the headquarters commanded by Yu Xuezhong, was Zhang Xueliang's secretary at the time of the Xi'an incident. In June, he visited Wan Yi. On 2 August, the night of the 'joint court martial', he once again went to the place where Wan Yi had been imprisoned, and revealed a major plan to him.

"Division commander Chang was found to have an incurable disease, and he was not able to survive for even a couple of days," Guo Weicheng told Wan Yi. "He wrote me something and said he would hand over the army to me after his death. If I should command the army, I would implement the *Eight Proposals* formulated by Zhang Xueliang. If everything was under control, I would send soldiers armed with pistols to rescue you, and you can help me manage the army." Guo Weicheng also asked Wan Yi if there were reliable and trustworthy people in the 111th division. Wan Yi briefed him.

From left to right, progressive military officer Sun Liji, Yu Wenqing and Liu Jie, formerly of the 57th corps of the Northeast Army and underground party member, 1963

After Guo Weicheng left, Wan Yi considered what he had heard to be of great significance. He believed it might not be easy for Chang and Guo to make it, and that the Eighth Route Army should be notified of this and get ready. Therefore, that same night, and at great risk to his own life, he managed to escape from prison, groped around in the dark for dozens of miles, and finally arrived at the station of the 3rd battalion 6th regiment 2nd brigade of the Eighth Route Army Shandong column. The army sent four cavalrymen to escort him to the brigade headquarters, where he was warmly received by the brigade commander, Sun Jixian.

Hearing this news, the Shandong branch sent Gu Mu immediately to receive Wan Yi. Gu Mu first sent cavalry to the 2nd brigade to escort Wan

Yi, and he went to Sanjieshou in person to await him. They finally met each other, feeling extremely excited. Wan Yi urgently updated Gu Mu about everything he knew, and suggested that he report to the superiors right away that something was about to happen to the 111th division. Hearing this, Gu Mu said: "Comrade Wan Yi, you just stay here and have a rest. You don't have to go to the branch because, if you did, other comrades would visit you. The top priority for you right now is to rest. I'm going to report to the branch what you just told me." The decision by Gu Mu to let Wan Yi have a rest immediately was based on his analysis that he would be greatly needed in the imminent action of the 111th division.

As expected, Chang Enduo and Guo Weicheng took actions earlier than scheduled.

On 3 August 1942, Guo Weicheng reached the 111th division in a hurry, and visited the division commander Chang Enduo who was in his sickbed, elaborating on Wan Yi's prison break and Yu Xuezhong's investigation on his visit to Wan Yi. After considering for a while, Chang Enduo said resolutely: "Let's do it right now, don't wait for me to die." He immediately gathered cadres above regiment commander level to come to receive orders.

The cemetery of General Chang Enduo in Huadong Martyrs' Memorial Park in Linyi

New Life of the 111th Division

Division commander Chang arrested Tao Jingkui and other diehard-faction officers right away, directed every regiment commander to strictly follow chief Guo's commands, and left 662nd regiment commander Sun Liji to assist in commanding the army. In the meantime, it was announced that the 111th division would be renamed 'Northeast Marching Army' along with the announcement of the 'four major proposals'. At 11pm on 3 August, Chang Enduo and Guo Weicheng launched an uprising for the sake of the nation. The commander of the 666th regiment, Guan Jinghuan, sent troops of two battalions to besiege the headquarters from the west, and disarmed the special task battalion of the headquarters. At dawn, the headquarters commanded by Yu Xuezhong and landlord forces were disarmed.

Due to the hasty uprising, the 111th division was in chaos. Some troops were transferred; Zhang Shaoqian, the 665th regiment commander, was ambushed and killed in machine gun fire; two battalions defected and ran away. The engineer battalion imprisoned diehard-faction officers who had been betrayed, resulting in the commander-in-chief of the war zone, Yu Xuezhong, disguising himself as an old farmer and running away. He resumed his duties, and on the next day gathered all defected troops to attack the 111th regiment in retaliation. Chang Enduo and Guo Weicheng ordered the troops to advance towards the anti-Japanese base area.

In a conference of the Shandong branch held on 5 August, a decision was made that Wan Yi and Wang Zhenqian (former leader of the 111th division work committee) should approach the station of the 111th division, and offer support according to prevailing circumstances. In his memoirs, Gu Mu mentioned that they specified that Guan Songtao (of Liu Jie's division) and Jiang Chao, along with the two companies, should come to the aid of the 111th division.

Wan Yi was conferred the title of lieutenant general in 1955

Guo Weicheng was conferred the title of major in 1955

On the afternoon of 8 August, more than 2,000 progressive anti-Japanese officers and soldiers of the 111th division reached the anti-Japanese base area of Lünan county, along with more than 1,200 rifles, 60 light or heavy machine guns, two artillery pieces, a radio set and horses. They were under the unified command of both the Shandong branch and the Eighth Route Army. On 9 August, Division Commander Chang passed away due to a deteriorating incurable disease.

The uprising troop restored its old unit designation of the 111th division, which was later renamed the New 111th division. Wan Yi was the acting division commander, and Guo Weicheng was the deputy division commander and head of the political department. The memorial service for the division commander, Chang Enduo, was held on 27 January 1943. Luo Ronghuan, along with other leaders and comrades attended to pay their respects, laid wreathes and composed elegiac couplets. Gu Mu's own elegiac couplet went: "Resolutely waging war against aggression / a strong advocate of unity / wise and experienced counsellor / laying down his life to work for the sake of the nation / a patriotic general was wounded. / Overcoming difficulties and resolving crisis / preparing to strike back / counting on our peers to keep up the hard work / remembering the heavy responsibilities on our shoulders / a loyal guardian we just lost."

The acting division commander, Wan Yi, took over the pistol that division commander Chang had used, and took a solemn oath: "Carry on the unfulfilled wish of revolution, shoulder the huge responsibility, and lead all officers and soldiers in the division to fight against aggression until the very end."

New Life of the 111th Division

General Jiang Chao, who became commander of the 113th division of the 38th corps, led troops to operate deep behind enemy lines in the second battle of the war of resistance against America to assist Korea. This blocked the line of retreat of the main enemy force and was one of his most brilliant achievements

Liu Jie towards the end of the anti-Japanese war

In October 1944, the New 111th division led by Wan Yi was re-designated as the Binhai division of Shandong military region affiliated to the Eighth Route Army. In November 1944, the 57th independent brigade led by Liu Jie, Jiang Chao and other officers was re-designated as Hailing independent regiment. After the Soviet Red Army was dispatched to northeast China, Wan Yi led the army in a march towards this region at the order of Commander-in-chief Zhu. Both sets of troops fulfilled their wish to fight all the way back to their hometowns, and became main forces of the 7th branch of the People's Army of the Northeast (later named the Northeast Democratic Allied Army). Afterwards, they became the 114th division of the 38th corps and the 339th regiment 113th division of the 38th corps respectively, and distinguished themselves in action in the war to resist US aggression and aid North Korea (the Korean war).

Senior comrades who worked in the Northeast Army and members of the party historical data group of the Northeast Army. Front row (from left to right): Yang Xiguang, Yang Zhengmin, Lü Zhengcao, Li Jue, Guo Weicheng, Xie Fang, Liu Ding, Feng Wenbin, Song Li, Gao Jinming, Gu Mu and Wan Yi; Second row (from right to left): Wang Qin, Zhang Huadong (fifth from the right), Yu Weizhe, Kang Boying, Wang Xiping, Miao Boran (second from the left); fourth right in the third row: Liao Gailong; fourth right in the top row: Sun Dasheng

Chapter 12

Bloodshed on Daqing Mountain

In September 1940, after Gu Mu completed the 'September 22' evacuation of communists and progressive forces of the 112th division, his identity became known publicly. After being transferred to the CPC Shandong branch, Gu Mu originally worked as first secretary of the subcommittee of the Shandong branch army, minister of the united front work department of the branch and minister of the united work department of the 115th division. He was also later appointed as secretary general of the branch. Within the branch office, Gu Mu was involved in managing government affairs, in charge of confidential work, drafted documents, communicated between superiors and subordinates to ensure effective information exchange, and worked as editor-in-chief of *Shandong Work*. In addition, he was in charge of taking care of the livelihood of institutional personnel. In particular, he collaborated with comrades in the catering division, and made every effort to ensure everyone had enough food.

Monument to the victorious siege of Daqing mountain

Chen Ming (comrade-in-arms of both Gu Mu and Mou Feng), who died a martyr's death in the siege of Daqing mountain, pictured with the late Xin Rui (taken from *Women's Anti-Japanese War Archives by Zhang Xi*). After Gu Mu was wounded, Secretary General Chen Ming of the provincial wartime work committee, directed the siege and relocation of the institution, and sacrificed his life bravely and gloriously. Xin Rui, Chen Ming's wife, threw a grenade in the siege and perished together with many enemies. She was the head of the same sisters song and dance troupe to which Mou Feng belonged

At that time, the CPC Shandong branch was stationed next to the provincial wartime work committee (equivalent to a provincial government), and they often marched or were transferred together. Institutions of the provincial wartime work committee were led by Chen Ming, a senior comrade who joined the party in 1925 with impressive accomplishments in theory, literature and art. Gu Mu held him in high esteem. Moreover his wife, Xin Rui, a talented woman born in Jinan, was the head of the same sisters song and dance troupe to which Mou Feng belonged. These two revolutionary couples built up a good relationship and special bond.

In early November 1941, Shunroku Hata, the commander-in-chief of Japanese expeditionary forces in China, assumed personal command of Linyi garrison. He gathered four divisions, three mixed brigades of Japanese army and Chinese traitors, with a total number of 50,000 people, and divided the troops into 11 columns. They charged towards the 115th division (the main force of the Eighth Route Army) and southern Liutian, Yinan county, where the Shandong branch institutions were stationed.

On 5 November, Luo Ronghuan decided to break out of the encirclement. Following his order, the army headed in the direction of Linyi, where the enemy headquarters were based, taking a great risk. As they were familiar with the terrain, the army was able to move rapidly and silently under cover of darkness. They almost had an encounter with enemy forces but finally arrived safely at their rendezvous at dawn.

At that time in the infantry ranks of the branch institutions, there was a German journalist, the great international communist warrior, comrade Hans Shippe. It had been more than a month since he had been transferred from the New Fourth Army to the Shandong branch, and he had interviewed Zhu Rui, Luo Ronghuan, Li Yu and other party, political and military leaders, and members of the 115th division. In this transfer operation, Gu Mu was assigned the task of looking after Shippe by Luo Ronghuan.

After successfully breaking out of the encirclement, Shippe said, with elation: "Tonight is the most unforgettable night of my life. This is much more meaningful and memorable than any single joyful evening party I attended in the west." He wrote a report entitled *Silent Battle* and published it in the first edition of *Soldiers News*, which encouraged and inspired soldiers' morale.

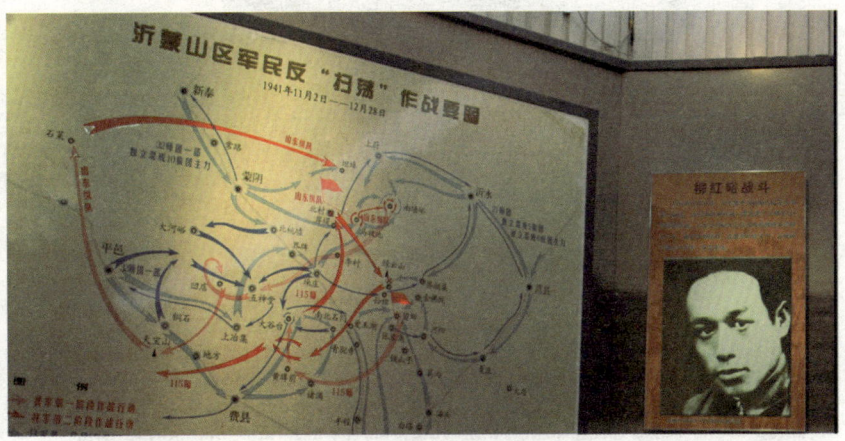

A military operation map of soldiers and civilians in Yimeng mountain area countering 'mopping-up' operations, displayed in an exhibition room of Huadong martyrs' memorial park in Linyi. On the right of the exhibition board, above the photo of Gu Mu, is a description of the battle of Liuhongyu

After breaking out of the encirclement in Liutian, party institutions and troops were circling around and confronting the enemy in the Meng mountain area. On 27 November, after a rapid overnight march, Gu Mu led institutions to Xisuo village, Shuanghouyazi town, Yinan county before dawn. They were about to take a rest when, suddenly, the enemy encircled them.

Gu Mu at the graves of comrades-in-arms Chen Ming and Xin Rui during a visit to Linyi, May 2005. The person in charge of the martyrs' memorial park wrote: "Tomb of martyrs Chen Ming and Xin Rui." These words were in Gu Mu's original handwriting. Back then, individual leaders within Huadong branch objected to the scale of the tomb, believing that it wasn't commensurate with the ranks of Chen Ming and Xin Rui, and they thought it wasn't appropriate to bury this couple together. Park staff put aside this issue for a time and, once the controversy had gradually receded, they inscribed these words and left out Gu Mu's name

A statue of Hans Shippe in the memorial square to commemorate victory in the Daqing mountain siege

Gu Mu received orders to conduct delaying tactics with the enemy to cover the withdrawal of the institutions. He assembled teams of security guards, seized favourable terrain and confused the enemy. This breakout of institutions was later known as the battle of Liuhongyu. The Japanese troops kept charging. Seeing security guards fall by the dozen, the guard company commander reported to Gu Mu: "The mission of delaying the enemy and covering the withdrawal has been accomplished. The order to outflank the enemy on both sides doesn't seem realistic, and we are also not sure if the direction of retreat of the institutions is safe or not. You had better catch up with the institutions and get transferred along with them." The guard company commander signalled several security guards to assist Gu Mu to withdraw in the direction where the institutions had been transferred. The guard company commander along with several soldiers headed straight to the other side of the battlefield, intending to lure the enemy away to cover their withdrawal.

Unfortunately, it was already too late. The enemy found not only the guard company commander, but also Gu Mu along with other guards. In the blink of an eye, bullets were flying towards them like hailstones.

All of a sudden, Gu Mu felt as if he had been punched in the waist, and fell to the ground. He managed to stand up and ran a couple of steps. With limbs feeling weak, he looked down, realised he had been shot in the chest where his clothes were saturated with blood, and he fainted on the spot.

Gu Mu was carried out on a stretcher and caught up with the troops. After examination, doctors said that the bullet had passed through his lungs, skimmed his ribs and came out the other side. Although he was severely injured and suffered from considerable loss of blood, at least his heart had managed to avoid a direct hit.

On the third day, a severely wounded Gu Mu was transferred to Daqing mountain along with the other troops. They once again encountered an enemy encirclement. During the fraught withdrawal, the institutions fell straight into the enemy's trap due to weak combat effectiveness. The battle was extremely fierce and intense. In order not to be a burden, Gu Mu ordered security guards and soldiers to take him by stretcher and hide him inside a tall haystack.

It was already night time when the battle concluded. Gu Mu felt severe pain from his wounds, and thought that he wasn't going to survive. He didn't want to burden the soldiers, so he let them rejoin the other troops. They didn't obey his order so Gu Mu insisted, angrily: "None of you can protect me here. You have to listen to me and catch up with the troops." Hearing this, the soldiers left, but the security guards remained. Gu Mu went on: "This is my order. No one is allowed to stay here, and none of you shall disobey my order."

Alone in the haystack, Gu Mu passed out for a long time. After he regained consciousness in the middle of the night, he realised that he was still alive, and struggled to crawl to a fellow-villager's doorway at the end of Shimen village. Then he fainted again. Later on, an elderly man woke him up, and fetched him a bowl of sorghum rice porridge. Before the encirclement happened, military doctors had instructed Gu Mu not to eat anything because they didn't know if his intestine or abdomen were wounded. But now, having been starved for three days, he had to ignore his doctors' instructions; he devoured the porridge. The elderly man again hid him in a haystack just outside the village.

Leaders' inscriptions displayed in an exhibition room of Huadong martyrs' memorial park. The one fourth from the right reading "I miss Yimeng mountain area" was written by Gu Mu, expressing his strong feelings as if they were etched on his bones and heart

Afterwards, the branch sent Chen Linhu, Gu Mu's fellow villager and comrade-in-arms in the apprentice soldier teams of the Northeast Army, to enquire about Gu Mu's whereabouts, and he finally found him. At that point, Gu Mu was suffering from a severe infection, and pus and blood were oozing from him. Military doctors gave him basic treatment. Afterwards, in light of the fact that the branch organs were still on the move, the superiors decided to hide Gu Mu in a 'fortress household' (safe house) in an enemy-occupied area to recover. Two weeks later, Gu Mu was able to walk with a stick thanks to the landlord's aunt and nursing assistant taking good care of him, and he insisted on reporting for duty. The nursing assistant couldn't talk him out of it, so she contacted the anti-Japanese government, and they sent two men to carry him back to the army on a stretcher.

Two days later, they managed to reach the place where the organs were stationed. On seeing Gu Mu, several military cooks were shocked. After a short while, they huddled up close to him and enquired after his well-being. This was because everyone thought Gu Mu had already died a martyr's death. Gu Mu was told that, after he had been shot, Chen Ming, Xin Rui, Liu Zichao, Zhen Lei and other senior comrades-in-arms who had taken his place to direct the transfer and breakout of the three organs had each died a martyr's death. Hans Shippe, whom Gu Mu was instructed to look after by Luo Ronghuan, had also died a martyr's death. Hearing this news, Gu Mu was overcome with grief...

An exhibition room of Huadong martyrs' memorial park displayed the inscriptions of some party and national leaders. The one written by Gu Mu was straightforward and revealed his true feelings: "I miss Yimeng mountain area." This was because Yimeng mountain area was a place on which he bravely shed his blood; a place where the spirits of his closest comrades-in-arms remain; and hundreds of thousands of people who genuinely and sincerely supported the Eighth Route Army and the CPC.

An anti-Japanese martyrs' memorial tower was built on Ma'an mountain (now known as Anti-Japanese mountain) of Ganyu county, Binhai base area, 2 August 1942. This photo shows party and political leaders after the inauguration ceremony. Back row (from third left): Luo Ronghuan, Li Yu, Chen Guang and Xiao Hua. Second left in the third row is Gu Mu

Chapter 13

Witnessing Liu Shaoqi's Thorough Supervision of Work in Shandong

On 10 April 1942, Liu Shaoqi came to Binhai, and prepared to take part in the seventh party congress in Yan'an while inspecting the Shandong anti-Japanese base area on behalf of the CPC. Initially, he lived in Zhufan village, Linshu county, later moving to Dashu village, Ganyu county. The Shandong branch assigned Gu Mu to accompany Liu Shaoqi.

Comrade Liu Shaoqi in Binhai

Liu Shaoqi's home in Dashu village, Ganyu county in the former Binhai base area. It has since been converted into a memorial building

At that time, comrade Liu Shaoqi appeared to be thin and weak, and frequently coughed while speaking. Gu Mu advised him to rest for a couple of days. Comrade Shaoqi replied: "Is this the right time for me to take a rest, considering the current situation and work status?" He continued to engage in intensive work without a pause.

After initial investigation and research, comrade Shaoqi formed his own opinion on the ineffective work that had been carried out in reducing rents and interest rates in Shandong base area. He thought that strengthening the implementation of policies to reduce rent and interest rates and improving the welfare of employees could fully mobilise the masses, thereby fully galvanising the nationwide war of resistance against Japanese aggression.

Gu Mu reported Liu Shaoqi's research report to the Shandong branch. Leaders and comrades of the branch absorbed Liu Shaoqi's instructions earnestly, and realised the significant connection between rent and interest rate reduction and the mass anti-Japanese movement, thereby improving awareness about the rent and interest rate reduction and the urgent need to implement it. On 25 April, the Shandong branch convened an expanded cadre meeting in Jiaolong bay, Linshu county, and approved the *Decision on Reducing Rent and Interest Rates, Improving Employee Welfare and Carrying out the Mass Movement*. In addition, the Shandong branch established Linshu and Lünan counties as pilots for 'double reductions', and drew more than 200 cadres from the leading party, political and military institutions and from the first branch campus of the Chinese People's Anti-Japanese Military and Political College. Split into two working groups, they left for Linshu and Lünan to pilot 'double reductions' and increased wages.

Gu Mu with his wife, Mou Feng, cradling their son, Liu Nianyuan, in her arms, 1944

In the process of implementing these 'double reductions', Gu Mu often accompanied Liu Shaoqi to conduct detailed surveys and guidance in villages located in Daxing, Dongpan, Xiazhuang and Jiaolong in Linshu county. In the process of this work, especially in helping the work group in Daxing to conduct surveys, Gu Mu made constructive suggestions on implementing 'double reductions' based on the actual situation in Linshu, which comrade Shaoqi acknowledged and approved. As a result, the 'double reductions' working group in Linshu decided to adopt an approach of breaking through in key areas. In particular, in Daxing district, they took the villages of Yandianguanzhuang, Daxing, Wangzhaizi and Beichen as the central task, and promoted the implementation of 'double reductions' in surrounding villages.

At the very beginning, the masses were sceptical about implementing 'double reductions', as they were afraid to incur the wrath of landlords. With keen insight, Gu Mu sensed this point. So he and Yuan Chenglong, leader of the work group, assigned staff to visit and communicate with poor peasants, tenant peasants and farm labourers. They told the masses that rent and interest rate reduction was a central task of the people's government. They also assured them that landlords and local tyrants would not be able to overturn the measure so long as the government existed. Working groups adopted further measures while the circumstances were favourable. On 3 July, a memorial meeting was held in Yandianguanzhuang to mourn victims of the masses who had been killed in 1938 by the KMT's Liang Zhongting, former head of Tancheng county. The Shandong branch, Binhai prefectural party committee, Linshu county party committee and leading institutions at all levels sent staff to attend the meeting, with more than 3,000 people from 44 villages in Daxing in attendance. Liu Baitao, the head of the county, delivered a speech. Three murderers who had sabotaged 'double reductions' were executed on the spot, and a reinforcement of the self-defence regiment was announced to guard the achievements of 'double reductions'. Afterwards, Daxing district held a grand parade of the self-defence regiment consisting of more than 2,700 militia. The second instruction brigade gave the conference three rifles and more than 30 grenades. These two meetings had a huge impact in suppressing arrogant feudal forces, highly motivating the masses and accelerating the implementation of 'double reductions' and higher wages. After hearing the work group's report, Zhu Rui, secretary of the Shandong branch, fully acknowledged the 'double reductions' of Daxing district. In late June 1942, the Shandong branch and Binhai prefectural party committee held a cadre meeting in Dongpan village, Linshu county to roll out more 'double reductions'. The focus of the meeting was to elaborate on the experiences of 'double reductions' pilot schemes.

The extensive implementation of rent and interest rate reduction widely improved people's lives. It also strengthened the organisation of the masses, reaffirmed the basic superiority of the masses and promoted construction of the party, political power, cadres and the army.

Comrade Shaoqi seriously criticised the Shandong United Front for rightist mistakes made during their work. At that time, in order to commemorate the first anniversary of the establishment of the 'Shandong self-defence and anti-Japanese force', Gu Mu had been ordered to make a speech at the meeting, and he asked comrade Shaoqi for further instructions. Unexpectedly, Liu Shaoqi became furious on several occasions, and Gu Mu was confused about his attitude. Later, he realised that comrade Shaoqi was against establishing this army. It was correct for the Shandong branch to adopt unified collaboration policies towards the 'Association of Shandong anti-Japanese comrades', which consisted of KMT members who were willing to fight

Luo Ronghuan and his wife, Lin Yueqin, in Shandong anti-Japanese base area

against the Japanese army, noted public figures and organisations of enlightened gentry. However, they were neither KMT soldiers nor armed forces. Enlisting these people and forming a new 'third party' army would create a heavy burden, and it was a clear example of a rightist mistake. Comrade Shaoqi dealt with this issue in person.

During his stay in Shandong, Liu Shaoqi directed the Shandong branch to publish *Resolution Summarising the Party's Work in Shandong over the Last Four Years During the Anti-Japanese War and Future Tasks*. This was followed by significant reports, such as *On Work in Shandong, The Mass Movement Issue, Strategy and Tactics of China's Revolution, Problems of Inner-Party Struggle, The Issue of Ideological Method* and *The Issue of*

After comrade Zhu Rui was transferred back to Yan'an, work of the party and the military (including the 115th division and Shandong military region) of Shandong were both under the command of comrade Luo Ronghuan. The former site (Beikuo, Rizhao) of the military work conference that determined this unified leadership has since been converted into a memorial building, and the name was inscribed by Chi Haotian. The courtyard and homes of Luo Ronghuan, Xiao Hua and other leaders were all provided by Mou Feng along with her family and relatives. In the eyes of the Japanese and traitors to China, this family was an 'eighth route nest'. (They bombarded this place, during which Xiao Hua managed to survive because he was outside enjoying the cool air. However, an elder member of the family was killed in the bombardment.) After their children joined the revolution, the family was much more like an 'eighth route nest'

Finance and Food Supplies. Regarding the ongoing expansion of an anti-Trotsky group that emerged in Huxi, Liu Shaoqi pointed out that unjust cases would be redressed immediately, mistakenly killed comrades would be subsequently reclassified as martyrs, relatives involved would be compensated, innocent comrades in custody would be released right away, and comrades who had left the army voluntarily would be reinstated and reassigned jobs.

In late July, comrade Shaoqi gave a speech in a cadres' meeting before he left Binhai. "Now is a critical moment for our work in Shandong," he said. "If you still insist on your old ways, I will give you a plaque in two years, highlighting two words: 'rightist opportunism'. In light of our fierce struggle against the enemy here in Shandong, we would suffer a serious setback if we emphasised that 'everything is subject to the united front' instead of focusing on construction of the party and the base area, and fighting the enemy."

In 1943, Zhu Rui was transferred back to Yan'an, and Luo Ronghuan assumed the position of secretary of the Shandong branch, presiding over all party, military and political work. He resolutely implemented the anti-rightist direction given by comrade Shaoqi. In the meantime, he also paid attention to prevent 'leftist' mistakes. For instance, after personally conducting the rectification campaign for a while, Luo Ronghuan reported to the CPC: "In circumstances where enemy-occupied areas are rampant, I suggest we temporarily put 'internal operations' aside." This was approved by his superiors. Gu Mu wrote about Luo's rectification

When Luo Ronghuan and Xiao Hua lived in Beikuo, Rizhao, encouraged by Gu Mu and Mou Feng, all of their landlords' six daughters joined the revolution. Here are five of the six Mou family sisters, in Shanghai, 1973. From right to left: Mou Dunhe (the fourth eldest sister), Mou Dunxiu (the fifth eldest), Mou Yanyu (the eldest), Mou Dunli (the youngest), and Mou Jian (also known as Mou Dunying, the second eldest)

campaign in his memoirs: "It not only improved cadres' ideological and political level, but also strengthened revolutionary solidarity from an organisational perspective. It made great achievements with almost no harmful consequences." In the days that he was following Luo Ronghuan, Gu Mu learned a lot. Having deep feelings and thoughts, he once said: "Comrade Luo Ronghuan adhered to the principle of proceeding from reality in everything, and insisted on the principle of seeking truth from facts. He is always my role model."

Chapter 14

In the Midst of Battle, Welcoming Victory in the War Against Japan

In the last year of the war of resistance, Gu Mu served as party secretary for the second prefecture in Binhai and political commissar of the military sub-district. The second prefecture lay in the southern part of the Binhai area, or Binnan, and so the committee Gu Mu served was called the Binnan local party committee.

Gu Mu volunteered to work at the grassroots level in 1944. His superior assigned him to be deputy secretary of Lunan district in October 1944, and he was then transferred to be secretary of Binhai second prefectural committee and political commissar of the military sub-district. Here, Gu Mu sits with comrade Zhou Yun at the edge of the River Shu in Binhai. Comrade Zhou sacrificed his life within six months of this photo being taken

In October 1944, shortly after Gu Mu took up his posts, his military sub-district, on instructions from higher command, carried out a large-scale military training exercise. In mid-November, it began an operation to retake areas that the enemy had been taking incrementally. The operation got underway smoothly, capturing Japanese puppet force strongholds in Linshanpu, Jiacang and Zhonggong. From there, it was possible to link up with main force units to take the county capital of Juxian. There, the head of the local 'peace preservation forces' under the Japanese, Mo Zhengmin, led an uprising of 3,000 people, arrested Yu Jingwu, a despotic landlord and head of the armed Wanxian society,[1] who had switched allegiance to the Japanese.

In May of the following year, Japanese forces launched a 'cleansing operation' against anti-Japanese base areas in Shandong, brutally advancing toward Jiaodong, Luzhong and Binhai. The Japanese deployed 100,000 troops in the campaign, and committed aircraft and military vessels for a combined 'land, sea and air' operation. Bursting with confidence, they advanced from the coast almost 20km in the direction of the threatened base areas. Units of the Eighth Route Army main force, with additional local units, bravely gave battle, attacking the enemy in a mobile and flexible manner. Masses of local militia added to the lethal assaults on the enemy. With the support of the populace, the struggle against the Japanese cleansing operation was finally victorious. By the end of May 1945, the Binhai district alone had captured a total of 140 Japanese army locations, large and small, and had wiped out 5,000 Japanese troops, including an Imperial Army brigade commander.

Gu Mu in 1945, the year of victory in the anti-Japanese war

In the Midst of Battle, Welcoming Victory in the War Against Japan

While the struggle against the Japanese cleansing operation was underway, Gu Mu was marching with the mobile command headquarters. He listened regularly to radio transmissions on his five-tube radio, and learned of current developments both worldwide and in the larger war within China. Soon, good news arrived. The Americans were engaging Japan heavily in the Pacific, Soviet Red Army forces were approaching Berlin, the Germans had surrendered – everyone hearing the news was overjoyed, realising that the final demolition of Japanese fascism could not be far off. On 5 August, Gu Mu made a report to his combined units on mobilisation efforts, saying: "The puppet forces have resigned themselves to the failure of their May 'cleansing operation', but they will still put up a last-ditch effort. From now on, our battles will be even more ferocious, on an even larger scale than the 'cleansing operation' and our struggles against it. All of us, civilians and military alike, must be courageous in the face of sacrifice, maintain our spirit of waging a final battle for a final victory, and smash an even larger-scale Japanese 'cleansing operation'.

Ma Bangcai (1926-1988), a militiaman from Mazhuang village, Caozhuang town, Linshu county in Binnan region, with his distinguished war record, was named 'the explosion hero' by Binhai military region in 1944. He was also awarded the title of 'militia hero' by Shandong military region

But events were moving even more rapidly than people's expectations. On 15 August, the emperor of Japan proclaimed his nation's unconditional surrender. The news was greeted with wild celebration when it reached Shandong. Colourful lanterns were lit everywhere, while dancing dragons and lions opened widespread celebrations. But some comrades remembered Gu Mu's words of 5 August, and turned to him now: "Commissar Gu, when do we begin the next battle against the Japanese 'cleansing campaign'?"

Gu Mu replied: "Well, I admit that I miscalculated the bigger military picture. But luckily my mistake didn't harm our work!"

"You said it! Let's hope you make more mistakes like this in future," they shouted back, laughing.

Chapter 15

Face to Face Alone with Hao Pengju

On 19 September 1945, Luo Ronghuan led 60,000 Shandong main force troops to the northeast, by sea and by land. Before this, Lü Zhengcao's units and the forces of Wan Yi and Zhang Xuesi had been pushing forward toward the northeast, announcing that they wanted to advance alongside Luo's forces.

Luo Ronghuan said: "I have thought about taking you to the northeast with us, but I believe that battle conditions here in Shandong are likely to be even more bitter, and we need to leave behind some of our core units. You have been working in Shandong for many years; you know the local situation. So I have decided that you must remain here."

By April 1946, Gu Mu had been named secretary general of the east China region. In the east China bureau, he had many opportunities to discuss the economic work going on in Shandong. For example, the founder of Beihai Bank, who had fled to his home district after the Japanese occupation of Qingdao, contacted the general manager of Zhonglu Bank, Zhang Yutian, to see if they could combine their organisations to form a new, jointly managed operation. Some comrades, blinkered by 'leftist' habits of thought, considered the plan absolutely unimaginable.

Gu Mu was keen to discuss what he had learned from his broad experiences in Shandong, but he understood that senior leaders in the New Fourth Army who had authority over local reconstruction and economic work might be sensitive about hearing his ideas. Gu Mu had been given his orders by the general political commissar, Luo Ronghuan, and he was eager to spread the lessons learned during his economic work in the base areas more widely. Nevertheless, he knew that moving too quickly was ill-advised. Among his peers in the east China bureau, the leader Gu Mu respected most was Comrade Chen Yi, known for his quick tongue and broadmindedness.

Gu Mu was named secretary general of the east China region in April 1946

In mid-June, Gu Mu asked Chen Yi to reassign him back to Binhai, but to take on even heavier military responsibilities. Chen Yi replied: "Who's going to take over your duties here as secretary general?" Gu Mu had an answer for that: "I've already discussed this with comrade Wei Wenbo [the head of the civilian transport department] and he's ready to take on two posts at once." Chen Yi said with a laugh: "You have come well prepared! All right, we can look into it." By July, Gu Mu had become the party secretary and district military commander, reporting directly to the east China bureau.

In January, 1947, the east China field armies' main forces scored a major victory in southern Shandong. Some 300,000 KMT troops, arriving both from the north and the south, had overrun the base area at Yimeng. At this critical moment, the Hao Pengju uprising occurred.

Gu Mu referred to Hao Pengju as "the shameless dragon of ever-changing colour". Hao had been the head of so-called 'Huaihai province' under Japanese occupation. After the Japanese army surrendered, Hao first committed himself to the KMT, but was soon dissatisfied; in January 1946, he brought his forces over to the New Fourth Army. After Gu Mu took up his position in Binhai, Chen Yi left it to Gu to manage the relationship with Hao. Seeing that the situation did not seem to favour the communists, Hao again secretly made contact with KMT military headquarters at Xuzhou.

Li Guodong, who had been Hao Pengju's logistics chief, was at a cadre training facility in the town of Zibo in Shandong, when he received a visit from Zhang Yaping, the head of the Lianyungang Revolution Commemorative Hall. Li said to Zhang: "Under our chiefs Secretary Gu Mu and Liu Baitao, our basic task right now is not to make any concessions to Hao Pengju. Once, one of his reactionary subordinates took me into custody. I decided to seek Hao out and talk sense to him. He admitted he was in the wrong, and finally had that officer shot. I again told him to make a full report of his actions."

In January 1947, in an effort to take care of the Hao Pengju matter once and for all, Gu Mu accepted Hao's invitation to a one-on-one meeting. Just before leaving for the meeting, he said: "If I don't return tomorrow, it means that Hao Pengju is definitely in rebellion. Report to Chen Yi, and annihilate Hao."

A photo taken in 2010 of Li Meilin, Gu Mu's guard for many years in the early part of the liberation war. He told the story of Gu Mu's brave decision to meet Hao Pengju alone. Li's son, Li Shuai, provided papers to the 'seminar on Comrade Gu Mu's struggle in Binhai revolutionary base area and the discussion forum on the theory of reform and opening up' (Lianyungang)

Gu Mu went to Hao's headquarters in the village of Xuban, Zhuting county, with three of his guards. As soon as he stepped inside, he sensed a pregnant stillness in the air. Hao welcomed Gu Mu with a hot pot feast, posting sword-bearing guards on either side of him. Sensing danger, Gu's own guards stood close behind him.

The hotpot bubbled and gurgled, and the room grew steamy. A pungent odour filled the air. A huge dog wandered in and out, opening its jaws and letting its tongue loll by Gu Mu's side. Li Meilin sent it off with a kick. Just as it was about to attack Li, Gu Mu deftly tossed it a piece of mutton, saying: "This might not fill you up, but you should stick with whoever feeds you." Gu Mu's light remark delivered a stern message. Hao Pengju ordered his guards to lead the dog away.

Gu Mu spoke plainly to Hao. "Chen Yi and you have an agreement to allow you to come and go as you wish. You have come to Binhai in grand style. If you want to leave, you'd leave in an above-board way. If I were you, I would think in the long term."

When the grand banquet had ended peacefully, Hao took Gu Mu out for a stroll along the dikes surrounding his ponds. Their guards kept a keen eye on them from a close distance. Hao's guards carried big swords and daggers, visible for all to see, looking murderous, as though they were about to grab a criminal. Gu Mu had noticed Commissar Zhu Kejing, and others whom he had dispatched to Hao's headquarters. Gu said: "Better take care: Hao wants to flee. We might be able to physically keep him here, but his heart wouldn't be in it. He can't get out of our Binhai, and Chen Yi wouldn't agree to that anyway. Take the necessary security measures to be ready for any sudden, violent incident."

On the night of 26 January, Hao Pengju raised his rebellion. Chen Yi received Gu Mu's telegram and sent two companies of his field army to join the First Regiment of troops from Binhai military district, who annihilated Hao's troops and two of his generals. Hao Pengju was taken alive.

Chapter 16

Suppressing Chaotic Struggle, Beating and Killing During Land Reform

On 4 May 1946, the CPC's central headquarters published *Instructions from Party Centre on the Question of Land Reform*. This famous document came to be known as the *4 May Instructions*. That July, after arriving in Binhai, Gu Mu quickly set about making careful arrangements to carry out the instructions. From his experience working with Liu Shaoqi in Linshu, Shandong province, to reduce land rents and interest rates, Gu Mu felt confident that he could implement the land reform mandate peacefully, in a step-by-step fashion. He decided that, in accordance with the differing conditions in the various counties that made up Binhai region, after a period of struggle aimed at 'investigating landownership and reducing rents', land redistribution in the old district would be fundamentally completed, and the inherited problems of land ownership would give way to the new challenges of maximising production. In the newly liberated areas, on the other hand, it was going to be necessary to harness all powers to motivate the masses to carry out land reform. In those contested civil war border zones, in order to proceed with land reform in the midst of armed conflict, the watchword would be: 'A gun in one hand, an abacus in the other.'

By the end of October, 84% of villages in the district had completed land reform and some 280 square kilometres of land had been redistributed to nearly 53,000 poor peasant households. The peasants, their lives transformed, hailed their improved fortunes. In a fervent movement of 'opposing Chiang Kai-shek and protecting our lands', 16,000 village youths joined the communist armies.

But because all this took place so quickly, the assault on the forces of feudalism could not be comprehensive. Not all of the land redistribution carried out by means of forcible 'struggle' against landlords was completely rational. In some places, bands of armed men connected to local landlords, calling themselves 'return our countryside units', viciously counterattacked. More than a few evil landowners and rural bosses plotted to 'overturn the heavens', restoring the old land deeds, assailing the new land calculations, and even killing land reform activists, village cadres and others working for land reform. By early 1947, another round of investigations of landlords and land ownership had begun. The *21 February Instruction* from the east China bureau, while affirming the achievements of the land reform campaign to date, nevertheless pointed out the mischaracterisation of certain weak points in the campaign as 'rich peasant deviationism'. Soon after, in the *7 July Instructions*, the party pointed out: "In carrying out the clearing of accounts, re-investigating the distribution of land, and readjusting or reassigning land rights, proceed to take action only after the voices of the 'poor peasant small groups' that we have organised are heard, and then only after the peasant associations have held their discussions and approved. No other organisations' permission is needed." It went on to state: "In the process of land reform, we must rebuild the party, reconstruct the cadres, reform our work style and reform all other party organisations." These instructions allowed 'leftist' errors that had already appeared during the first half of 1947, as land reform had proceeded with the second 'investigation of land titles', to become even more serious. In area after area, land reform discarded the leadership of the party, returning all powers to the peasant association, and making the most destitute peasants and tenant farmers the masters of all that went on, even including random beatings, random killings and random expulsions of entire families. This actually damaged the spirit of activism among the masses.

One day towards the end of July, Gu Mu travelled incognito to the village of Zhumei in Junan county to have a look around. He discovered that the misdeeds of the landlord who had been beaten to death had not merited his killing; actually, a small number of village cadres and 'activists' had feared that land reform might be reversed, with catastrophic consequences. To Gu Mu's way of thinking, this was a case of incomplete motivation of the masses, because policies had not been clearly conveyed and land reform tasks had not been carried out with sufficient attention to detail. Because of this, land reform had simply lost contact with the vast majority of the people, and had fallen into the trap of focusing only on poor peasants and tenant farmers. When he got back, the local party committee urgently sent a message to all counties and districts to stop that kind of behaviour immediately. In August, the clear message went out: "Letting the peasants manage their own affairs does not mean ignoring the leadership of the party." The orders continued: "Correct the practice of 'sweeping everything out the door at one stroke', indiscriminately lumping all landlords together without distinguishing 'great' from 'petty' landlords or 'ordinary landlords' from 'evil strongmen'."

In September, he issued a severe order regarding the manner of judging landlords and evil strongmen. In October, he demanded the thorough correction of the error committed by a few rural cadres of killing landlords at their whim. In December, the power of execution was taken away from the counties and returned to the higher district level, with the solemn warning that "those who make the error of killing people will pay a severe price". After much hard effort, the problems that had emerged during land reform in Binhai were rectified in good time.

Chapter 17

Chen Yi Assigns Top Talent to Support the Battle Front

During the war of liberation, all manner of local work was subordinate to the task of supporting the fighting fronts. Everything was for the front, and everything was for victory.

In early 1947, when Chen Yi passed through Binhai while directing the military campaign in southern Shandong, he assigned special tasks to Gu Mu. He said: "The war in Shandong is widening. The work in the rear areas to support the fighting front must keep pace, making sure that when we need soldiers we have soldiers, when we need food we have food, when we need

Chen Yi, field army commander of east China, and the deputy commander, Su Yu

labourers we have labourers, when we need stretchers we have stretchers. Fulfilling these tasks must start in Binhai. Central and southern Shandong have seen much war for many years and have suffered great destruction; it will be hard to find additional manpower or material assistance for the front lines from there."

Gu Mu replied: "We will resolutely carry out Leader Chen Yi's orders." Chen Yi said with the hint of a smile: "In the army, there are no jokes. If the front line fights badly, my head is on the line. If the work of supporting the front lines is done badly, your head is on the line, Gu Mu!" Gu Mu replied with a smile: "Take comfort, Leader Chen; we will certainly perform our part well. That's all there is to it: we will completely carry out our tasks."

Gu Mu with some of his comrades during the war of liberation in Dadian, Binhai, in March 1946. Dadian was the headquarters of the 115th division of the Eighth Route Army. Third from the left is Liu Baitao, Binhai's deputy commissioner who would later become commissioner; second from the right is Zheng Zijiu, who served as party committee secretary in Rizhao and Hailing counties, independent regiment political commissar of Hailing county, and prefectural party committee secretary of Binhai

Chen Yi Assigns Top Talent to Support the Battle Front

Gu Mu and Su Yu, July 1946

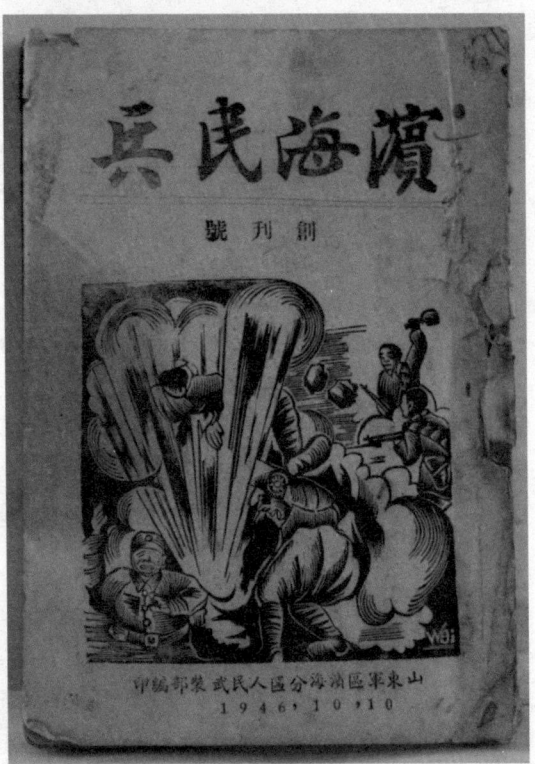

The first issue of *Binhai Militia* in Binhai liberated area

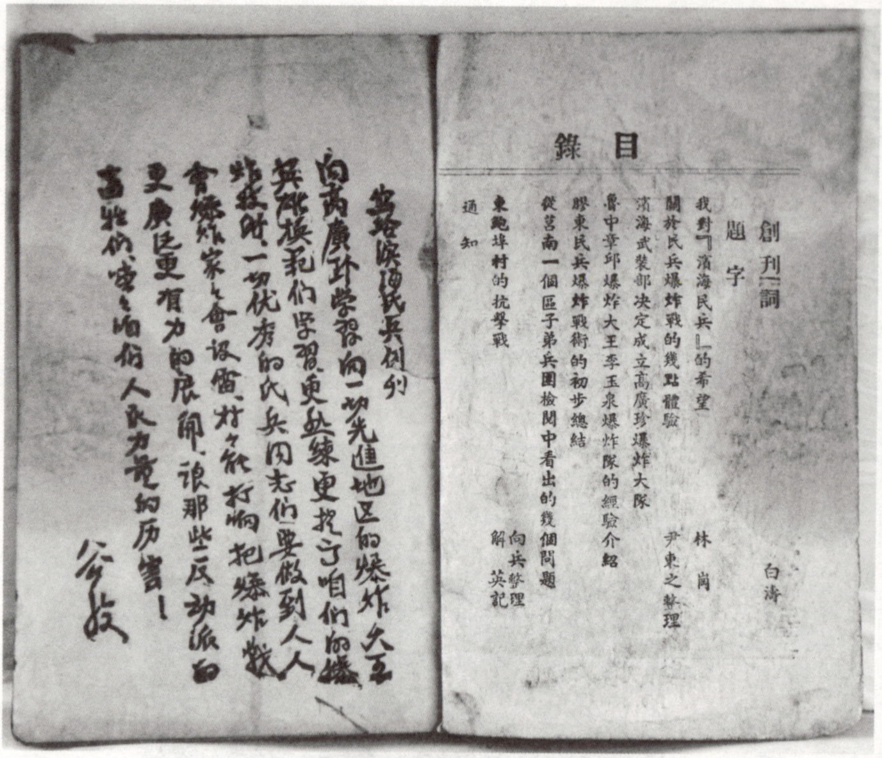

为滨海民兵创刊

向高广珍学习 向一切先进地区的爆炸大王英雄模范们学习，更熟练更提高咱们的爆炸技术，一切优秀的民兵同志们要做到人人会爆炸，家家会设备，村村能打响，把爆炸战更广泛更有力的展开，让那些反动派的畜牲们，尝尝咱们人民力量的厉害！

谷牧

目錄

創刊詞 白濤
題字
我對「濱海民兵」的希望 林岗
關於民兵爆炸戰的幾點體驗 尹東之整理
濱海武裝部決定成立高廣珍爆炸大隊
魯中章邱爆炸大王李玉泉爆炸隊的經驗介紹
膠東民兵爆炸戰術的初步總結
從莒南一個區子弟兵團檢閱中看出的幾個問題 向兵整理
東鮑埠村的抗擊戰 解英記
通知

Gu Mu's inscription and the contents page of the launch issue of *Binhai Militia*

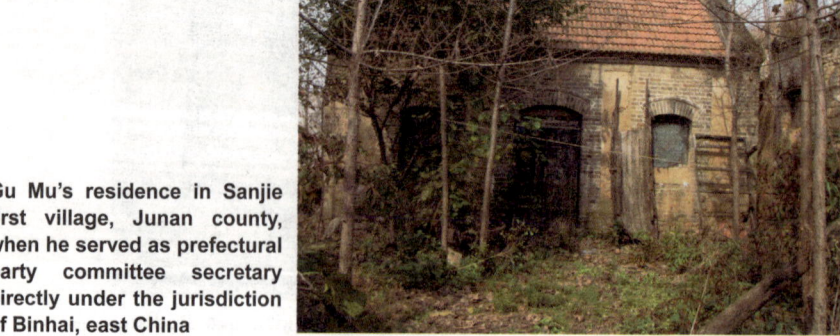

Gu Mu's residence in Sanjie first village, Junan county, when he served as prefectural party committee secretary directly under the jurisdiction of Binhai, east China

Chen Yi Assigns Top Talent to Support the Battle Front

Gu Mu with Fu Qiutao, Li Leping, Zhang Guangzhong, Zhao Zhao and Xie Hui in 1947. A note handwritten by Gu in his later years can be seen on the right of this photo

The district party committee, on Chen Yi's orders, created the Binhai commission for supporting the front lines, later called the front line support command, under the leadership of Xie Hui. The deputy secretary of the district party committee, Sun Hanqing, became the political commissar. The frontline support command in turn set up an organisation department, and units handling materials, transport, publicity and education, as well as a special district transport brigade for military grain, with four sub-units, mobilising approximately 20,000 civilian workers, 17,000 small carts and more than 1,600 shoulder poles for transporting supplies. Each county and district had its own unit for dealing with the tasks of supporting the front. Efforts were organised under a 'civilian labour system' with battalions, companies, platoons and squads forming a civilian labour force that allotted stretchers, small carts, shoulder poles and so forth so they could be deployed easily whenever needed.

From late 1946 to March 1947, Binhai district's support of the Subei campaign, the central Shandong campaign and the Laiwu campaign, mobilised more than 533,000 civilian labourers, transported 14,000 tonnes of grain and produced 700 tonnes of pancakes. The populace contributed 23 tonnes of vegetables, fish, dough, peanuts and soybeans.

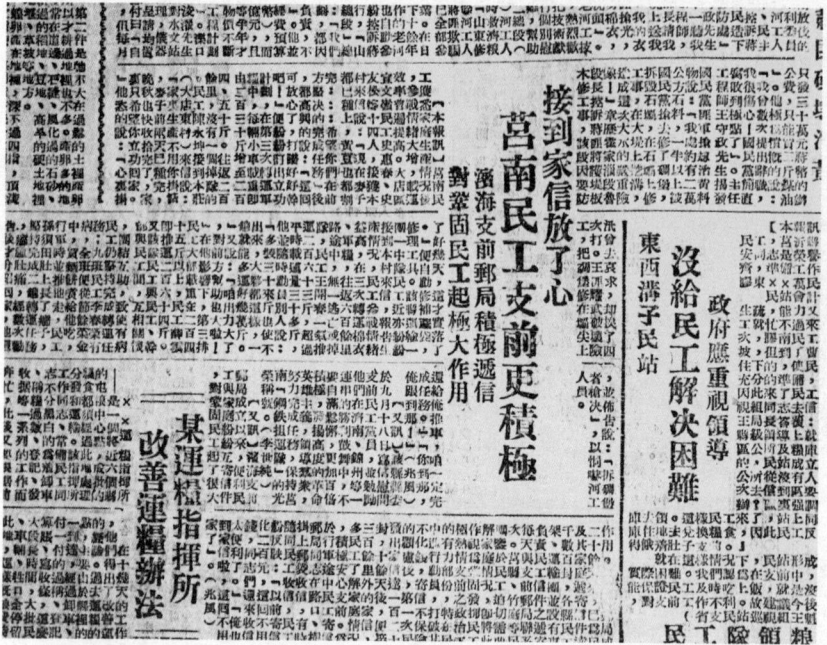

A report on Binhai's support work for the front line appeared in *The Masses Daily* on 6 November 1948

During the battle to relieve Mengliangu, Binhai district mobilised approximately 100,000 men to carry out civilian war tasks.

During the Huaihai campaign, Binhai mobilised 570,000 people, provided 18,500 tonnes of processed grain, transported 17,500 tonnes of grain, produced 600,000 pairs of military footwear, sewed 200,000 flour bags, maintained nearly 1,800km of roads, and carried out hurried repairs on 194 bridges.

The three-year war of liberation was a victorious conflict that depended on the utmost civilian support for the fighters on the front lines. It was thus also a war in which the people sought and gained their own liberation.

Chapter 18

The Story Behind a Rare 66-year-old Portrait of Chairman Mao

The great Huaihai campaign started on 6 November 1948. At dawn, the KMT's 44th division, which had been holding Haizhou district, released its grip and began to withdraw to the west. Forces from the Binhai liberated area in Shandong and the Huaihai liberated area in Jiangsu joined in attacking the enemy.

The commander of the KMT's 44th division, Yang Buren, was a particularly villainous traitor. Originally called Wang Hongming, he was a cadre at regiment level in the Eighth Route Army. He was the worst of the group involved in the elimination of counterrevolutionaries in Huxi in 1939, responsible for the deaths of more than 300 cadres from Jiangsu, Shandong and Anhui. Then he fled, aware of the gravity of the crimes for which he was responsible. In August 1941, in Binhai, he rebelled and went over to the Japanese, becoming head of a Japanese commando squad in Xinpu. That was when he changed his name to Yang Buren. He did a great deal of harm to communist forces and bases.

Once the war was over, Yang Buren changed sides again, joining up with the KMT. In the spring of 1947, holding the rank of major general, he escaped to the area around Haizhou, Donghai and Ganyu, hooking up with his old forces and recruiting army deserters to launch an assault. The forces of Haibin military subdistrict launched an assault on Yang Buren's bases at Xiakou, Wangdongsha and Dingzhuangzi on 12 October 1947, annihilating the first battalion of Yang's troops. By 1948, Yang Buren had moved to the KMT's 9th pacification area, commanded by Li Yannian, and then went on to become commander of the 44th division in Haizhou district. He treacherously poisoned the minds of the people, constantly vilifying the Communist Party and conducting all sorts of false publicity campaigns.

By the time the 44th division withdrew to the west, Yang Buren had managed to attract many students from the Donghai normal school and several enemy secret agents, with whom to continue his destructive activities.

As Yang Buren moved west on 6 November, armed clashes flared in Xinpu and Lianyungang. Enemy agents fanned the flames; hundreds of people joined in a rampage of looting of army and administrative offices and granaries. The looting escalated to attacks on roadside stores, warehouses and homes. In the midst of this unprecedented outburst of looting and chaos, even the provincial Donghai normal school was not spared.

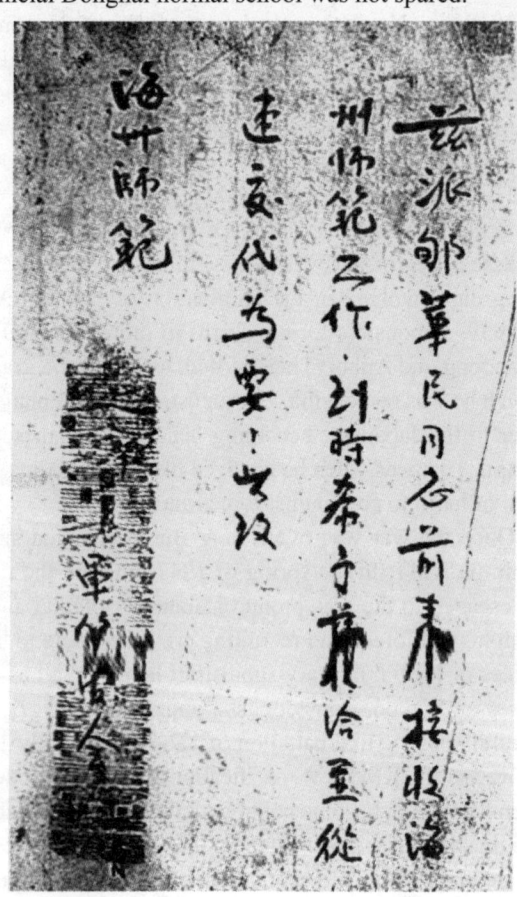

Gu personally wrote a letter of introduction for Xun Huamin to take control of the school

The Story Behind a Rare 66-year-old Portrait of Chairman Mao

By 7 November, the PLA had taken control of an area encompassing Xinpu, Haizhou and Lianyungang. Gu Mu received the order to prepare to take governing control of the entire area. To assemble personnel for the job, he specially ordered Liu Baitao, a prefectural commissioner in Binhai district, to bring Xun Huamin, who had been heading Binhai middle school in Ganyu, to report to him. The two men talked through the night. On 8 November, when Gu Mu assumed his duties in charge of the Xinpu-Haizhou-Lianyungang (Xin-Hai-Lian) region, Xun Huamin joined him in the lead vehicle in the motorcade. Gu Mu knew that Xun Huamin was a veteran party cadre from revolutionary times, and a graduate of Donghai normal school. Gu Mu put Xun in charge of Donghai normal school, and assigned him responsibility for getting students of the college back into their classrooms without delay.

The East Asia hostel in Xinpu, where the administrative organs of the Xin-Hai-Lian area were based

Gu Mu, when he served as secretary of the Xin-Hai-Lian special region committee, also held the post of political commissar of garrison command

Once Gu had assumed his duties in Xinpu (at that moment, administrative organs of the Xin-Hai-Lian area were based in the East Asia hostel in Xinpu), he assigned two others to assist Xun Huamin. The first was Yang Zhuming, from Haizhou. Yang had earlier been a teacher in Binhai middle school; when Gu Mu gave him his new assignment, he was working as a deputy district director in Haizhou district. The other was Zhang Jiping, of Shuyang, a schoolmate of Xun Huamin then in charge of cultural education in the Xin-Hai-Lian special area.

Xun Huamin, Yang Zhuming and Zhang Jiping arrived at Donghai normal school and viewed the utter destruction of the old school; they were deeply saddened. All the windows in the administrative offices had been stolen. Inside, nothing remained – the tables, chairs and blackboards had been stolen or broken, while all boxes and cupboards were empty. But worst of all, there was no sign of any students. Hua and his comrades fretted miserably through the night. The next day, they reported to Gu Mu with their thoughts on rebuilding: the top priority was reconstructing the school building, temporarily relocating classes to the Confucius temple and recovering the school's lost property. The next task was to call on the

The Story Behind a Rare 66-year-old Portrait of Chairman Mao

Gu Mu with his mother and eldest son in Xinpu, 1948

teachers and encourage them to return to work. Third, through various channels, the students had to be drawn back to their studies. If there were not enough students, other upper middle schools could be combined with the normal school. The fourth task was to request the cultural affairs office of the district party committee to transfer a number of mid-level cadres from Binhai middle school to the normal school. And finally, they called for the fastest possible announcement of a call to enrol new students.

The next day, 9 November, the establishment of the Xin-Hai-Lian special district military control commission was formally announced. Three days later, all schools in the cities published a call for students to return to school. And on 14 November, Xun Huamin was declared the new head of Donghai normal school.

Gu Mu paid great attention to conditions in Xin-Hai-Lian special area. In his memoirs, he wrote in detail about the problems encountered when he first entered the area, and the measures he undertook to deal with them: eliminating armed banditry and protecting social order; restoring road, water and rail transportation; restoring mine production; securing water and electricity supplies, currency and finance, distributing land among the peasants, agricultural production, emergency and disaster relief, supporting fighters on the front lines, and handling his military administration duties by day and by night. Not only for the party, but for every person, this was a new beginning. To arrive at this starting point involved the sacrifice of many people. Today, we must consider longer-term, larger and more important questions, such as education.

Jiangsu Provincial Donghai normal school traced its origins to Haizhou in 1802, where its first predecessor was the Shishi academy. In 1906, after the elimination of the imperial examination system, this traditional Confucian academy was reorganised as Haizhou middle school, later becoming Jiangsu No. 11 middle school. After that, it became the District Donghai middle school and normal school, part of Jiangsu University district, and then changed its name to the North Jiangsu No. 2 normal school. It was the highest-level education institution in the Xin-Hai-Lian area. It produced many talents over the years, including the early champion of 'industrialisation for national salvation', Shen Yunpei, educators Jiang Wenyu, Dong Huai, Zhu Zhixian and Liu Baichuan, the painters Zhu Dequn and Yan Han, revolutionaries Chen Weida and Hui Yuyu. As Gu Mu saw it, the rapid reopening of the schools, the recovery of confidence among teachers, the peaceful resumption of classes and the image of students quietly seated at their desks reading and listening to their teachers represented more than just a restoration of order and proper procedures; it was symbolically important in determining the success or failure of the party's efforts to govern the cities it had taken. It was absolutely necessary that Donghai normal school raise its banner again!

Xun Huamin and his two partners did not disappoint Gu Mu's expectations. They immediately set to work by stimulating student activists to action, reaching out to those students who had scattered to the four winds to bring them back to school and recovering lost school property. They mobilised students from Donghai No. 2 middle school, Lede middle school and the National Lianyun No. 21 middle school to come to Donghai normal school and attend classes. The education and cultural bureau at the provincial level transferred a number of teachers and advanced students from Binhai middle school. Donghai normal school quickly put together a party small group under Xun Huamin. The tasks of rebuilding were quickly accomplished, and fully fleshed out. When Xun Huamin made his reports to Gu Mu, realistically reviewing the work of "restoring the school and restoring the students", Gu Mu instructed him: "This is pretty much what I expected. Do not be disheartened – it is even more important not to let up in your efforts. Continue your work with even greater attention to detail and persuasiveness. Take 'thought work' straight into the hearts of the young students." As for the teachers and students who had fled west or south, Gu Mu said: "They are like floating duckweed in a rain storm. In reality, they have lost the ability to control their own destinies. Their biggest hope is that this reborn school can now extend a helping hand to them, helping them to escape from the hardships and misfortunes of their lives." He said firmly: "To do this work well, it must be of assistance to the armies. The party committee of our Xin-Hai-Lian special region can work in liaison with the armies, helping you to do your work well. Donghai normal school has to work actively on liaison with the armies to the south. With a lot of hard work, the students will trickle back to school." After Gu Mu paid prompt tribute to the achievements of Xun Huamin and his team, he discussed the students who were still fearful of the Communist Party and uncertain about making a commitment. "Do not be too harsh on them. Give them travel money and travel passes, and let them make up their own minds. That way, in the end, many students will be able to separate fact from fiction, and they will return to school."

Late in November, all the preparatory work for the reopening of Donghai normal school was finished. On 25 November, the military administration decided that the new school would formally reopen for classes. On that date, Gu Mu called Xun Huamin and Zhang Jiping to his office. He made clear that he fully appreciated their hard work. He said: "School is going to reopen tomorrow. This is a big day for education in our Xin-Hai-Lian area, and a big day for our entire special district." On that day, Gu Mu had to attend an important meeting at military district headquarters and was not able to join in the formal ceremonies celebrating the reopening of the school. He was filled with regret that he could not see Donghai's teachers and students with his own eyes, and made a special point later of visiting students and teachers at Donghai normal school on more than one occasion. Later on, he wrote, in his own hand, letters of appointment and letters of recommendation for Xun and Zhang. As he said to them: "Tomorrow, when those official letters of appointment that I wrote come into effect, will be a day to commemorate." And then he affixed the seal, reading 'Xin-Hai-Lian military control commission, East China South Central Shandong military district, Chinese People's Liberation Army'. Then, Gu Mu took a picture of Chairman Mao that he had brought with him from Shandong and had been hanging for a long time in his own office, and gave it to Donghai normal school's director Xun Huamin, with the solemn words: "In future, I look forward to seeing how you have managed this school."

The picture was a line drawing, sketched in pencil on yellowing paper with the words 'Chairman Mao Zedong'. Printed portraits of party leaders at that time were made by the renowned painter Liang Binghong[1] in Shandong in 1947 and were circulated widely from Shandong military district.

At this particular time, portraits of Chairman Mao of such high quality and originality were extremely precious. Xun Huamin profoundly understood the boundless hopes and trust that lay behind this portrait, and felt within himself the birth of a divine mission.

Ten days after its formal reopening, Donghai normal school moved out of its temporary quarters in the Confucian temple and returned to its original school building. Several days later, a jeep pulled up in front of the school. Gu Mu, dressed in grey military clothes, kept his word and came to have a personal look at the students and teachers. Principal Xun Huamin allowed a few advanced students, including Ge Weizhen and Luo Minggan, to act as Gu's guide. In front of a classroom, Secretary Gu looked at the students attending class and said quietly: "We should not get too close to the classrooms; speak softly, so as not to disturb anyone." When he arrived at the auditorium, he noticed the portrait of Chairman Mao that he had donated. He looked at the picture for a long time. Principal Xun said: "Chief, I hung the portrait of Chairman Mao that you gave me here in the auditorium, so that all the teachers and students might see it. I say with deep emotion: this is the beginning of an entirely new era. We will treasure this portrait and hand it down through the generations."

Chapter 19

Three Successive Reports Receive High Marks from Chairman Mao

In December 1948, the Xin-Hai-Lian special zone was created, with county-level subordinate offices in Xinhai and Lianyungang. Gu Mu served as party secretary and, at the same time, as political commissar for the so-called 'security sector'.

China's revolution had taken huge new turns. From the stage when the countryside had surrounded the cities to the new stage in which liberation forces took control of the cities themselves was an unprecedented and novel situation. Party central authorities constantly called for everyone to review what had happened and what lessons could be learned. For much of the year, Gu Mu set about personally making reports to higher party committees regarding conditions in Xin-Hai-Lian. In total, he sent four reports.

In April 1949, as a result of persuasion from underground party members, Liu Nongjun, the regimental commander of the third regiment of the KMT's paratroops, which was known as Chiang Kai-shek's 'bodyguard', led an uprising of his regiment. The troops sailed landing craft tank No. 102 to the coast of Lianyungang, using flags to signal their intention to switch allegiance before sending people ashore to make contact with the communists. Gu Mu helped them settle down and, later, he was appointed by the East China Field Army to help incorporate these troops into the army of the CPC. This is a report on the uprising in the 20 July 1949 edition of *Dazhong Daily*

On 12 February 1949, sailors on the KMT warship Huang'an staged an uprising in Qingdao. The troops arrived in Lianyungang on the following day. Following the uprising, the Huang'an made a great contribution in the battle of Yijiangshan island. Along with another warship, it sank the KMT destroyer Taiping and other vessels. After the establishment of the PLA Navy, the Huang'an was renamed the Shenyang. Gu Mu is pictured here with the Xin-Hai-Lian special committee in a meeting with the Huang'an mutineers

Gu Mu in Jinan, summer 1950

Gu Mu, in the early period of the founding of the New China

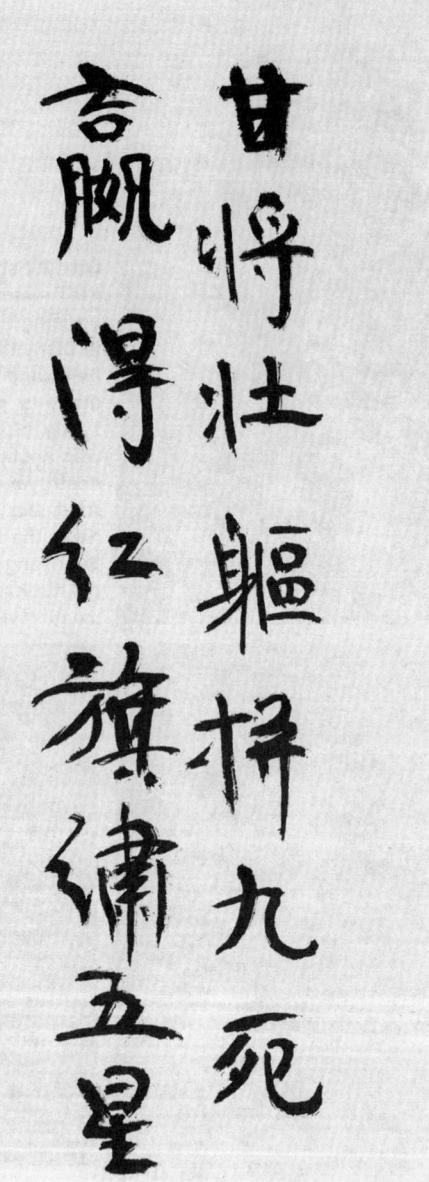

Gu Mu's calligraphy: "Willing to die nine times for the five stars on our national flag"

Three Successive Reports Receive High Marks from Chairman Mao

In these reports, Gu Mu rather bluntly stressed two points. First, as to the immediate tasks upon entry into the cities – restoration of production, restoration of employment and restoration of schools – Gu argued that these tasks were crucial to establishing revolutionary order and organising the masses. Second, he argued that success in the work of taking over administration required that leadership be drawn together and unified. All cadres assigned to urban work had to study hard and stress the maintenance of discipline.

The basic experiences that Gu Mu was summing up in Xin-Hai-Lian provided invaluable lessons for this early stage of control.

On 18 November 1949, Gu was suddenly appointed party secretary of Jinan, and soon after became Jinan's mayor as well. In these new offices, Gu Mu adopted the spirit of the second plenum of the seventh party congress, and worked at effecting the key transition in the party's work. That meant restoring production, supporting and assisting the forces on the front lines, stabilising prices, reinforcing the dikes on the Yellow river – it was a great deal of work.

Gu Mu's wife, Mou Feng, was an outstanding student of the former Jinan middle school for girls. She took her second son back to Jinan, and she is pictured here holding him in the company of her third younger sister Mu Nairong (right)

A trial for counterrevolutionaries conducted by the public in Jinan

But what really gained him attention in higher political circles at first was his success in suppressing the reactionary secret society known as the Yiguandao, something that no others had dared to attempt (Beijing and other places suppressed the Yiguandao later). Later on, during movements known as the 'three antis' and the 'five antis', Gu Mu drafted three summations, all of which were well received by Chairman Mao, who ordered party units everywhere to "perform as shown in these reports. All must carefully study the experiences of the Jinan comrades."

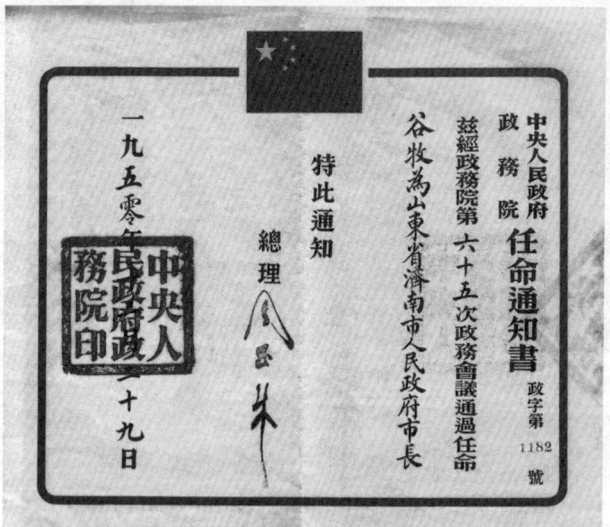

Premier Zhou Enlai issued this appointment letter for Gu Mu, 1950

Three Successive Reports Receive High Marks from Chairman Mao

Jinan had long been the centre of secret society activity, with more than 30 different groups on the ground. Among them, Yiguandao and the 'Sacred brotherhood of the heavenly way for all those with a single heart' had both become dependents of the Japanese invaders and later collaborated with the KMT's infamous central statistical bureau secret police by participating in so-called 'United society for infinite virtue and national salvation'. That group carried out various secret police activities nationwide, with extreme viciousness.

On 5 April 1950, Gu Mu personally drafted a report on the work of "suppressing reactionary forces", and again received Chairman Mao's strong approval.

On 15 April, at 2am, Gu Mu had just gone to bed when his secretary banged on the door of his sleeping quarters inside his office. "Great news," he cried. "Chairman Mao has given his approval to our reports!"

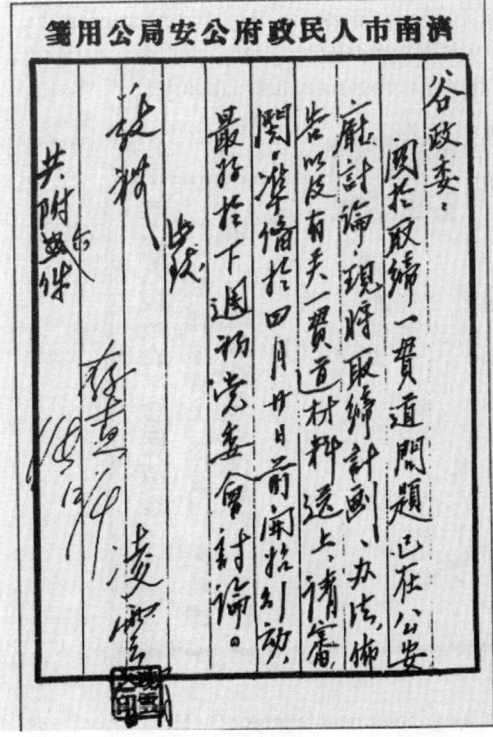

Ling Yung's letter to Gu Mu. Ling was head of the Jinan public security bureau

Early that morning, the head of the city's public security bureau, Ling Yun, arrived with the report that Chairman Mao, on 13 April, had read Gu Mu's 5 April report. Mao said: "This report from the party committee in Jinan, *Suppressing Reactionary Forces*, is excellent. Have the party committees in all large and medium-sized cities read it carefully and proceed as shown in the report."

Gu Mu and Ling Yun, head of the Jinan public security bureau, decided after consultation that they would first tackle the Yiguandao, and move on to attacking all reactionary secret societies. The chief of the Jinan Yiguandao was apprehended on 19 April with nine of his subordinates, thus taking out each and every top leader in the group. The huge quantity of documents seized included KMT-issued materials such as *Basic Guide to Defending Against the Communists, Analysis of the Bandit Traitors' Warfare Methods* and blank forms used for applying for KMT membership, all of which laid bare the evil and reactionary face of the enemy. Smashing the Yiguandao was a big step forward in establishing social stability and reassuring the people about their own security. It did not take long for the influence arising from the Jinan experience to spread across the whole country.

Mao Zedong wrote an appointment letter for Gu Mu

Three Successive Reports Receive High Marks from Chairman Mao

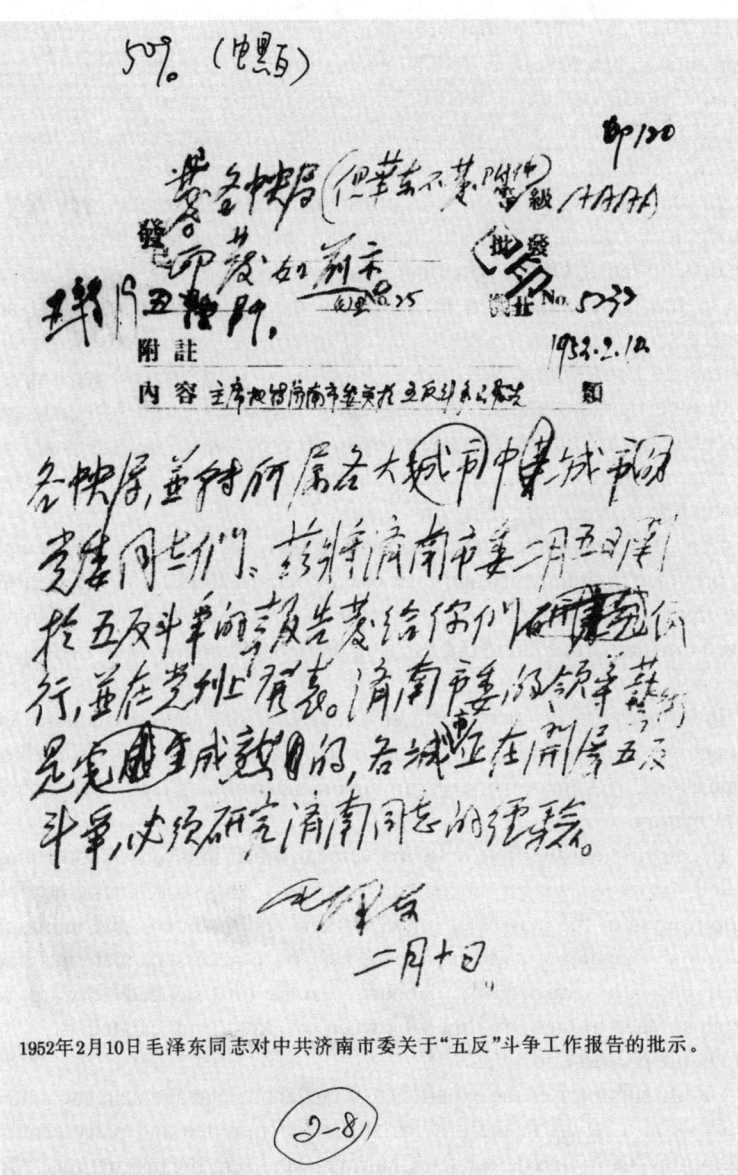

1952年2月10日毛泽东同志对中共济南市委关于"五反"斗争工作报告的批示。

Chairman Mao's instructions to Jinan provincial party committee on the 'five antis' struggle, 10 February 1952

In 1951, the CPC commenced the big 'three antis' movement against corruption, extravagance and bureaucratism. On 27 December of that year, Gu Mu penned a report for the Shandong party committee and party central authorities. He summed up the experiences and the lessons learned thus far in the 'three antis' movement in this way: "On the one hand, the top leadership must take responsibility, leading the way as the movement extends downward through all levels, reaching deep into our leadership ranks. On the other hand, we have to make sure that the masses grasp the policies adopted by the party directly. We leaders must act with discretion, never lightly accepting informers' accusations or blindly extracting confessions. We have to bind together informers' accusations with investigations and fact-finding, and make sure that punishments and re-education are linked; that's the way to prevent chaos."

On 6 January 1952, the party central authorities transmitted Mao Zedong's message approving this report:

"To all central authorities, for transmission to all local bureaux, as well as province, municipality and district party committees: This report from the Jinan party committee is excellent. Please have all large and medium-sized city units read it and publish it in party publications. Mao Zedong, 6 January."

In January 1952, party central authorities put out instructions on launching the 'five antis' movement, aimed at bribery, tax evasion, theft of state assets, evasion of work, skimming on materials and theft of economic information.

In carrying out the 'five antis' movement, Jinan improvised something called 'worker-manager encounter sessions'. This combined the full mobilisation of the masses of office workers and labourers, and thorough efforts at elucidating party policies. Then, once necessary materials had been basically grasped, the labour organisations stepped forward to organise face-to-face meetings between workers and capitalists. This technique proved effective.

Gu Mu summarised the experience of the labour-management encounter sessions in a report to the provincial party committee and party central authorities. Only five days later, Chairman Mao sent his instructions: "To all central authorities, for transmission to comrades in all large and medium-sized city party committees: I am sending you this report on execution

Three Successive Reports Receive High Marks from Chairman Mao

of the 'five antis' programme in Jinan; you should emulate its example and publicise it in party publications. The Jinan committee's leadership is very sophisticated. As you carry out the 'five antis' struggle, all cities must carefully read and learn the experiences of the comrades in Jinan. Mao Zedong."

Gu Mu when he was party secretary and mayor of Jinan

In mid-February, Xiang Ming, second secretary in the party's Shandong bureau, passed on to Gu Mu a telephone message he had received from Liao Luyan, the party's head of the office of policy research in Beijing: "The chairman has decided that Jinan shall become a designated point of liaison with party central authorities." Next, Gu Mu got a phone call directly from Liao Luyan, asking Gu Mu to submit information on the 'two movements' situation in Jinan immediately and directly to Liao's policy research office. With that, reporting by telephone to party central authorities became a nightly homework assignment for the Jinan party committee.

Chapter 20

Calmly Reining in a Deviation to the 'Left'

By night, Gu Mu raced to Jinan on a hand-powered railway cart to take up new duties. The party secretary of Jinan, Liu Shunyuan, had suddenly 'resigned' and departed. A gaping hole had suddenly opened at the very top of the political structure in Jinan.

Liu Shunyuan was a highly principled 'old revolutionary'. Working at Lüda in Liaoning in 1946, he had struggled against Soviet Red Army violations of discipline and Soviet 'big power chauvinism'. Stalin took a dim view of Liu's behaviour and put pressure on Liu Shaoqi during Liu's visit to Moscow. Word that Liu Shunyuan was in difficulty began to seep out. A few people began looking for damaging information on Liu Shunyuan to use against him.

At about that time, a Soviet delegation arrived in Jinan for a visit. Party central authorities ordered Liu Shunyuan not to involve himself in receiving the delegation. An administrative cadre with evil intentions awaited his moment, and disclosed the damaging information Liu's detractors had dug up to a provincial party committee leader. The cadre magnified the seriousness of Liu's supposed

Gu delivers the opening speech at a people's representative conference in 1950 attended by people from all walks of life in Jinan

misdeeds and alleged that a number of industrial production accidents had resulted from Liu's lackadaisical handling of class enemies.

This party leader was already prejudiced against Liu Shunyuan, and took the materials he had received to a full party committee meeting, where he attacked Liu Shunyuan. The two men launched into a savage argument. That led to an urgent order by the east China bureau for Gu Mu to head for Jinan in the middle of the night.

As he hastily took up his new duties, Gu Mu believed he could have avoided intervening in the Liu Shunyuan matter. What he did consider supremely important was that the leadership team remained united, and that discipline be upheld in the execution of orders from the leadership. After investigating the situation, Gu Mu concluded that if he did not get rid of those who had attacked Liu Shunyuan, all sorts of bad things would happen.

The committee members of Jinan people's government, 9 September 1950. Front row from left to right: Dong Yan, Ling Yun, Shi Leiguang, Gu Mu, Zhang Dongmu, Liang Jiqing and Wu Minggang. Middle row: Ai Luchuan, Qi Jilin, Ma Junren, Xu Meisheng, Qi Ming and Shen Ying. Back row: Huang Cangxi, Hua Zixiu and Liu Jianfei.

At that time, there were two key symbolic factors in determining each cadre's fundamental 'party character' and 'faithfulness to party principles'. One was the cadre's attitude regarding the USSR. The other was the cadre's zeal with regard to class struggle.

Gu Mu, though, kept to the principle of seeking truth from facts, and calmly distanced himself from cadres who displayed this kind of 'leftism'.

The party leader who received the incriminating materials about Liu Shunyuan was an old friend of Gu Mu from the war years, and had great faith in Gu Mu. At Gu Mu's insistence, he took a careful look at the situation, and agreed to transfer elsewhere the individual who had provided the damning materials on Liu Shunyuan.

In 1952, the focus of the 'five antis' movement shifted to the business world. After several years of cooperation, Gu Mu had a high opinion of the leader of the Jinan federation of industry and commerce, Zhang Dongmu. Zhang had worked closely with the party during the initial phase

Gu Mu, who was vice chairman of the CPPCC national committee in Jinan in 1989, with comrades who were in charge of the provincial and municipal people's political consultative conference. From left to right: Zhang Dongmu (Jinan's vice president of the Chinese people's political consultative conference (CPPCC)), Gu Mu, Lu Maozeng (chairman of the CPPCC of Shandong province) and Liu Yaohua (chairman of the CPPCC of Jinan)

of economic recovery after liberation. During the Korean war, Jinan had contributed funds for the purchase of 27 airplanes, of which 23 were bought with money contributed by the federation (Miao Hainan and Zhang Dongmu each personally contributed funds for an airplane).

Zhang Dongmu drafted a report on the federation's response to the 'five antis' campaign. Gu Mu read it and did not change a single word, expressing his strong confidence in this vice mayor of Jinan who came from the Jinan federation of industry and commerce.

For his part, Zhang Dongmu looked upon Gu Mu as his leader and teacher, deeply admiring him for his leadership skills and his high policy standards. Late in his life, he recalled an incident: "During the 'three antis' and 'five antis' campaigns, Gu Mu one day was in the middle of a meeting of Jinan municipal council when some unit called to ask what should be done with an inscribed plaque in their possession that contained 'feudal' content. Those at the meeting took two positions: most argued that, since the revolution had been successful, feudal items like this should be destroyed; others disagreed. The two sides could not decide, so they turned to Gu Mu.

"Gu Mu slowly replied: 'They can't smash the plaque, and they can't burn the plaque. We're in the middle of carrying out the 'three antis' and 'five antis' campaigns. If we make ourselves 'anti' everything that comes along, the 'three antis' and 'five antis' campaigns will dissolve into chaos.' Hearing Gu Mu's words, everyone in the room nodded in agreement."

Chapter 21

Mao Zedong Takes Gu Mu with him on his Special Train

In early 1952, Chairman Mao went south on an inspection visit, and passed through Jinan. Without getting off the train, he had a meeting with Shandong provincial leaders, and took Gu Mu along with him for the trip to Xuzhou in northern Jiangsu.

This was the first time Gu Mu had met Chairman Mao.

Mao said to Gu in a friendly manner: "I've been reading your reports. The work in Jinan is going very well indeed." Those warm words put Gu Mu at ease.

Mao listened to Gu Mu's brief oral presentation, and then changed the subject, ranging over many things.

"Where does the name Jinan come from?" he asked.

Gu answered: "Because it lies south of the Ji river."

"Then why is there no longer any sign of the Ji river?"

Gu Mu knew the historical reason for this: when the Yellow river changed its course, it swallowed the lower reaches of the Ji. But he could not tell whether Chairman Mao had other reasons for asking the question, so he hesitated.

"The old course of the Ji river in Shandong was overcome by the Yellow river. You can find that in many books," Mao continued. "As the saying goes: 'When you come to a new capital, ask about the local customs; when you enter a new state, inquire as to what is prohibited.' When we're doing local work, we have to understand local conditions, both at present and in the past."

Next, Mao asked: "Where was Zhuge Liang from?"

"Zhuge Liang was from Linyi, in Shandong, but he later moved to Xiangyang in Hubei."

"How did he get the name Zhuge?"

Gu Mu was stumped.

"Have you read *The Three Kingdoms* by Chen Shou? You should check out the *Biography of Zhuge Jin*. Kong Ming's ancestral surname was Ge, originally from the city of Zhu. Later, he moved to Yangdu [the ancient name for today's Linyi county]. But in Yangdu, Ge was already one of the most common surnames, so the arrival of a newcomer with the same name was not welcomed. Therefore, Kong Ming, because he came from the city of Zhu, changed his name to Zhuge..."

Later on, Gu Mu consulted the historical records and confirmed that Mao Zedong was right on all points.

When they sat down to eat, the first course to be served was fish.

Mao turned to Gu Mu and asked: "Which fish would you say is best?"

Gu Mu had grown up on the coast, so he named a few sea fish he liked.

Mao responded: "Don't the books say that the perch from the Song river is the best of all?"

Gu Mu replied: "Oceans occupy two-thirds of the earth. The varieties of sea fish are far more numerous than those of freshwater fish."

Mao replied: "I have eaten all sorts of fish, and freshwater fish are still the best."

Gu Mu looked carefully at Mao, and offered a circuitous response. "Mr Chairman, there are delicious freshwater fish and there are delicious saltwater fish. But the most delicious fish of all are those that are born where the salt water and the fresh water meet. A fine example of that would be the sea bream of Jiaodong, here in Shandong."

"So you are pretty knowledgeable about fish," Mao observed. "You might become a natural scientist. But I still prefer freshwater fish."

Mao thus praised Gu Mu, but was not to be swayed in his own preferences in fish.

Just as he was about to eat a mouthful of rice, Mao caught sight of a long range of barren hills. Suddenly he said: "Why are there no trees on those hills?"

"There used to be trees on those hills, but all were lost in time of war," Gu replied.

"That is one reason. In our Soviet base area, when the KMT had us encircled, they destroyed many trees, but before long new ones grew. Your hills here basically have no trees at all!"

"In the south," Gu replied, "trees grow very quickly. Shandong's climate is dry, and that affects the growth of trees up here."

"You are not entirely correct," said Mao. "In olden times, Shandong was rich in forests. Think of what *The Water Margin* says about Jingyanggang, where Wu Song fought the tiger. There were plenty of trees…"

This conversation with Chairman Mao, on the train during Mao's trip to the south, taught Gu Mu a great deal. Later, he expressed his feelings in writing:

"In that conversation with Chairman Mao about tree-planting, perhaps he was criticising me for not paying enough attention to afforestation and not pursuing the idea with greater energy. Regrettably, at that time I didn't have a deep grasp of what he meant, and so I could only carry on a superficial conversation with him about this and that. But when we came to discussing the history of our revolution in Shandong, I raised the idea that the party history was not correct in its recounting of how the Wang Ming line had caused the complete elimination of our party in the 'white' areas we didn't control. I pointed out that, if we had lost all our underground agents in the white areas, then where, after Han Fuju's flight early in the war of resistance, would all the communist leaders for the war in Shandong have come from? After I raised this point rather sharply, Chairman Mao didn't take it to heart."

Chapter 22

Chen Yi Deploys his Commanders to Assist with the 'Five Antis' Campaign in Shanghai

In February 1952, Gu Mu was transferred to Shanghai to become head of the Shanghai municipal party committee's publicity bureau. In December of that year, he and Pan Hannian were appointed deputy secretaries of the Shanghai party committee.

Prior to Gu Mu's transfer, the 'five antis' campaign had not been going well in Shanghai, China's premier industrial city. The central party

Gu Mu accompanies Chen Yi to receive the married couple Xiao Hua and Wang Xinlan, who came to Shanghai for a meeting, and General Wang Zonghuai. From right to left: Zhang Yan, Yang Chun, Chen Yi, Xiao Hua, Wang Xinlan, Wang Zonghuai, Gu Mu and Mou Feng

Gu Mu votes in Shanghai municipality's first people's congress

authorities, the east China bureau of the party and the municipal party committee all saw that, if current trends continued, the result would be chaos. They hastily set about organising their forces to save the situation. Along with Gu Mu, Chen Pixian and Wang Yiping were sent to the city. Chen Yi personally selected Gu Mu, whose reports on the 'three antis' and 'five antis' campaigns in Jinan were famous everywhere.

Chen Yi wanted Gu Mu's help in strengthening the leadership of the 'five antis' campaign. Together, they imposed strict controls aimed at curbing the rampant 'left' deviation. They worked in great detail. Mayor Chen Yi first came forth with a public report on mobilisation, making clear official policies, hammering home the prohibition of excessive violence and calming the agitated mood of the city's capitalists. He ordered that the 'five antis' campaign stick to the five designated objectives, and not expand into other areas.

Gu Mu in Shanghai, 1952

According to Chen Yi's instructions, top executives at 303 industrial and commercial enterprises were to be dealt with by combining 'strict education', 'unification of production' and 'allowing them to transition in safety'. They were to be allowed to criticise one another, and were to be treated with dignity. Subjecting them to unbearable savagery was forbidden.

Many people found that these methods of 'martial drama but civilised singing' exceeded their expectations. A few tried to play fast and loose, and they wound up losing everything. In the final disposition of their cases, those entrepreneurs who had shown relatively good political attitudes were treated leniently. For example, the municipal party committee designated the family of Rong Yiren as 'essentially law abiding entrepreneurs'. Chairman Mao said: "Ease up a bit; drop the 'essentially'. Just say 'law abiding family'.

Four fellow students from Rongcheng in Shanghai in 1952. From right to left: Cao Manzhi, Wang Yiping, Li Yaowen and Gu Mu. At that time, Cao Manzhi was expelled from the party and removed from his position in the 'three antis' campaign, Gu Mu and Wang Yipin had just arrived to start work in Shanghai, where they met with Cao despite the political pressure

Chapter 23

Learning from Premier Zhou

At the beginning of 1953, Gu Mu assumed the additional position of secretary of the industrial production working committee under Shanghai municipal communist party committee, with responsibility for both industry and transportation. At the outset, Gu Mu was a novice when it came to large-scale industry. But he energetically went out to visit enterprises to increase his understanding and to look more deeply into the various problems.

At that time, many districts were engaging in the Soviet-derived 'one man leadership' system. Gu Mu's view was that a system of orderly rules and improved direction had to rest ultimately on the foundation of a spirit of dynamism among all staff and workers. Strengthening administrative management in turn could only be guaranteed through the unified leadership of the party. Thus, the path to achieving good outcomes lay in drawing upon the experiences of arousing and relying upon the masses, as learned in the years when Shanghai was a revolutionary base; in strengthening systems of responsibility; in carrying out reasonable reforms; and in competently handling both safety and welfare tasks.

At that time in Shanghai, the machinery sector was grievously short of business orders. Gu Mu went looking for business at the machine building ministry in Beijing and the machine building bureau in Shanghai, and quickly enabled Shanghai plants to supply important machinery and equipment to the large First Auto facility in Changchun and to major water conservancy projects at the Foziling, Meishan and Guanting reservoirs.

Before 1953, the system of 'unified purchase and distribution' of processed industrial products by the state that acted as the sole agent of privately-owned enterprises was already fairly well developed. The first five-year plan called for a major increase in the proportion of firms organised under 'joint public-private management'. Starting in the second half of the year, Gu Mu took on the task of furthering the transition of factories from purely private ownership toward state capitalism.

On the surface, many private factory owners welcomed the new arrangements, which involved setting up joint government-private ownership of their enterprises. But in their hearts, they remained suspicious. After thorough investigations, the enterprise committee said to the municipal party committee: "Actively cultivate the right conditions, but advance step by step." The municipal government tightened its oversight of the work of the government production administration bureau by using special representatives for the biggest companies, and 'in-plant representatives' or 'coaches' for medium-sized and small enterprises. Within the factories, joint 'committees for production enhancement and economisation' were set up, embracing factory owners or their agents, party representatives, representatives of the Communist Youth League and representatives of the mass of the workforce. These committees discussed problems such as how to reorganise production management and wages and benefits for white- and blue-collar workers. People in the business sector approved these measures warmly. Gu Mu regularly discussed matters with Rong Yiren and others and came up with timely solutions.

In November 1953, Premier Zhou Enlai came to Shanghai to see how the work was going, and heard a number of reports. Pan Hannian reported on market conditions, while Gu Mu reported on industry and transportation. The materials they prepared were vast and complex. Some of the numbers were jotted down on note pads; others were simply in the heads of Han and Gu. The premier absorbed everything in great detail and shot forth some comparative analyses. Han and Gu turned to some statistics, and the premier suddenly expressed his uneasiness. "The numbers you're using don't match with the statistics you quoted earlier," he said. Embarrassed, the two men hurriedly re-examined their figures. Premier Zhou laughed and said: "Don't go looking for the mistake. I've already recalled it." After that, the numbers the premier stated and the numbers in Gu Mu's and Pan Hannian's work books agreed.

Premier Zhou said: "Working on reconstruction is harder than fighting war. The top leaders need to get involved in this, so that they can be experts themselves, rather than amateurs." Gu Mu recalled later: "His remarks taught us an important lesson. In the long years ahead when I held leadership positions in economic work, I always made it a point to be sure I understood the latest conditions. I tried to grasp the latest knowledge. For every economic issue I worked on, I had to grasp the relevant numerical data and understand how the data changed over time, hold the data in my mind and grasp that information in the broader context. When reporting to the premier, there was no room for 'probably,' or 'maybe'. We had to be ready to talk very, very concretely."

Chapter 24

Deputy Secretary of the Third Department at the State Council

In December 1954, Gu Mu was brought to Beijing to become deputy secretary of the third department of the state council and, concurrently, deputy chairman of the national construction commission. Both of these bodies reported to Vice Premier Bo Yibo.

The third department was the state council's agency for assisting in developing heavy industry and observing and examining the progress of the sector. It was also the state council's liaison agency for the ministries of non-ferrous metals, coal and chemicals, as well as the first and second ministries of machine building, plus large-scale construction projects and the construction commission itself. One of Gu Mu's biggest tasks, when he arrived at the third department, was to formulate development guidelines for technology improvements in the heavy industry sector.

That task originated in Chairman Mao's directives on technology work and on the tasks of the educated professions – so called 'intellectuals'.

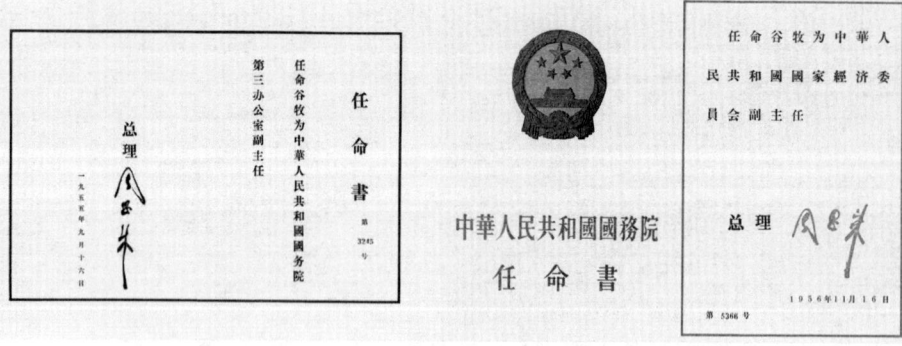

Two appointment letters issued by Premier Zhou Enlai to Gu Mu

> 关于改进工业管理体制的规定
> (一九五七年十一月八日)
>
> 我国是社会主义国家,我国的建设是有计划的建设,全国各地区各企业的生产和建设工作都必须服从国家的统一计划,决不可以违反国家的统一计划,我们现行的工业管理体制基本上是符合这种要求的。但是,从目前情况看来,现行工业管理体制存在着两个主要的缺点。一个是有些企业适宜于交给地方管理的,现在还由中央工业部门直接管理;同时,地方行政机关对于工业管理中的物资分配、财务管理、人事管理等等方面的职权太小。另一个是企业主管人员对本企业的管理权限太小,工业行政部门对于企业中的业务管得过多。这两个主要缺点限制了地方行政机关和企业主管人员在工作方面的主动性和积极性。在国家的统一计划以内,给地方政府和企业以一定程度的因地制宜的权力,是完全必要的。这种国家统一计划范围内的地方政府和企业的一定程度的机动权力,正是为了因地制宜地完成国家的统一计划,这是国家统一计划
>
> * 这是陈云同志为国务院起草的文件,经国务院全体会议第六十一次会议通过,一九五七年十一月十四日第一届全国人民代表大会常务委员会第八十四次会议原则批准,自一九五八年起施行。本文原载一九五七年十一月八日《人民日报》。

Gu Mu and **Chen Yun** jointly drafted *The State Council's Regulations on Improving the Industrial Management System*

Gu Mu instructed all ministries and commissions under his department to come up with planning guidelines for their respective sectors, conferring on multiple occasions with Xu Chi on the heavy industry ministries, with Shen Hong and Zhou Jiannan from the first ministry of machine building, and other vice ministerial-level officials. He also assembled a set of individuals who possessed both strong technological understanding and good writing skills, to form a 'small group' tasked with producing written materials. Working overtime for two months, they managed to put together a planning report in broad outline form. Later on, this report was integrated into Premier Zhou Enlai's *Long-Term Guidelines for the Development of Science and Technology, 1956-1967*.

Because of the economic blockade imposed by imperialist countries, the Shanghai economy ran into severe difficulties. With the service and commercial sectors in Shanghai depressed, and given the low levels of technological development, shortages of trained manpower and a lack of industrial experience in China's hinterland, Chen Yun called for the transfer of a portion of Shanghai's industrial sector into the interior, to kill two birds with one stone.

Gu Mu assumed responsibility for carrying out these policies on the ground. In and around 1955, a total of 270 facilities in light industry, textiles, apparel, and food and beverages were moved to Henan, Shaanxi, Gansu and Inner Mongolia. As many as 210,000 people were relocated from Shanghai, including more than 23,000 engineers, 80,000 technologically skilled labourers and another 50,000 in fields such as design, architecture and factory installation. This first instance of the large-scale transfer of technologically-skilled migrants was a significant factor in advancing the economic development and industrialisation of the interior.

Gu Mu and his wife Mou Feng, 1956

Chapter 25

Deeply Respecting Zhou Enlai's Opposition to Impetuous and Rash Advance

Late in 1955, the state economic commission (SEC) was created from the third, fourth and sixth departments of the state council, and charged with responsibility for formulating the nation's annual development plans. Bo Yibo chaired the new commission, and Gu Mu became one of its vice chairmen.

Gu Mu's entire family, Beijing, 1958

At that time, work on the second five-year plan was underway. Vice Premier Li Fuchun began the work in August 1955, and Premier Zhou Enlai himself put a great deal of effort into it. That November, Chairman Mao led in the promulgation of the *17 Articles on Agriculture*. Soon after, at a meeting of the party politburo, Mao criticised 'conservatism and right deviationism', drastically raising numerical targets for the 1956 annual plan and causing many of those working on the second five-year plan to jump on to the bandwagon. A new set of ill-grounded and inflated numerical targets went up to Mao, who approved them in April 1956. That meant trouble for all the carefully laid plans for balancing material supply and demand in the new five-year plan.

125

Gu Mu, May 1959

On 8 February 1956, Zhou Enlai issued a warning during the 24th plenary session of the state council: "Do not be bedazzled by surface signs of blazing activity… Do not randomly get into things that have no basis in reality and no solid foundation. Do not move at crazy speeds, or there will be enormous peril."… "The minds of many leaders have become overheated. They must bathe in ice water and come to their senses."

On 11 May, Zhou, at another plenary state council meeting, bluntly pointed out: "It is already eight or nine months since the campaign against conservatism and 'right deviationism' started last August. We must not continue on this path any longer." In another report, Zhou, along with Li Fuchun and Li Xiannian, said: "In this time of fighting conservatism, we must also fight against the other deviations – rashness and impetuosity."

On 4 June, Liu Shaoqi chaired a session to discuss the draft national budget. On 12 June, when Zhou Enlai chaired a plenary state council session, they both pushed for reductions of inflated and unrealistic targets, saying: "The demands of a few hotheaded activists are not the demands of the entire populace."

On 15 June, Li Xiannian issued, on behalf of the state council, a document entitled *Regarding the Final Accounts for 1955 and the National Budget for 1956*. In it, he pointed out: "The results of this 'advancing impetuously' cannot assist in the development of our socialist endeavour, and will only lead to losses."

On 20 June, *People's Daily* issued a message from the party's central publicity bureau, produced at the request of Liu Shaoqi, and then published the article as an editorial under the names of Liu and Premier Zhou Enlai. It was entitled *As We Oppose Conservatism, We Must Also Oppose Blind Impetuosity*.

Liu Shaoqi looked over the revised draft editorial and wrote: "After the chairman sees this, pass it to Hu Qiaomu." Mao, for his part, simply wrote the words: "I won't read this."

It was under these circumstances that Premier Zhou expressed himself: "Our economic plans have to be based on a solid and dependable foundation. To plan our productive strength, we must rely on a broad-based and balanced style of thinking that takes account of people, finance and materials."

When the eighth party congress convened, the premier presented his *Recommendations Regarding the Second Five-year Plan*. According to Gu Mu's memoirs: "After three years of setbacks occasioned by the Great Leap Forward, Chairman Mao said: 'Comrade Zhou Enlai oversaw the formation of the second five-year plan in 1956. Most of its directives, for example in the steel sector, were achieved with three years to spare. This is extremely good!'"

But that was later. At the time, the wild pursuit of hyper-fast development had not yet hit the brakes. That was clear during formulation of the 1957 single-year plan. In that period, party and government leaders such as Zhou Enlai, Liu Shaoqi and Chen Yun remained relatively clear-headed, and spoke up many times to oppose the hyper-active pursuit of inflated targets that they saw around them. Even though this stance by Zhou and others angered Chairman Mao, they earned Gu Mu's deep admiration and respect, and became his role models. Around this time, while discussing steel production quotas, Gu Mu got into a bitter argument with a provincial party secretary in the east China bureau (for details, see page 190 of *Gu Mu's Memoirs*, published by the Central Documents Publishing House in 2009).

Chapter 26

Rethinking the Campaign to Make Iron and Steel, in a Specialised and Professional Way

Gu Mu had welcomed Zhou Enlai's opposition to the blind pursuit of inflated goals, and revered Zhou for his views. He despised those whose standpoints waved in the wind and tried only to side with the top leadership. In his memoirs, Gu Mu wrote about the entire campaign to 'smelt iron and make steel', objectively examining the spirit of specialisation and the professional ethics of each of the leading figures in that movement.

From 5-23 May 1958, the second plenum of the eighth congress of the CPC approved the general line, 'In accord with Chairman Mao's motion, the party central authorities call for all-out efforts to strive for the top and build socialism even more rapidly in every province and every locality'. It also called for simultaneous advances in every direction: industry and agriculture; centrally-run and locally-run industries; large, medium-sized and small industries. It criticised those who opposed 'impetuous advances' and called for attaining, within only five or seven years, the earlier objective of 'overcoming Britain in steel production in 15 years'. Another excessively high demand was to 'achieve the basic transformation of our backwardness through three years of bitter struggle'. Along with such bizarre slogans as 'One day is equal to 20 years', the plan was heavily biased toward subjectivity, in complete rejection of the laws of economics. It created enormous political pressures with its language about 'raising the capitalist white flag of surrender'.

In reality, by early 1958 the national economy was already stumbling into the mire. Both the Nanning conference that January and the Chengdu conference in March gave evidence of the triumph of a kind of metaphysical thinking, while the idea of 'opposing impetuous advance' was heavily criticised. On 20 March, the ministry of metallurgical industry sent a document entitled *We Can Speed Up the Development of the Iron and Steel Industries* to the party central authorities, and a separate report detailing enormous increases in non-ferrous metals production. These messages received Mao Zedong's high praise, and they were distributed accordingly within the government and party. With that, the frenzy to 'overcome Britain' became white hot.

In his memoirs, Gu Mu wrote later: "Because the date for overcoming Britain in iron and steel production kept on being moved forward, from 15 years to 10 years to five years, the production targets for 1958 kept rising as well. The SEC [then in charge of setting and realising the growth targets established in each annual plan] sent a report to the party central authorities in April, on the basis of the reports it was receiving from the provinces, projecting annual steel production of 7.11m tons. After the second plenum of the eighth congress on 7 June, the metals ministry reported to the party central authorities that annual steel production would reach 8.2m tons. Ten days later, a leading comrade reported to the politburo on *Conditions Surrounding Implementation of the 1958 Plan and Prospects for 1959*, projecting 1958 steel production of 9m tons. After another three days, on 20 June, after Bo Yibo had reviewed and edited it, the SEC's *Summary Report to the Party Central Authorities* raised 1958 steel production to 10m tons and projected 25m tons of steel production in the following year. "With three more years of hard struggle, on top of the last two years, we will be able to catch up with and out-do Britain in the production of iron, steel and other key products, while finishing the task of building a complete industrial structure." Chairman Mao authorised this report to be circulated through all channels.

Gu wrote: "At the expanded politburo meeting in Beidaihe in late August, iron and steel quotas were raised again, this time to 10.7m tons (double the previous year's quota of 5.35m tons). We heard that this had been decided in a conversation between Chairman Mao, Bo Yibo and Wang Heshou, and then discussed by the relevant leading party figures. They all read the publicity documents with a big show of enthusiasm, and proclaimed that, once the new targets were announced, nobody should change a word. To them, the difference between 10m tons and 10.7m tons was nothing – a rounding error. In any case, not a single person in the central committee meeting raised his voice to disagree with these wild targets. We had only just begun to work on building the industrial sector of the economy. With regard to the simple question "How are iron and steel forged?", many central and local cadres were completely in the dark. They knew nothing about the complex and difficult processes relating to coal, electricity, transport or machinery – all vital to the building of an industrial economy. Asking them for intellectually discriminating opinions on these things was out of the question. Even those members of the state council or central government ministers who had some grasp of these matters failed to provide cool consideration; they failed to discuss actual conditions in a spirit of 'seeking truth from facts'. They could find no openings to speak about actual realities. All they did was heat things up further and raise the stakes. With this thinking pattern of 'impetuous advance' sweeping over the entire party, raising troublesome questions was naturally difficult, even perilous. But, looking back on all this, we must today draw some important lessons: be respectful of history, and squarely face up to reality."

In his memoirs, Gu Mu added: "At the time of the Lushan plenum, I went to a meeting called by the premier. The meeting ran from noon to about 4pm. A number of ministries – metallurgy, coal, machinery, transportation and commerce – made reports. After the meeting broke up, the premier held a small session with comrades from the SEC and the state planning commission. He wanted us to really analyse the current situation, and to formulate measures that could actually solve problems. At the meeting, the premier talked about some of the twin phenomena of excessive grandiosity and divorce from reality. He spoke with feeling and sadness. He said: 'Sometimes, Chairman Mao, when he receives your reports, gets inspired. Sometimes he asks others for their opinions. If the words he utters are clearly understood, everyone would carry them out to the letter. Because his every word is taken as an official order, the chairman cannot simply talk casually with you as he might like. What a way for the chairman to spend his days! When we meet, all we can do is spend a few minutes in small talk about the weather. Or else, after just a minute or two of paying attention to something, he opens his mouth and issues an order. What kind of intraparty democracy is this? Actually this is just like sealing the chairman's mouth!' He went on: 'On last year's doubling and redoubling of iron and steel targets, originally it was the chairman who asked for others' opinions.

But we hadn't done any investigation or analysis. The whole party rose up as one. This was a terribly serious lesson for us.'"

Under those conditions, the premier could not have been more sharply critical. But in his memoirs, Gu Mu has no fear of offending anyone. He looks back on that stage of history with practical realism, clearly recognising the premier's demands that cadres with leadership responsibilities preserve the spirit of specialised expertise and maintain high standards of professional ethics.

Primitive steelmaking in China

Chapter 27

A 'Small Group of 10' Works to Reverse the Nation's Economic Travails

The tragedies of the 'Great Leap Forward' had an educational effect on the entire party. On 24 December 1960, the party central authorities called a working conference in Beijing to discuss and adopt an eight-character guiding formulation: 'Realign, Firm Up, Fulfil and Raise Higher'.

At this meeting, Deng Xiaoping represented the party secretariat. He announced the formation of a 10-person 'small group' with responsibility to organise all the economic agencies and industrial and transportation organs to put into action the new guidance from the central committee. The 10 members of the small group were Bo Yibo, Gu Mu, Wang Heshou, Zhang Linzhi, Lü Zhengcao, Zhao Erlu, Liu Lanbo, Peng Tao, Chen Zhengren and Sun Zhiyuan. Deng's instruction to the group was: "When Bo is present, he leads. When Bo is not present, Gu Mu is to lead."

Zhou Enlai personally arranged for the small group to set up offices on Yangfengjia Street, opposite the north gate of the Zhongnanhai leadership compound. During the day, ministers all worked at their regular ministerial jobs. But at night, they came together at the small group office. Soon after, Bo Yibo fell ill, and Gu Mu took charge of its work.

What lay before the small group was nothing less than a complete redirection of the nation's production. At that time, materials were in short supply. The functions of the economy were under extreme stress. Every problem the small group had to tackle was a matter of life or death for the people. For example, on one occasion, Shanghai had only two days' supply of coal reserves. Anshan Iron and Steel Company shut down its furnaces. People felt suffocated by the endless crises falling upon them.

Premier Zhou's written instructions to Gu Mu. The letter reads: "Comrade Gu Mu: please study and discuss the issues that need to be addressed in the 1962 non-ferrous metals plan. Financial group — Zhou Enlai 15 February"

The hardest part was that the problems in the iron and steel, coal and machinery sectors formed a vicious circle. Gu Mu later said: "If we wanted to protect levels of production and quality in iron and steel, the metallurgical industry ministry and its agencies asked us to protect the quantity and quality of coal production. If we wanted to protect coal, the coal ministry told us they had to protect mining operations as well as supplies of transportation equipment of sufficient quality. If we wanted to protect the equipment needed in mining, the machine building ministries demanded that we protect both the supply and the quality of the necessary steel. Going round and round like this produced a vicious circle. Our work was extremely difficult."

Solving the coal supply issue was the most pressing challenge in dealing with production problems in the industrial and transport sectors and, indeed, in the entire economy. In April, Gu Mu went on an inspection visit to the Jingxi coal bureau outside Beijing. He learned that many underground miners had left their jobs. The most urgent matter was the living conditions of staff and workers. "Their grain allocations were inadequate. They had no miner's clothing, no soap for washing. There were no medicines for the sick. The underground miners had no spirits to drink when they were above ground. It was extremely difficult to maintain the necessary numbers employed in the mining industry."

So, when he got back, Gu Mu sent up a report, recommending that special supplies be directed to the nation's miners. Zhou Enlai and Li Fuchun paid very careful attention to this report and circulated it as a central government formal document. Subsequently, Gu Mu was assigned to write and circulate, under the name of the state council, a paper entitled *Several Decisions Regarding the Improvement of Supplies for Production Workers in Mines Directly Controlled by the State*. This increased the amount of food grain for miners, raised their grain, oil and cotton rations, guaranteed that workers could keep their own household implements, and even went so far as to specify that two bottles of liquor per month would be supplied, in principle, "to workers in iron ore and coal mines".

Liu Nianyuan, Gu Mu's eldest son, joined the army in 1962 and went to Tibet, where he worked and fought for 15 years. In 1962, Wan Li also sent his eldest son, Wan Do'ao, to set an example by working in the countryside. These two actions were praised by Premier Zhou at a state council meeting

During difficult times, Gu Mu still tried to be a good father. Here, he enjoys a visit to the park with his small daughter

During that period, the members of the '10-person small group' were themselves on short rations, experiencing real hunger. With Premier Zhou's permission, the ministers who went to work at the commission at night were allowed to purchase one bowl of noodles without providing grain coupons that otherwise were required for all grain-based foods. Every night, as the group met, the premier sent his secretary Gu Ming to listen in, in order to gain a timely understanding of the situation. Sometimes, the group listened to reports from the field. It could take several days to work through a problem. Often, Gu Mu would return to his dwelling late at night, have something to eat, take a sleeping pill and lie down, only to hear his red telephone ringing. When he picked up the phone, Premier Zhou would be on the other end. Gu would look at his watch; it was two or three in the morning, and again he would throw himself, on an empty stomach, into his duties.

Chapter 28

Daqing Experience Helps Create Industrial and Transport Political Units

The realignment measures Gu Mu instituted gradually took effect. At the end of 1963, the Daqing oilfield was completed. That winter, Gu Mu led an SEC delegation to an on-site conference held at Daqing by the party's northeast bureau. It was the third time Gu Mu had gone to the front line at Daqing to see for himself. He gained a comprehensive understanding of the Daqing experience, and sent reports on it up to the state council and party central authorities. In mid-December, when the SEC convened its own national conference on industrial and transportation work, key topics were a study of the Daqing experience and consideration of ways of building further upon Daqing.

On 16 December 1963, Chairman Mao wrote a comment on a report from the ministry of metallurgical industry: "At this time, because the industrial

'Mud dwellings' and dry brick buildings where workers lived during the early days of the search for oil

ministries are actively calling for learning from the People's Liberation Army (PLA), the great achievements of the ministry of petroleum ought also to make their mark." He proposed that the national industrial ministries and agencies "learn from the PLA, setting up political affairs units at each level and using special personnel to provide political guidance".

In February 1964, Gu Mu was assigned to set up a 'party central industry and transport political section'. A set of high- and middle-ranking political cadres and cadres with industrial skills were transferred from military posts to the new organisation, and assigned to leading roles at the party central industry and transport political section, and at political offices in each separate industrial or transport ministry and in the major mines. Of the three deputy chiefs of the party central industry and transport political section, Li Renlin and Deng Dongzhe came from the Beijing and Fuzhou military districts, while Zhong Min came from Fujian province.

The party central industry and transport political section no longer exists. Many organisations today trace their origins to that institution, and perform many of its former functions. Two of China's greatest leaders in the area of economic development, Yu Qiuli and Gu Mu, were able participants in the effort to put military-style political work into effect. Yu Qiuli had served as political commissar of the 358th brigade during the revolution and had creatively developed the 'recollecting hardships and three investigations' programme,[1] which had a profoundly transformative effect on the thinking of PLA troops and rapidly increased their fighting effectiveness. Chairman Mao called this "a new type of movement for the entire army". And when Gu Mu was working on military transportation he, too, depended on the political work performed by party personnel, transforming the spirit of the soldiers in northeast China army units and boosting their fighting strength in a big way. In the first 10 or so years of the PRC, a unique period in building the planned economy, the experiences of political work and political organisation played a major role. These 'spiritual treasures' had a big influence on succeeding generations.

Chapter 29

A Visit to Peng Dehuai amid 'Third Line of Construction' Upsurge

On 27 May 1964, as the CPC politburo was hearing reports from the field, Chairman Mao made a statement: "We must work on three lines of strategic dispositions, and must strengthen the 'Third Line' to defend against enemy invasion." That August, the central party secretariat discussed the question of the Third Line. Mao advanced the idea further: "First, we must concentrate our powers to build the Third Line, guaranteeing necessary inputs of labour, materiel and funds."

Early in 1965, Mao decided that the state construction commission in Beijing ought to be in overall charge of the Third Line project. He therefore re-established the construction commission, and made Gu Mu its chief. The main tasks of the state construction commission were the formulation and execution of plans for basic economic construction work nationwide, especially for the strategic base areas of the southwest and northwest, and for other key bases in rear areas along the First and Second Lines of Construction.

In late August and early September, Gu Mu chaired a national conference on the work of transferring assets to new locations in the interior. The conference decided to move 500 production centres from coastal locations to Third Line locations, mostly military industries, their associated metals plants, machinery and electronic materiel, high-energy fuels, rubber products, and factories producing civilian-use products sorely needed in the interior locations of the Third Line. Along with these industrial transfers, the conference decided to move certain technology services vital to national defence and related science and technology research units into the interior.

To put all these plans into effect, Gu Mu travelled to southwest China for his own inspection. At one meeting in Chengdu, he specially sought a meeting with comrade Peng Dehuai.

At that time, the elderly Peng was vice chairman of the southwest area construction commission. Gu Mu noticed that, while he was speaking from the dais, Peng remained seated below the speaker's platform. Gu felt very uncomfortable. So he interrupted his speech and descended to stand in front of Peng. "My respected elder Peng," Gu Mu said. "How is it that you have come all the way here? Please – you should go home and rest. I will personally report to you on what we discuss at today's conference." Peng responded, brightly and generously: "You are the head of the national construction commission. I am only vice chairman of the southwest regional construction commission. Naturally, I must come to hear your report."

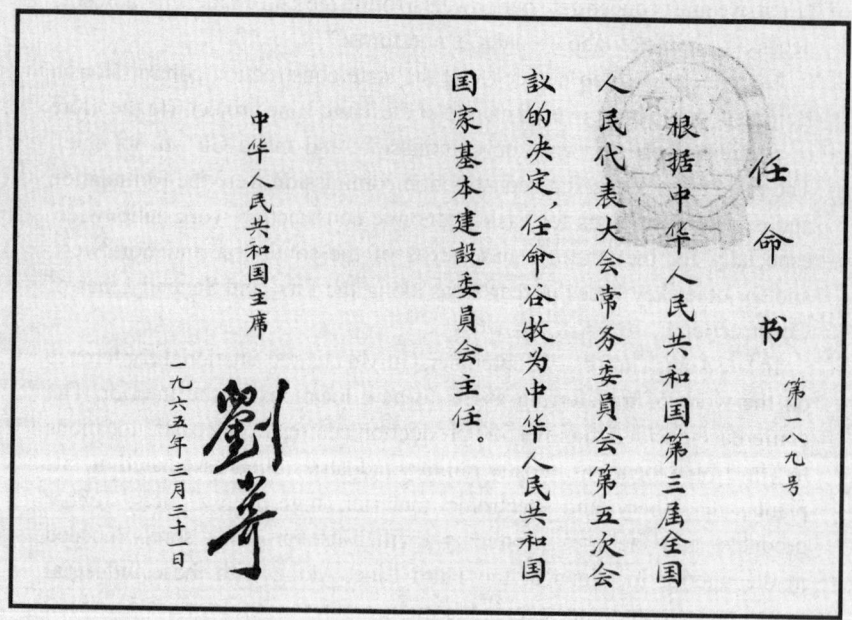

Gu Mu's appointment letter, issued by Liu Shaoqi

That evening, Gu Mu went to pay a call on Peng Dehuai. In Gu's view, Peng was the cornerstone of the entire modern system of secure military logistics developed by the PLA during the Korean war. During their conversation, Gu Mu asked Peng to take responsibility for all the logistical backup for the Third Line programme. From this heart-to-heart conversation with Gu Mu, the old marshal understood that the party central authorities still cared about him. He was stimulated, and immediately asked to work with his old command, the railway troops. Gu Mu was deeply concerned about Peng Dehuai's advanced age and fragile health, and gently refused. "It is best that you remain here in personal charge," he said. "When we go to Beijing for the annual conference on material allocations, I'll make sure to arrange proper physical examinations for you."

On 12 November 1965, in the metallurgical headquarters of Panzhihua, Sichuan province, Li Jingquan accompanied Deng Xiaoping and others to inspect the planning model of Panzhihua steel works. Front row from left to right: Xu Chi, deputy director of the metallurgical department; Deng Xiaoping, general secretary of the central committee; Li Jingquan, first secretary of southwest bureau of the CPC and director of the southwest Third Line Construction committee; Lü Zhengcao, railways minister and first political commissar of the Railway Corps; Yu Qiuli, first deputy director of state development planning commission; Gu Mu, director of the state infrastructure commission; Sun Yong, section chief of central guard bureau

A group photo at the Panzhihua Iron and Steel plant in Dukou city. Front row from left to right: Li Jingquan, Deng Xiaoping, Zhuo Lin (Deng Xiaoping's wife) and Wang Tengbo (wife of the first secretary of Yunnan provincial party committee, Yan Hongyan). Back row from left to right, Xie Beiyi, Yu Qiuli and Gu Mu

Li Jingquan and Gu Mu hold discussions in Panzhihua, Sichuan, November 1965. From left to right: Li Jingquan (first secretary of southwest bureau of the central committee of the CPC), Gu Mu (director of the state capital construction commission), Cheng Zihua (secretary of southwest bureau of the central committee of the CPC and deputy director of the Third Line Construction commission) and Lü Zhengcao (minister of railways and first political commissar of the armed Railway Corps)

A Visit to Peng Dehuai amid 'Third Line of Construction' Upsurge

Gu Mu's words bore an unspoken meaning. The armed Railway Corps were created during the Korean war. With his old troops, Marshal Peng Dehuai would unquestionably find a warm welcome. But this would not be helpful in addressing Peng's political exile. The old general caught Gu Mu's meaning in an instant. He later told his niece, Peng Gang: "That was my happiest day since I was attacked at the Lushan plenum in 1962." He went on, emotionally: "They depended on us in war; now, faced with these huge construction tasks, they are again looking to me, an old and experienced 'knowledgeable cadre'."

Over his lifetime, Gu Mu had many encounters with Peng Dehuai, in addition to their night-time conversation in Chengdu, in which he acted with great concern for the proprieties (for example, with respect to the physical examinations he arranged for Peng during the annual conferences in Beijing). His behaviour toward Peng was a reflection of his own superior qualities and his political perceptiveness. Premier Zhou Enlai was also of this view. At Gu Mu's funeral, standing before the portrait of Gu Mu, the daughter of He Long recounted this act of kindness. Apparently, prior to the 'Cultural Revolution', both Zhou Enlai and Marshal He Long had been in contact about making these dignified arrangements for Peng Dehuai.

Chapter 30

Showing his Originality in Revolutionising the Design Field

The economy had just been returned to its original state, and the 'leftist' political wave had surfaced again. At the 10th plenum of the eighth party congress in late September 1962, Chairman Mao said: "Class struggle must be talked about every year, every month, every single day." The plenum blasted the so-called 'black secret wind', the 'individualist wind' and the 'reversal of verdicts wind', each reflecting a bitter internal battle among opposing party factions. Gu Mu immediately knew that this kind of talk would have an effect on economic production. He took some heart from another comment by Mao: "Do not relax your work because of class struggle; our work must always be at the top of our priorities." Gu Mu said: "From 1963 on, the socialist education movement [originally known as the 'four cleanups movement'] quickly spread from the cities to the countryside. At that time, cadres at our level had differing views of the movement, but they could only register their unanimous support of the party centre. Many times they had to act under the orders of the centre, making only small and flexible adjustments to match local conditions, but in their hearts they felt deeply anxious and they trod with extreme caution, afraid that they might slip on the ice at any moment. In the factories under my jurisdiction, the 'four cleanups' and 'designing a revolution' were precisely like that."

In the winter of 1964, Gu Mu and the party secretary and vice minister of the ministry of water conservancy and electric power, Liu Lanbo, led a work team to Beijing to carry out 'socialist education' at the Shijingshan electric power plant. The work style of the plant's party secretary, Li Ximing, was careful and thrifty, and he received the visitors' support. Gu Mu and Liu Lanbo prioritised improving the relationship between the party and the populace, and between cadres and ordinary people. While pushing ahead on the production front, this had the effect of protecting Li Ximing and other cadres while not resurrecting the then-current political technique known as 'organising the ranks by class'. This brought good results.

At that time in all of China there were more than 250 units doing prospecting and design work, of which 170 belonged to the central authorities. How was socialist education to be carried out in the design institutes? These organisations brought heavy concentrations of highly educated people whose thinking habits and work styles were far different from those in the farms and mining enterprises that Gu Mu knew well.

In October 1964, Gu Mu and the deputy chairman of the SEC, Song Yangchu, after much consideration, came to realise that, in the winter of 1963, some of the design units had promoted a revolutionisation in terms of staff thinking, engineering design and organisational structure of these design units. In other cases, design professionals stepped out of their office buildings and institutes to work side by side with labourers at the project sites in order to come up with ways of economising and speeding up the design process. Gu Mu presented these ideas on revolutionising the design system to the party committee in the SEC. The political section in the central party's department of industry and commerce put its name on a report forwarded to the central party secretariat. From there, Peng Zhen, who handled day-to-day work for the central party secretariat, forwarded the document to Mao Zedong. On 1 November, Chairman Mao sent this instruction: "Comrade Peng Zhen, please tell comrade Gu Mu he should, before the national design conference meets next February, make sure that all design organisations fully throw themselves into the mass revolutionary movement, with full and uninhibited discussion. In three months, great results can be achieved. Ask Comrade Gu Mu to get started immediately, and to check repeatedly on the work of his subordinates. Supervise them and push them. Sum up all experiences. That is what I will be looking for!"

On 2 November, Gu Mu convened cadres handling capital construction tasks at a total of 19 agencies from the industrial, transport and national defence sectors, and conveyed Chairman Mao's orders that they set in motion the revolutionary transformation of the design system. In his report that evening, he wrote: "The revolution in our design work is an important element in our socialist revolutionary movement. Tasks such as identifying classes and then reorganising the ranks of design institute staff can begin after an appropriate interval following the current phase of our work."

The central committee of the CPC issued and distributed Gu Mu's *Report on the Movement to Revolutionise Design*

中共中央批转谷牧关于
设计革命运动的报告

（一九六五年六月十四日）

各中央局，各省、市、自治区党委，中央各部委，国务院各部委，各人民团体党组，军委总政治部：
　　中央批准谷牧同志在全国设计工作会议上《关于设计革命运动的报告》，现将这个报告发给你们，希中央和地方各有关部门研究执行。
　　全国各设计单位根据毛泽东同志的指示，开展了群众性的设计革命运动。很多设计人员下楼出院，到生产前线去，到基建现场去，进行调查研究，总结经验教训，就地解决问题，这是设计方面一个很大的改革和进步。半年多来，运动的发展是健康的，并已经取得了显著的成效。
　　设计革命运动的做法是：放手发动群众，充分发扬民主，领导带头检查，主动承担责任，启发设计人员自觉革命；并且运用解剖麻雀的方法，总结经验教训，批判资产阶级思想；同时组织设计人员下楼出院，深入现场，联系实际，同工农群众相结合，促进思想革命化，改进工作作风；最后把思想革命落实到设计工作的改革上去。

On 8 November, Peng Zhen again conveyed Mao Zedong's instructions to Gu Mu: "Peng Zhen, please tell Gu Mu that his plans are fine."

Between December 1964 and January 1965, Gu Mu held four discussion sessions, each resulting in a brief report to party central authorities and other relevant organs. After watching all this, Zhou Yang wrote to Gu Mu: "Your method here is good. I'm in the middle of figuring out how to carry out socialist education in the education and culture sector, and your approach has given me food for thought."

From 15 March to 3 April 1965, the national design conference convened in Beijing. During its sessions, Gu Mu presented two reports to the party central authorities. Deng Xiaoping remarked: "The design units have taken in hand the task of revolutionising their design work by means of the 'four cleanups'. Their path is an active one, and I strongly approve it." Liu Shaoqi said: "The revolutionisation of the design sector has been carried out correctly… This is the way things should have been done in the first and second five-year plans."

In 1965, a year of portents of storms just ahead, Gu Mu's handling of the revolutionisation of the design sector drew the attention of Mao Zedong, Liu Shaoqi and Deng Xiaoping. Thanks to his 'revolutionising the design sector' as a substitute for the socialist education movement, and also to his agility with respect to 'placing class struggle in the forefront', we can say, objectively speaking, that Gu Mu actually brought about some tangible work results.

But later, Gu Mu thought again about the negative effects this had created. "It was unsuitable to use a political mass movement to solve real-world problems in the design sector. For example, reforming the regulatory systems got mixed up with other matters subject to ideological study. Especially while we were denouncing the thinking habits of the bourgeoisie, we hurt a great many key technology cadres, and had a bad influence on their work and their spirit of activism. From this we need to draw the appropriate lessons."

Chapter 31

Organising Military Units to Carry Out Capital Construction

In June 1965, while travelling from Chengdu to Panzhihua, Gu Mu received an order to join Yu Qiuli in accompanying Premier Zhou to Hangzhou, where Zhou was to make a report to Chairman Mao.

On the appointed day, Chairman Mao was in a good frame of mind. "I've read Yu Qiuli's report," he said, "and Gu Mu's report on the Third Line." Yu and Gu Mu both indicated that they wished to talk about some other matters. Gu Mu went into greater depth on certain Third Line issues that the written document had not covered in detail, especially the problems of poor transportation routes in the remote mountainous Third Line areas, which made transportation of very large pieces of equipment extremely difficult.

This rubbed a raw nerve with the chairman. "Are you telling me that my decision was in error?"

Gu replied: "My meaning was that we have to put transportation at the top of the priority list." Mao approved, and ordered him to get to work on that at once. He also ordered Gu Mu to carry out semi-annual examinations of the Third Line programme.

Gu Mu, 1965

Organising Military Units to Carry Out Capital Construction

Gu examines construction work in a Third Line area. He is pictured here with Song Ping and Gao Keting in Niqiu mountain, Qinghai province, in 1965

Gu Mu at the Liujiaxia site in Gansu province, August 1965

Gu Mu inspects imported drilling equipment with comrades including Lü Zhengcao, Song Yangchu, Xie Beiyi, Lü Kebai and Gu Ming, October 1965

As the Third Line programme developed, a strategic reorganisation took place in the ranks of the labour battalions working on major state construction projects. As many as a million workers were transferred to the interior from the coast, and from cities to remote mountain districts. Sichuan province alone assembled 600,000 construction workers. With that came all sorts of new problems of living arrangements for the families back home, education for their children and so forth. Just arranging for annual visits back to the workers' families imposed all sorts of demands on a transportation system already severely over-stretched.

Gu Mu thought long and hard. The Third Line was a very long-term responsibility. It was not clear that the accustomed military-style method of conscripting labour or drafting soldiers for labour, as was done with the railway troops or the engineering project troops, was what a new programme such as the Third Line required. Deng Xiaoping vigorously agreed with Gu, and went a step further by proposing to organise specialised construction brigades, under the slogan of 'Workers and soldiers joining together, able to labour and able to fight, with labour as the main task'. After more than a year of preparatory work, the PLA basic construction engineering forces were formally established, under the leadership of Lieutenant General Li Renlin. Gu Mu added the position of political commissar to his responsibilities. The first group was divided into five branches (corresponding to divisions), each comprised of four large units (corresponding to regiments). At its height, the basic construction engineering forces comprised 32 branches and 156 large units, totalling 490,000 people. At the beginning, neither Deng Xiaoping nor Gu Mu could have predicted that the biggest historic contribution these forces would make would be to complete all the major construction projects of the Third Line on time and according to quality specifications, while avoiding the local factional strife and chaos of the 'Cultural Revolution'.

A stone bridge connecting two tunnels of the Chengdu-Kunming railway. The bridge was built by workers using local materials

During the 'Cultural Revolution', the Third Line of Construction advanced continuously, even in the face of extreme hardships. The state invested approximately Rmb120bn in the programme, carrying out large construction projects, with a heavy emphasis on military industrial sites, in Shaanxi, Gansu, Ningxia, Qinghai, Yunnan, Guizhou and Sichuan, as well as in western parts of Henan, Hubei and Hunan. Because the Third Line was conceived in excessive haste, and on too vast a scale, and suffered from the depredations of the 'Cultural Revolution', the programme involved many heavy losses. But in the end, the Third Line of Construction zones established a broad range of industrial projects, and gradually created a new industrial base. Five new railway lines, including the Chengdu-Kunming line, opened for traffic, making a fundamental change in the historic isolation of the southwest because of inadequate transportation systems. The southwest became a base for all manner of highly specialised

Gu Mu with comrades including Deng Xiaoping (front row, third from left), Li Fuchun (front row, fifth from left), Cai Chang (front row, fourth from left), Liu Lanbo (front row, sixth from left) and Lü Dong (between Liu Lanbo and Gu Mu). They are standing in front of Chairman Mao's former residence in Yangjieling, Yan'an, November 1965

defence industries, driven by the transportation, energy and basic industry sectors. The Third Line programme brought a major improvement in the geographic disposition of the nation's productive capacities, promoted the development of many provinces' and regions' economies, and built a strong foundation for China's industrialisation as well as the subsequent programme known as 'the great opening up of the western region'.

On the eve of 'Cultural Revolution', Gu Mu with Li Fuchun (centre) and Liu Lanbo (right)

Chapter 32

Early in the 'Cultural Revolution', with Liu Shaoqi at the Grassroots

In December 1965, Luo Ruiqing was denounced. From March to April of the following year, the political climate quickly heated up. Peng Zhen, Lu Dingyi and Yang Shangkun were all investigated and denounced. At an expanded politburo meeting in May, the four men were either fired or transferred from their posts. This was deeply shocking to Gu Mu. He could not fathom its meaning.

The expanded politburo meeting then passed the 'May 16 announcement'. Gu Mu attended the meeting. What stunned him the most was Kang Sheng's personal attack on Marshall Zhu De. Gu Mu thought to himself: "The political life of those at the top has gone extremely awry."

At the end of the meeting, Gu Mu went to Zhu De's residence to express his warm regards. Zhu De said: "Now I'm called the 'black commander'." In the past, as a gesture of respect, Gu Mu had on several occasions entreated Zhu De to provide him with a sample of Zhu's calligraphy. Zhu had promised to oblige, but until then had never done so. Now, under a political cloud, Zhu De said to Gu Mu: "Do you still want to own an example of my calligraphy?" Gu answered without hesitation: "Of course I do! In the past, you kindly said you would present me with your calligraphy, so it's not appropriate to press you again about that now."

After *People's Daily* published Nie Yuanzi's big-character poster, all classes ceased at Beijing's colleges and middle schools, and big-character posters cropped up everywhere. Liu Shaoqi decided to send party working groups to the colleges and schools. That led to endless conflict between groups of students who defended the working groups and those that opposed them.

In late July 1966, Gu Mu was ordered to go with Liu Shaoqi to the Architectural Engineering College, a unit under jurisdiction of the state construction commission, for a visit to the 'grassroots'. He went there with Liu Shaoqi three times, either in the afternoon or the evening. In his speeches there, Liu Shaoqi mainly articulated his thoughts about the 'Cultural Revolution' that he arrived at while managing tasks at party central authorities, such as "Do not surround the homes of the 'black gangs'" and "Do not hold raucous shouting sessions". Liu Shaoqi said calmly: "Now, as to how to carry out this 'Great Proletarian Cultural Revolution', you are not very clear and you lack information. The questions you ask of us, I tell you frankly, I'm not sure how to answer. I think that more than a few comrades in party central and in the working groups don't know how to answer either... Our grand old revolution has run into some new problems."

This kind of talk by Liu Shaoqi reflected the perplexity with which veteran cadres viewed the 'Cultural Revolution'. Gu Mu empathised with them. After a while, Liu Shaoqi said that he would no longer be going to the Architectural Engineering College, and asked Gu Mu and Qi Benyu to wind things up there. Qi Benyu did not go. In a large meeting with teachers, students and workers at the college, Gu Mu still noted that Liu Shaoqi's repeated visits to the 'grassroots' were an indicator of Liu's concern for the college, and told his audience that Liu's most important instruction was for everyone to seriously keep to their studies. Gu Mu sincerely tried to express Liu's own voice, in an attempt to clear away the problems that had cropped up at the school. But later, these words were turned against Gu Mu, and used to denounce him publicly as a 'guardsman of the bourgeois headquarters'. The 'revolution faction' forced Gu Mu to write a 'confession', which, along with Liu Shaoqi's forced self-criticism, was broadcast throughout the whole society.

Chapter 33

A Talk with his Son, a Red Guard

When the 'Cultural Revolution' began, Gu Mu's second son, Liu Huiyuan, was a middle school student. As rebellion erupted among young people, the boy was electrified, especially by the widely reported conversation between Chairman Mao and his nephew, Mao Yuanxin.

One day, the boy said to his father: "Father, it's not really important, but not only am I the secretary of my Communist Youth League branch, but some of our comrades at school are organising a band to conduct class struggle. I'd like to have a conversation with you 'comrade to comrade'."

Liu Huiyuan argued that his grandmother had often listed the excesses committed by poor and lower-middle peasants during land reform, with terrible effects. Gu Mu replied: "It is very possible that some of those leftist excesses did occur during the land reform period." Agitated, the boy responded: "Father, what do you think is going on these days?" Gu Mu said: "I am a cadre of the revolution. Under no circumstances is it right for a son to rebel against his father."

In his heart, Gu Mu grew alarmed. He found out that his son was friends with Zhang Xiaobin, Bu Dahua and Luo Xiaohai, students from the Tsinghua University-affiliated middle school who had penned the infamous big-character poster 'Long live the spirit of rebellion', and that Liu was a leading figure in the Red Guards at that middle school. His son, along with Lai Ruirui of the Beijing Aeronautical Academy (son of Vice Minister Li Jifa of the ministry of construction materials), was drafting documents on preparations for establishing the Red Guards at Beijing's universities.

Gu Mu knew the situation was very serious. Patiently, he turned back to his experiences during land reform. He told his son of his own situation during an inspection of Zhumei village that year. He said to his son sincerely: "At the moment when a movement arrives on your doorstep, the first people to act may be unprincipled nobodies from within the mob. One has to be skilled at recognising them for what they are, and getting people like that under control. You must motivate and cultivate the worthy and dependable ones."

Talking of his own mother, Gu Mu went on: "A girl from a wealthy or middle-income rural family could not suddenly be forced to have the mentality of a poor or lower-middle peasant. But she has been a good mother. She firmly believes that what her son does is right, and that her boy and his friends are to be trusted." Gu Mu's wartime comrades, such as Wang Yiping and Cao Manzhi, when they had no other place to hide, would flee to her house to recover from illness; they all called her their godmother. She made

Mao Zedong meets representatives of activists in the Railway Corps. He said: "We need to build our railways in a greater, faster, better and more economical way." Pictured next to Mao is the Railway Corps' commander, Li Shouxuan. Second from the right is Commissar Cui Tianmin, and far right is Deputy Commander Guo Weicheng

her contributions to the revolution. Gu Mu said: "How can you demand that I draw the line separating myself from a woman as fine as this?"

This conversation shook Gu's son deeply, and helped to strengthen his ability to think independently, to keep him from getting too excited, and thus to avoid being sucked into the savage factional struggles bursting out around him. Not long after, through Gu Mu's arrangements, the boy left Beijing for Xichang, in southwestern Sichuan, to seek out and report to Guo Weicheng, the deputy chief of the Chengdu-Kunming railway headquarters. After six months in the seventh division building the Chengdu-Kunming railway, both Gu Mu and Guo Weicheng were subject to political denunciation, and it was no longer possible to protect Gu Mu's boy in that faraway location.

Chapter 34

A Contest For Power at a Forum on Industry And Transportation

In September 1966, at the suggestion of Li Fuchun and with the approval of Chairman Mao and Premier Zhou, Yu Qiuli and Gu Mu were assigned to help the leaders of the state council deal with economic tasks. At that moment, some of the 'Cultural Revolutionaries' were fearful that things were not disorderly enough, and were scheming to spread the fires to the government's industrial and transport agencies, by stirring up students to go to the mines and make common cause with the miners. Many cadres from economic affairs offices and enterprises in industry and mining were subjected to violent 'struggle', and the apparatus for directing production was on the verge of total paralysis.

Premier Zhou was gravely worried. He said to Yu Qiuli and Gu Mu: "If the foundations of the economy can remain calm, the whole economy can be held together. But once those foundations are disordered, there will be no way to mend it." The premier wanted both men to help by 'guarding the pass' and maintaining stable economic work. Gu Mu was ordered to get the necessary forces together to produce a detailed plan for railway transport. He also wrote a series of directives forbidding the disruption of orderly rail and waterborne transportation.

In early October, Gu Mu reported to the premier about the difficulties besetting the railway and water transport sectors. The premier was deeply alarmed at the prospect of a rail shutdown or heavy disruptions to rail traffic. Then, early in November, the whole nation was shaken by the 'Anting incident' in Shanghai, and the situation rapidly led to the full-scale seizure of power by 'Cultural Revolution' radicals – the so called 'January storm'.

Seeing the situation spin out of control, Gu Mu recommended to the state council that, at the upcoming national planning conference, the first item on the agenda should be a brainstorming session on how to go about conducting the 'Cultural Revolution' in the industrial and mining sectors. He had just begun to assemble a team to work on preparatory documents when, on 13 November, Chen Boda issued a draft version of *Twelve Articles Concerning the 'Cultural Revolution' in the Industrial and Transportation Sectors*.

Cadres from all across China and from ministries and agencies under the state council responsible for these two sectors gathered in Beijing for a forum that opened in the Jingxi hotel on 16 November. Everyone at the meeting knew that, if the 'Cultural Revolution' swept into the industrial and transportation sectors, the outcome was impossible to predict. They were furious at the central leadership figures who had brought about this 'Cultural Revolution'. But they did not dare to stand up publicly against the flow of the 'Cultural Revolution' tide.

Instead, they opted for flanking tactics, such as proposing a number of editorial changes to Chen Boda's *Twelve Articles*. They wrote a piece arguing that: "For 17 years, the industrial and transport sectors have operated fundamentally in accord with Chairman Mao's revolutionary line." They put out a directive ordering students not to head for the mines to make common cause with the workers there. Further, at Yao Yilin's suggestion, they added the line: "The spirit of this document is appropriate for the financial and commercial sectors as well." Through these edits and emendations, Chen Boda's original *Twelve Articles* turned into a different document, the *Fifteen Articles on Industry and Transport*.

The *Fifteen Articles* had just been finalised when, on the afternoon of 21 November, Chen Boda called Yu Qiuli and Gu Mu on the phone and brought them before him. In a rage, he quoted them a few lines from *Letter to Ren An* by the great Han dynasty historian, Sima Qian. Gu Mu knew these passages by heart from childhood. The gist of *Letter to Ren An* was that all those petty functionaries who wrote essays, or worked on history, or studied the movements of the heavenly bodies, or practised divination, or performed ritual sacrifices to the ancestors, were disdained over the generations as nothing more than the lowest of the low. Seeing that Gu

A Contest For Power at a Forum on Industry And Transportation

Mu was holding his tongue, Chen Boda went on. "The common people despise the powerless scribblers writing their documents," he said. "In the past, Deng Xiaoping was despicable. Now, it is you who are despicable, for making my *Twelve Articles* unrecognisable!"

Chen Boda would have nothing of Gu Mu's attempt to explain, so Gu and Yu Qiuli left the room. In due course, Gu Mu reported all this to Premier Zhou. The premier said that he didn't remember those particular passages from Sima Qian very clearly, and asked Gu Mu to write them down.

At 10pm on 22 November, Li Fuchun phoned Gu Mu to inform him that Chairman Mao had issued an instruction fundamentally affirming the opinions of Gu Mu and others regarding proposed changes in Chen Boda's draft document. It then dawned on Gu Mu why the premier had subtly allowed him personally to transform the original meaning of Chen Boda's document. At the beginning, Chairman Mao had clearly understood what was on Chen Boda's mind. But Zhou Enlai had skilfully found Chen's 'acupressure points' of greatest vulnerability.

From 4-6 December, Lin Biao led an enlarged politburo session at the Huairen hall. Reports from the earlier forum on the industrial and transportation sectors were presented, and the *Fifteen Articles* was debated.

Gu Mu argued that, first, there was no such thing as a 'black line' in the two sectors; second, there was no problem of leadership powers not residing in the hands of the proletariat; and third, continuity and coordination in the industrial and transportation sectors required that production should not be interrupted. These three factors clearly showed that the Cultural Revolution in industry and transportation was utterly different from the 'Cultural Revolution' in education and culture. Moreover, the situation in the industrial and transportation sectors had to be distinguished from the situation within other organs of the party or the government. It was essential to proceed in stages, Gu argued, one batch of problems at a time, while ensuring eight hours of productive work each day, and conducting the raucous activities of the 'Cultural Revolution' after the work day had ended. Gu pointed out especially forcefully that, in the effort to strengthen teams at all levels of government to raise production and construction, it was absolutely essential that cadres in trouble for 'committing errors' not be fired from their positions en masse.

When Gu finished his report, a storm of criticism descended on him. Wang Li said: "Your report contains a number of mistakes, and it fails to carry out the 'Cultural Revolution'." Zhang Chunqiao charged: "Your words speak only for a handful of capitalist running dogs." Jiang Qing called Gu Mu "completely counterrevolutionary". Chen Boda, in a fury, demanded: "Why did you not discuss this with me in advance? Are you trying to launch a sneak attack?" Kang Sheng said: "In a country that is becoming revisionist, it is the economic foundations, not the cultural and educational sectors, that are of prime importance. To destroy the deep roots of capitalism, it is imperative that the 'Cultural Revolution' be carried out with even greater intensity in the industrial and transport sectors."

On 6 December, Lin Biao summarised at the close of the expanded politburo meeting. "The forum on the industrial and transport sectors was badly run and was in error. The thought processes at that meeting were incorrect. A 180 degree turn is required."

Throughout the politburo meeting that ran over three days, Zhou Enlai, Li Fuchun, Li Xiannian, Ye Jianying and Nie Rongzhen all had little to say. When Lin Biao finished speaking, Zhou said: "Gu Mu and his colleagues only have one supreme concern, and that is that the political movement will have an impact on the national economy. And if the economy runs into difficulties, that in turn will affect the progress of the 'Cultural Revolution'."

Several days later, Zhou Enlai called a meeting to discuss whether and how widely to distribute the documents produced by the industry and transport forum. Gu Mu stated his view: "Approval of full distribution of the *Fifteen Articles* will certainly be heavily criticised. But I want to see distributed only the criticisms aimed at me. Don't get into all those other irrelevant matters, like Wang Li's mentioning comrade Tao Zhu by name."

After a little while, Marshal Nie looked at him and said: "Don't talk nonsense. I do not approve the circulation of this paper. I completely oppose circulation. Comrade Gu Mu is the only one with sufficient understanding of these questions to discuss them. It is not a question of making errors that will have subsequent damaging effects. All he did was revise the original draft! This draft was badly composed, and has to be significantly revised or completely rewritten. Circulating it in this state will only bring about far worse results and will plunge us further in the direction of disorder and conflict."

Marshal Ye Jianying, Li Fuchun and Li Xiannian agreed completely with Nie. The several figures in the room from the central 'Cultural Revolution' leading group continued to throw up specious arguments, but the premier had the final say: "The *Fifteen Articles* will not be circulated; all cadres who have come to Beijing to discuss the matter must go home; only the standing committee of the politburo will be authorised to discuss this in the future."

Nevertheless, on 19 December, the party central authorities did distribute widely Chen Boda's *Fifteen Articles* along with another document, both calling for the extension of the 'Cultural Revolution' into the industry, mining and agriculture sectors. From that moment on, the 'Cultural Revolution' spread to industry and transportation, finance and commerce, agriculture, science and technology, and other fields. Industrial and mining enterprises were plunged into upheaval and peril.

Meanwhile, the rebel factions put up big posters on street corners quoting the enlarged politburo meeting criticisms of the industry and transport forum and of the *Fifteen Articles*. For Gu Mu, as he tried to maintain production, this meant even more hardship.

Chapter 35

Becoming a Junior Partner in the 'February Countercurrent'

Amid these terrible conditions, Gu Mu still made a trip to southwest China from the middle of December 1966 to the end of January 1967, to observe the progress of the Third Line of Construction. What he found throughout his journey could be called 'extreme dangers, and perils on every side'. For example, the general supervisor at the Panzhihua steel industry base, Vice Minister of Metallurgical Industry Xu Chi, was beset by chaos, and could only invite Gu Mu to meet him in the little town of Miyi. The chief of Shuicheng Iron and Steel in Guizhou, Tao Ticheng, warned Gu Mu: "This place is not safe; we must not stay here long. Hurry up!" And, sure enough; the next day the rebels forcibly seized control; Tao Ticheng was later tormented to his death by the rebels.

In the eyes of the rebels, since Gu Mu had come to the southwest so soon after being criticised at the enlarged politburo meeting, he must have been trying to escape his fate, so they sent repeated telegrams ordering him to return to Beijing to undergo criticism. In his memoirs, Gu Mu later said: "Even though my heart was bound to the work of the Third Line, returning to Beijing to take part in the 'February countercurrent' was still an honour!"

Gu returned to Beijing at 11am on 30 January. As he stepped out of the plane, he was seized, bound and detained by men from the rebel faction.

On the morning of the next day, Gu Mu was subjected to 'struggle' for five hours. The premier had sent a special emissary to be present, and after his vigorous intervention, Gu Mu was sent to the north gate of Zhongnanhai.

Gu Mu had frequently travelled between Beijing and the Third Line in the southwest. He had worked as hard as he could to belittle and weaken the 'Cultural Revolution's' work at the grassroots. What he had not foreseen was that the rebel factions and their powerful political allies behind the scenes had already built a network and had dug a whole series of pitfalls for Gu Mu. His seizure at the airport in Beijing was just the first sign of this. Soon, a volley of attacks from hidden positions was launched against him.

In early February, the rebel faction at Beijing Chemical Industry College took up the cry: "The crime of Gu Mu's opposition to Chairman Mao." In his diary for 7 February, Gu Mu wrote: "In recent days, the Beijing Chemical Industry College has announced that I am a counterrevolutionary element. The first criminal charge is that I once said, in some party meeting, that Chairman Mao was not quite right in the head. Such talk was common among small groups of people, but I have no memory of that."

In those ferocious months of the 'Cultural Revolution', everyone knew what would become of those who were publicly denounced for 'Opposing Chairman Mao'. Gu Mu struggled and floundered until he found a way of getting a message to Li Fuchun. Zhou Enlai and Li respectfully explained things to Chairman Mao: the trusted aide to some leading figure who had been overthrown had intentionally sent a distorted and inflated bill of particulars against Gu Mu and passed it to the rebel faction. Chairman Mao quickly understood what was going on. What Gu Mu had feared most – the explosion of Mao's fury – did not happen. But in Mao's eyes, Gu Mu was no longer the same person he had once praised and rewarded.

The rebel faction was furious. On 10 February, two bands of people entered Gu Mu's home and confiscated his property, carting off the safe where Gu Mu kept his important papers. When Zhou Enlai learned of this, he sent a personal emissary to the state construction commission with a private letter ordering the return of the documents. The long night passed, and on the next day the documents were returned. This enraged the rebels even more.

During the meeting on the night of 11 February 1966, Ye Jianying had placed the blame on Kang Sheng, Chen Boda and Zhang Chunqiao: "You have brought chaos to our party. You have thrown the government into disorder. You are bringing chaos to our industry and our agriculture. You are determined to throw the military into chaos as well. What do you think you're doing?"... "Your coup in Shanghai – now you're calling it the 'Shanghai Commune'! Something as big as that affects the entire national order. Changing the name of the Shanghai authority without any discussion by the politburo – what do you think you're doing? Can there be a revolution without party leadership? Do you want us to have no military at all?"

Marshal Xu Xiangqian said: "Our military is the mainstay of the dictatorship of the proletariat. As you create chaos in our military, do you or don't you want the armed forces to be that mainstay?"

Nie Rongzhen also spoke: "You can't take down the elders, so you go after their children and denounce them as criminals. Brutally persecuting veteran cadres, assaulting those who are already helpless – you really have evil intentions!"

On 12 February, the rebels of the construction commission invaded the small meeting hall within the Zhongnanhai compound. Gu Mu was 'struggled against' for two hours. Around 2pm, Li Fuchun and Li Xiannian listened to the 'charges' against him, and the battle came to a temporary halt.

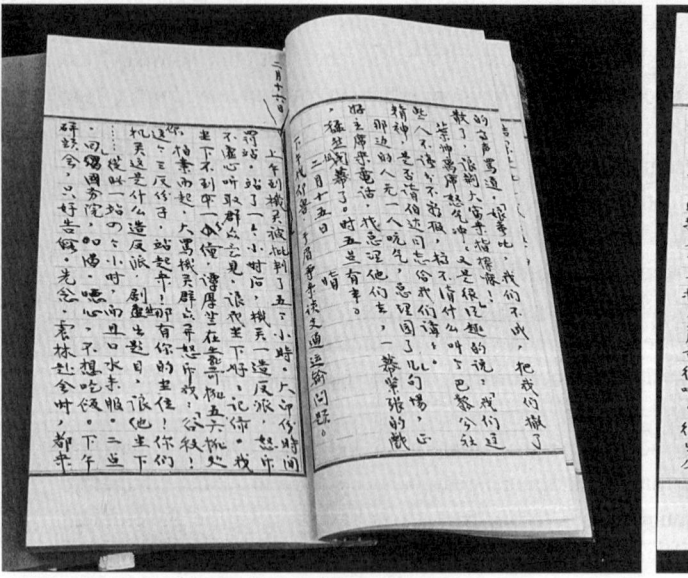
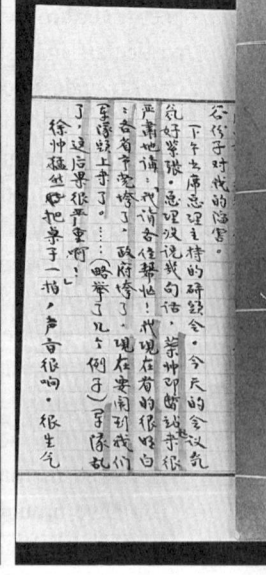

Gu Mu's diary entries for 14 and 15 February 1967

Becoming a Junior Partner in the 'February Countercurrent'

On the following day, 15 people from the office set up to reorganise workers in the basic construction sector into soldiers came to Zhongnanhai to struggle against Gu Mu for his errors pursuing that work. The criticisms lasted all morning. Someone from every part of the office of worker reorganisation delivered a denunciation. This was all obviously orchestrated.

That night, Li Fuchun rushed to Gu Mu a special bulletin containing a letter of petition. A special call for action against Gu Mu had appeared. His 'hat' (the charges against him) were great: "Viciously slandering Chairman Mao, while heaping praise on Liu Shaoqi."

On 14 February, Zhou Enlai held a brainstorming meeting of the politburo. Both sides went at it again. The meeting ended when a phone call from Chairman Mao arrived. In his diary, Gu Mu wrote this with respect to the politburo session: "14 February. Weather clear. I went to the meeting called by the premier in the afternoon. The climate at today's meeting was very stressed. The premier said a few words, and then Marshal Ye stood up and solemnly said: 'I ask for everyone's help. I now realise that the party has collapsed in all provinces and cities of the nation. The government has collapsed. The frenzy is about to engulf our armed forces. If chaos erupts in the military, the consequences could not be more severe!'

"Marshal Xu Xiangqian furiously pounded the table. 'If we have done so very badly,' he said in a loud and angry voice, 'we can walk away from this. Let Kuai Dafu run the place!'

"Marshal Ye Jianying rose from his seat, sputtering with fury. He addressed Chen Boda sarcastically: 'Our group is illiterate. We don't read newspapers. We have no idea what the 'spirit of the Paris Commune' might be. Perhaps comrade Chen Boda would care to present an instructional lecture to us?'

"Those on the other side were silent. The premier tried to find a compromise. Just then a call from Chairman Mao came in, and the premier left. The curtain fell abruptly. It was 5:30pm."

On 16 February, Gu Mu endured a vicious struggle session organised by Tan Houlan of the Beijing Normal University rebels and rebels from other organisations, forced to stand continuously for five hours. He endured the worst abuse, and was deprived of water. Gu Mu's gruelling trips to the far southwest caused him ceaseless struggle and denunciation by the rebels.

Standing on his feet for five straight hours, suffering badly from arthritis, caused Gu Mu unbearable pain.

In the afternoon, he returned to Zhongnanhai, thirsty, sick at heart and close to collapse. Physically and psychologically he had reached the limits of his endurance. Gu Mu later recalled: "It was probably comrade Yu Qiuli who reported our situation to Li Xiannian and other leaders. In the afternoon, Li Xiannian and Tan Zhenlin, before they went to a short meeting of party central authorities, came to see me and were deeply moved by what they saw…"

Possibly because of what they saw when they visited Gu Mu before their meeting, they were uncontrollably angry. Tan Zhenlin opened fire first at the short meeting. "Why has Chen Pixian not been allowed to attend this meeting?"

Zhang Chunqiao answered: "The masses did not agree that he could come to Beijing."

Tan shot back: "You are 'the masses'! Masses! What 'masses' are you talking about? Do you still want the leadership of the party?" The more he spoke, the angrier he became. "Our fishing fleet is producing nothing. I ordered them to sea and they told me I was suppressing the revolution! Whenever they found an opportunity, they criticised me. You are at war with senior cadres everywhere, beating veteran cadres everywhere. Jiang Qing wants to paint us all as counterrevolutionaries."

Xie Fuzhi interjected: "Comrade Jiang Qing and the central 'Cultural Revolution' group are still protecting you."

This made Tan Zhenlin even angrier. "I have no use for her protection. We didn't make our revolution for Jiang Qing. You are trying to destroy the veteran cadres wholesale. The rectification and salvation movement in Yan'an hurt so many people. But this movement today is the most vicious in the history of our party, worse than anything that has come before."

Banging the table with his fist, Tan stood up. "According to you, we should let you and your group take over! I have had it. I will work no more. Cut off my head. Throw me in prison. Strip me of my party membership. I will still fight on to the end!" With that, Tan picked up his satchel and walked out.

Chen Yi called to him: "Don't leave. Stay here to fight the battle with your colleagues!"

Li Xiannian said: "The whole nation now is wrapped in forced confessions, struggles directed not only at veteran cadres but at their children, and at the military. At military headquarters in the western suburbs, even the teenagers are being seized!"

The overthrow of large numbers of veteran cadres had begun with an editorial in the party journal *Red Flag* in 1966. The premier said to Kang Sheng and Chen Boda: "On something as big as this, you still had no consultation with us and never gave us a draft to look at?"

Chen Yi added: "Even now, can you not figure out who is a revolutionary and who is not? Years ago, Wang Ming proclaimed himself a completely correct revolutionary. He said something about 'Remote mountain valleys are never going to produce Marxism-Leninism...' Years later, what became of him? Now we still need to see, in the end, who it is who opposes Chairman Mao. Who is correct? History provides the truth; if we continue down this path, what is our party going to become? We may all weep bitterly, but there will be no place for us to go."

Yu Qiuli responded: "The rebels at the state planning commission subjected me to struggle sessions twice a week. They never apologised to me. I will not show up."

Zhou Enlai, who had called the meeting, took no sides during the bitter exchanges among the veteran cadres, and never tried to relieve the sullen atmosphere in the room. At the end of the meeting, moreover, Zhou Enlai broke with his usual custom and did not make a report to Chairman Mao.

Early on the morning of 19 February, Mao called a meeting and criticised Tan Zhenlin, Chen Yi and others in the harshest terms for negating the 'Great Proletarian Cultural Revolution'. He said: "I have waited for you people for three days and you have not come. If this is the way it is, I will go back to Hunan, Chen Boda will go back to Suzhou and Jiang Qing will remain in Beijing. You can all criticise and pillage." The meeting with Mao resolved that Chen Yi, Tan Zhenlin and Xu Xiangqian would 'take some time off to reconsider'.

Between 25 February and 18 March, the politburo convened seven times for 'meetings to criticise political life'. The 'Cultural Revolution' small group furiously counterattacked to turn things around, calling the forum meeting on 16 February "the most serious anti-party incident since the 11th plenum of the eighth central committee in 1956". Zhou Enlai himself was forced to apologise. Yu Qiuli and Gu Mu were declared "the tiny group of conspirators in the February countercurrent". From that moment, the politburo ceased to function. In actuality, the central 'Cultural Revolution' small group took over the functions of the Communist Party politburo.

Chapter 36

Struggled Against by Day, Working at Night

Having declared Gu Mu to be a 'junior partner in the February countercurrent', the rebel faction's struggle against him grew steadily fiercer. Getting any work done grew even more difficult. But whenever Premier Zhou met with representatives of the masses from any government agency, he always asked Yu Qiuli and Gu Mu to go with him. He said: "Yu and Gu are fine comrades, and they have the approval of Chairman Mao. If they were not members of Mao's top team, would I be bringing them with me to this meeting? In a country as large as ours, there are innumerable jobs to attend to. I need their assistance. This has been approved by Chairman Mao, too."

Under these tremendous pressures, Gu Mu even saw his home invaded and his possessions confiscated on eight occasions during the Cultural Revolution. During the day, he was forced to attend criticism sessions; at night, he returned to work. Sometimes, at struggle sessions, he was pushed forward and down with his body bent, forced into a 'jet plane' position. Yet, at other times he sat in plain view receiving field reports and helping Premier Zhou manage the economy.

At about that time, both Yu Qiuli and Gu Mu left their residences to live within Zhongnanhai. Each time that Gu Mu left Zhongnanhai to go to his office, Zhou Enlai sent a special liaison person with him, and came to a 'Three must not happen' agreement with the rebels. But did those rebels honour such rules? Was two hours in a struggle session sufficient? Most struggle sessions ran for four or five hours, not including all the hurling of abuse and insults, or the head-jerking, or the painful arm-twisting, or the forced stooping or the kicking. Worst of all was the four or five hours of water deprivation, the desperate thirst, the head-spinning dizziness.

Once, Gu Mu returned to Zhongnanhai, his entire body close to collapse. Sometimes he could not even manage to get a bit of food down his throat. Li Fuchun could not stand to watch. He told the premier: "Gu Mu has gone out to be 'struggled' three times each week. His body can take no more. He can't get his work done – even if it's down to just one or two struggle sessions a week!"

The premier replied: "One time, two times – he should not even go once. Next time someone calls for him to go out, I must give my personal permission."

During that period, the premier wanted Gu Mu to take charge of the transportation system. To support him in this work, the premier specially arranged for Gu Mu to stand on the Gate of Heavenly Peace during the May Day celebrations. But shortly after the celebrations ended, big posters went up on Beijing's streets bearing the slogan: 'Down with the big counterrevolutionary Gu Mu!' In 1936, Gu Mu had been arrested and imprisoned by the KMT's military investigations unit. The CPC had later cleared him of any wrongdoing, but the rebels made much of it. Zhou Enlai remarked: "What's done is done. Just carry on with your work as usual."

Gu Mu's whole family once lived in building No. 19 in Baiwanzhuang's Shen district, Beijing

The fury over Gu Mu's 'counterrevolutionary' misdeeds continued without letup. In August, the 'secret agent' incident occurred. The rebels discovered that, early in the war of liberation, there was a KMT secret agent with the rank of colonel whose name was identical to the name Gu Mu took during Gu Mu's underground work in the 1930s. The name was Liu Mansheng. So, without any research or analysis, the rebels threw charges against the wrong man. It was hard for Gu Mu to defend against these mixed-up charges. Zhou Enlai told him: "If you say you don't know, I can help you find out. But for the time being, you had better not leave Zhongnanhai for your office. Why not stay inside the compound and help me with some of my work here?"

After that, the rebels put together a 'Grab Gu Mu unit'. They set up a position at Zhongnanhai's north gate, baying and howling. This went on for three months. But Zhou Enlai protected Gu Mu, not once letting him leave the compound.

In early April 1968, Li Fuchun said to Gu Mu: "The military has established basic control over the state construction commission." Li and Zhou Enlai decided that Gu Mu could safely return to his work place. On the eve of Gu Mu's departure from the safety of Zhongnanhai, Li Fuchun grasped his hand and said: "The premier has allowed me to convey his special farewell as you depart. You must take good care, and steel yourself."

Gu Mu's face burned; a tear almost fell from his eye. Li Xiannian was still angry about the slandering of Gu Mu as a KMT secret agent. "You were secretary general to the east China bureau of the party, were you not? Confidentially, if you had been a KMT agent, how could the party have won its east China victory?" Li went on: "Why would the KMT have used someone with the modest rank of major in their secret police to fill the high party posts you held in our east China bureau?"

Chapter 37

The Premier Issues Orders for Harbour Construction

During the 'Cultural Revolution', every unit had a special place for detained 'capitalist running dogs' and other 'cow spirits and snake ghosts'. It was known as the 'cowshed'. Gu Mu lived for a year and seven months in such a 'cowshed', 'receiving criticism from the masses' and 'gaining the compassion of the masses'. Once the questions about his past were thoroughly examined, in November 1969, he was further investigated at the state construction commission and at the May 7 cadre school. After that, he was sent down to a basic construction site in Jiangyou county, Sichuan, to be 'forged' in a unit under the command of the first battalion of the basic construction engineering forces. In July 1970, he was sent to the Jianghan oil field at Qianjiang, in Hubei, to 'gain grassroots experience'.

In February 1972, US President Nixon visited China, opening a new chapter in Sino-American relations.

Formerly, because the Taiwan Strait was a war zone, China's maritime transportation was very backward. In the thaw of Sino-American relations, Premier Zhou Enlai saw an opportunity. He promptly recalled Gu Mu, who was still cooling his heels at the Jianghan oil field, to return to Beijing to work with Su Yu on the work of ports and harbours construction. The premier said: "Strengthen construction of our ports. The economy needs this. Our foreign trade needs it. Victory requires it. How can we proceed if we don't take this on? It is long overdue. We must transform the face of our ports and harbours in three years."

Except for the time he had spent being 'forged' as a common labourer, Gu Mu had not actually performed work of any kind for a long time. Receiving the premier's commission, he resolved to do something great

The Premier Issues Orders for Harbour Construction

in his later years. He would not miss the opportunity presented to him by changes in the international situation.

Before Gu Mu received his orders, Su Yu had been in charge of port and harbour construction. For Gu Mu to join the veteran cadre Su Yu was an assignment not to be missed. After a while, Su Yu fell ill and had to step back, leaving most of the burdens on Gu Mu's shoulders.

In order to carry out Zhou Enlai's instruction to "change the face of our ports and harbours in three years" and to turn this goal into concrete programmes, Gu Mu set out to array all his forces as soon as he took on the job.

First, he asked the state council to approve the setting up of a leading small group on port and harbour construction under the state council, comprised of responsible people from the various relevant agencies and equipped with an administrative office to handle day-to-day tasks. The principal coastal provinces, municipalities and autonomous regions where port development was most prominent were to establish related entities, so as to create a seamless work system from top to bottom.

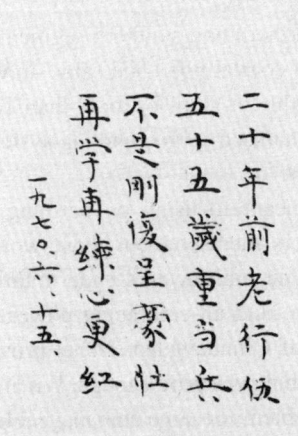

Gu Mu in military uniform, when he worked at a basic construction site. In 1970, he sent a copy of this photo to each of his children. On the left is a light-hearted poem written by Gu

The 'five good soldier' certificate of Liu Liyuan, the third son of Gu Mu (the character for 'Yuan' is written incorrectly and was the result of a printing mistake by an army clerk). At that time, Gu Mu disagreed with Lin Biao's formalistic actions in the army (Gu Mu's old leader Marshal Luo Ronghuan thought little of the idea of 'One sentence is worth ten thousand'). But Liu Liyuan, who had always been naughty as a child, was actually rated as a 'five good soldier', which really pleased Gu Mu and his wife

Second, he divided the work into northern and southern segments. He carried out research on the expansion of coastal ports and came up with a plan for the construction of 44 new berths for ships of more than 10,000 tons; the building of 150 additional mechanised cargo handling systems at the ports; and nine new docking facilities.

In the past, running ports simply meant focusing on berthing slots and basic construction work on the piers themselves, without worrying about cargo-handling areas or materials or public works under municipal government control. That meant no one held all-embracing power. This problem was visible to all at the port of Qinhuangdao, Hebei province. Balancing state investment and state planning was hard enough. When local investment was added to the mix, the problems became unmanageable. Gu Mu issued instructions: a fee of Rmb1 was to be collected on every ton of cargo handled by the ports, as a 'port construction equipment fee'. This idea was first applied in Qinhuangdao. Gu Mu totalled up the numbers: "With this fee, Qinhuangdao can generate several million renminbi each year; it can certainly manage a number of tasks."

The Premier Issues Orders for Harbour Construction

A Gu Mu family portrait taken in 1973. It was purely accidental that the whole family were gathered together. Gu Mu (front row, right) had just completed his work in the local government and was appointed by the premier to take charge of port construction. Mou Feng (front row, left) was ill and had returned to Beijing from the May 7 cadre school in Jiangxi province for examination and treatment accompanied by their daughter, Liu Yanyuan (middle row, left). Gu Mu's first son, Liu Nianyuan (back row, centre) and his wife Jin Jianhua (middle row, centre) came back from Tibet after their daughter was born. Gu Mu's second son, Liu Huiyuan (back row, left), was a soldier and had just completed a mission to escort weapons to Pingxiang, Guangxi province, before they were supplied to the Viet Cong. He was returning via Beijing and asked for permission to visit his parents and grandmother (front row, second from right). She is holding her first grandson, Liu Shilai. Gu Mu's third son, Liu Liyuan (back row, right), was a leading player in the 38th Army's football team and was due to play in a match in Beijing. Gu Mu's fourth son, Liu Xianyuan (middle row, right), was asked by the Haoliang River fertiliser factory in Heilongjiang construction corps to study in Beijing

As he approached his tasks in port and harbour construction, Gu Mu considered the limits of further development of Shanghai, the nation's biggest port. He suggested the rapid development of new ports near Shanghai, and for the purpose he selected two locations for further research: Ningbo, in Zhejiang province, and Zhapu, south of Jinshanwei in greater Shanghai. Zhapu was the location that Dr Sun Yat-sen had selected, in his *Outline of National Construction*, for the development of a great 'oriental port' (though it presented serious silting problems). Gu Mu's thoughts about these ancillary ports were later put into action.

Premier Zhou Enlai took a personal interest in port development. His important instructions gave rise to a host of equally important questions that needed to be resolved in a timely fashion. On 1 February 1975, a gravely ill Premier Zhou chaired his last state council session. Seeing Gu Mu, the premier eagerly asked for the latest news on port and harbour construction. In his report, Gu Mu stated: "Our original goals can be achieved. Please put your mind at rest, Mr Premier." Relieved and encouraged, the premier went a step further: "How will it be in 1980?" And he instructed Gu Mu to turn his attention as well to the challenges of airport development.

Chapter 38

Working with Deng Xiaoping to Redirect Industry and Transportation

In May 1973, Gu Mu was reinstated as head of the state construction commission (at that time, the title was chairman of the revolutionary committee, which meant that Gu now chaired the party's core small group within the commission).

In January 1975, at the first session of the fourth national people's congress, Gu Mu was appointed vice premier of the state council.

Gu Mu in Beijing, 1975

For Gu Mu, the most important thing that happened in 1975 was joining Deng Xiaoping in the huge process of 'reorganisation'. Reorganisation started within the organisational apparatus of the industrial and transportation sectors. The very first system to undergo reorganisation was the railway sector. Deng Xiaoping put Gu Mu in charge of the project.

Gu Mu immediately put the state planning commission, the ministry of railways and other agencies to work studying the issues, and drafted a *Decision on Strengthening Our Work on the Railways*. On 5 March, this document was circulated as *Central Document No. 9 for 1975*. Minister Wan Li thereupon took a leading small group on an inspection tour to key rail centres in Xuzhou,

Taiyuan, Zhengzhou and Changsha. By April, a number of extremely serious bottlenecks had been completely cleared up.

In the last days of March, Deng Xiaoping chaired a state council meeting, at which he said: "The spirit contained in *Document No. 9* should not be used only for work on the railways; it is appropriate for all industrial agencies." Gu Mu was in the middle of strenuous efforts to deal with major outstanding problems afflicting industrial production and construction. Deng Xiaoping's directive provided him with a clear path forward. He decided to put the reorganisation of the steel industry, which carried significance for the entire industrial economy, at the top of his priority list.

Late in April, at a state council business session, Gu Mu said: "Today, the main reasons for the iron and steel sector's failure to advance are internal, not external. We have to make a big effort to eliminate these problems."

Deng Xiaoping nodded in agreement: "The time has come for us to decide to resolve outstanding problems in iron and steel." Deng called for a national iron and steel conference, and assigned Gu Mu to assemble appropriate materials for the meeting.

Some state council leaders and staff in 1975. Front row from right to left: Yu Qiuli, Wang Zhen, Wu Guixian, Chen Yonggui, Ji Dengkui, Su Zhenhua, Gu Mu and Kang Shi'en

From 8-29 May, the iron and steel industry conference convened in the Qianmen hotel in Beijing. The conference revised the party central document, *Instructions on Making Strenuous Efforts to Achieve This Year's Iron and Steel Production Goals*, and published the result as *Central Document No. 13 for 1975*.

On 22 May, Deng Xiaoping chaired a regular meeting of the state council, and listened to Gu Mu's report. In his report, Gu Mu strongly argued: "If we want the iron and steel sector to advance, we are going to have to solve the 'revolution' problem at a number of major enterprises. We must strenuously oppose factionalism and pay close attention to the veteran cadres and personnel with scientific and technical skills. We will have to realign the leadership teams and strengthen the authority structures in charge of production." Deng Xiaoping affirmed Gu Mu's views.

A week later, on 29 May, Ye Jianying, Li Xiannian and Wang Zhen attended the ongoing iron and steel conference. Deng Xiaoping first called for Chairman Mao's 'three instructions' ('study theory', 'peacefully unite' and 'elevate the national economy') to be "the guiding principle for our work in the period ahead". Gu Mu later said: "This was our response to the 'Gang of Four' and it represented the first alteration of the 'Cultural Revolution' banner, 'Take class struggle as the 'guiding principle'."

Once that meeting was over, work began on the reorganisation of the leading teams at the ministry of metallurgical industry and a number of large enterprises. Tang Ke was reassigned from the ministry of petroleum to oversee leadership reorganisation at the ministry of metallurgical industry. He removed a representative of the army and another leader, and sent work groups to Anshan Iron and Steel, Wuhan Iron and Steel and other large enterprises to oversee implementation of *Document No. 13*. Because the span of the iron and steel industry's production was so vast, the state council also formed a 'small group on the reorganisation of iron and steel', with Gu Mu at its head. Lü Dong and Yuan Baohua became its deputy chiefs. Once reorganisation began, results quickly materialised. At Anshan Iron and Steel, Wuhan Iron and Steel, Baotou Iron and Steel and Taiyuan Iron and Steel – all of which faced severe production shortfalls – output was restored to planned levels by June.

While reorganisation was underway, Gu Mu further organised geological experts across the nation to prospect for rich new sources of iron ore and other mining raw materials. Unfortunately, the reserves they discovered were insufficient for large-scale development. Recognising this, Gu Mu and a group of experts came to the conclusion that China should build very large steel mills near coastal ports so as to make use of imported iron ore. This was the genesis of the huge Baoshan Steel complex later built in Shanghai.

From 16 June to 11 August 1975, the state council held a number of brainstorming sessions on planning. Gu Mu handled the drafting of the state planning commission document, *Some Issues Regarding the Faster Development of Industry*. The document finally encompassed 20 articles, and was known more simply as the *Industry Twenty Articles*. On 18 August, Deng Xiaoping chaired the meeting at which the *Twenty Articles* draft was debated. Gu Mu then made further revisions.

Originally, the plan was to send the document to party central authorities for approval and distribution. But suddenly everything changed. Not only were the *Twenty Articles* never distributed; the following year, that document became the target of criticism by the 'Gang of Four'.

Not long after National Day, the political climate suddenly turned cold. The ministry of coal called a reorganisation meeting and invited Gu Mu to speak. But while his address was in preparation, Li Xiannian urged Gu Mu to use plenty of quotations from Chairman Mao. Gu Mu was mystified. Li Xiannian replied impatiently: "We have erred in a big way, by suggesting that production was more important than revolution!"

At the end of November, party central conveyed Chairman Mao's latest instruction: 'Counterattack the rightist reversal of verdicts'. With that, Deng Xiaoping was removed from most of his tasks, and left only to 'specially deal with foreign matters'. Reorganisation itself at that point was totally shut down.

Chapter 39

Gu Mu Becomes a Top Target for 'Gang of Four' Attack

On the morning of 5 January 1976, the mortally ill Zhou Enlai underwent one final surgery. Gu Mu and Wang Zhen went together to visit him in hospital. Their hearts were stricken at the sight of the premier's emaciated visage. But with the 'Gang of Four' also in the room, Gu Mu struggled to contain his grief. When he got home, his wife saw that his eyes were red and swollen. "Old Gu, what's the matter?" she asked. Gu answered simply: "The premier is in bad shape," and began to weep and groan.

On 8 January, Zhou Enlai's heart ceased to beat. Immediately afterwards, Deng Xiaoping was removed from all positions.

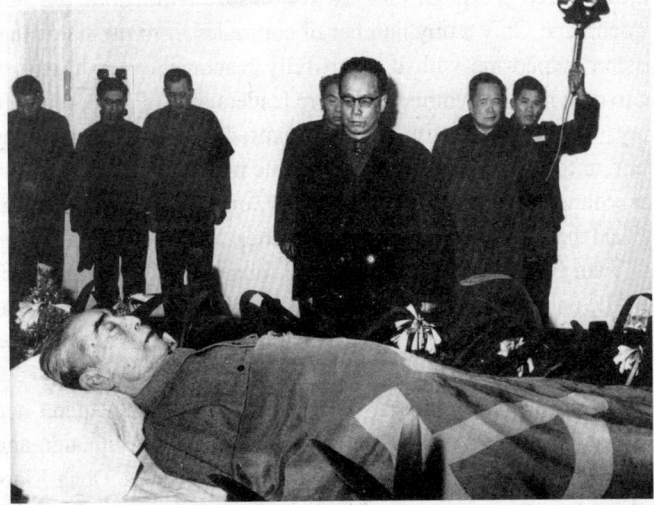

Gu was deeply grieved to say goodbye to Premier Zhou Enlai, his mentor and dear leader of the nation

The 'Gang of Four' set out immediately to turn everything around. Amid their clamour to 'criticise Deng, and counterattack against the rightist reversal of verdicts', the normal orderly functions of society and of work were thrown into chaos. At the Zhengzhou railway bureau, the villainous leader Tang Qishan disrupted normal operations on dozens of railway lines, spreading disorder over half the country.

Many of the veteran cadres were appalled by all this. Ye Jianying, confined to the sidelines, went to visit Gu Mu at his home. To prevent anyone else from hearing him, Marshal Ye turned up the volume on the radio to block out the sound of his own voice, and listened as Gu Mu explained how far the economic disruption had spread. When Gu Mu was finished, Ye Jianying said: "This is a disaster. The best we can do is to try to minimise the damage. You have a very heavy burden."

And so, Gu Mu became the target of some of the 'Gang of Four's' heaviest attacks. The documents he had produced, including *Several Issues Regarding the Strengthening of Industrial Development*, *A General Outline of the Work of our Party and our Nation* and *Several Issues Relating to Scientific and Technical Work* were slandered as 'the three big poisonous weeds aimed at restoring capitalism', and were fiercely attacked.

Gu Mu offered a straightforward response: "I did draft the *Several Issues* document. Only a tiny number of comrades from the state planning commission helped me with it. I am fully responsible for it, and it has nothing to do with the commission's core leadership." Gu Mu wanted to go to a 'May 7 cadre school' with the other comrades involved in drafting this document, to try to avoid the full force of the blast directed at him.

What wounded Gu Mu the most was that, once more, he had to pretend that he had had another epiphany and utter 'criticise Deng Xiaoping' slogans. Yuan Baohua visited Gu Mu and found him deeply torn. He told Gu Mu: "If, under present circumstances, we have to say things that are untrue to our hearts, comrade Deng Xiaoping will understand why when he hears them."

On the evening of 13 March, Gu Mu was ordered to attend a party politburo meeting, and to report on the 'criticise Deng' campaign and the production situation in the industrial and transport sectors. Deng Xiaoping also took part in the meeting. Gu Mu had taken on the vast reorganisation tasks in industry and transport under Deng's leadership; what went on in his heart cannot be put in words. "I have not done a good job at 'criticising Deng'," he said, "because Comrade Deng Xiaoping and I are of one mind. I simply cannot find the dividing line that would separate his thoughts and mine."

When Gu Mu had finished, Zhang Chunqiao accused Gu Mu of merely touching on small matters and avoiding serious issues in his statement. Zhang was bent on settling old scores. He argued that, since 1970, the problems in foreign trade had recurred; that Gu Mu on several occasions had spoken to him in a hostile manner; and that Gu Mu dared to say what Deng Xiaoping himself had not dared to say. The atmosphere was very intense.

Chapter 40

'If I Don't Enter the Bitter Sea, Who Else Will?'

Everyone agrees that Gu Mu made a huge contribution to the later 'reform and opening-up process'. In fact, as Gu Mu himself saw things, the last phase of the 'Cultural Revolution' actually strengthened the state council's leading role with respect to the economy. His contributions to the larger destiny of the party and the nation were even greater, and demonstrated even more clearly his abilities. Facing the final strengthening of his enemies, the 'Gang of Four', this cadre, with his extensive experience and leadership skills in dealing with economic work, now displayed the qualities of a politician as well.

On the evening of 31 May 1976, Gu Mu went to a politburo meeting to give a work report. He arrived a little early. Jiang Qing walked in and saw Gu Mu, and asked in a sharp voice: "Why was a set of imported chemical fertiliser equipment sent to Daqing? I order you to remove it!"

Gu Mu looked at her coldly and said: "This was not my decision. If you want to make accusations, you had better ask the politburo for its decision."

Jiang Qing railed on and on. Hua Guofeng, who had become Premier Zhou's successor, walked into the room. After figuring out what was going on, he said gravely: "This was approved by Chairman Mao himself."

Jiang Qing spluttered and walked out. But Zhang Chunqiao was not appeased. "I oppose what you-all are doing," he said, "dragging in the name of Mao Zedong to oppress us."

To the 'Gang of Four', Gu Mu was one of their opponents, who stood in their way as firmly as a fort at the head of a bridge; only after they got rid of him would they be satisfied. The cadres who took Gu Mu's side, with his best interests in mind, urged him to take some time to rest in hospital. Gu Mu, though, was absolutely clear; that would not do. If he were seen to be slacking, the 'Gang of Four' had long been prepared to take him before the state council and bring in their own people to take over his important economic work. At that time, Yu Qiuli was recovering from serious illness. Li Xiannian, who had already been shunted to the sidelines, once again warned Gu Mu: "Whatever you have to do, do not let them take control of the state council."

Ye Jianying said to Gu Mu: "During the anti-Japanese war, the political authority we established in some villages in contested areas displayed 'two faces' – one for us and one for the enemy. You had better do that again this time."

Gu Mu gritted his teeth and stiffened his resolve. The words of Premier Zhou, quoting a familiar Buddhist phrase signifying self-sacrifice for the good of others, echoed in Gu Mu's ears: "If I don't enter the bitter sea, who else will?" The example of the premier's practical approach shone before his eyes.

Gu Mu liked the painting *Pine Tree on Mount Tai*, which was drawn by the young artist Wang Lu. He always hung it above the bookshelves in his study, which was known as the 'nine rattan cane study'

In the most difficult times during the 'Cultural Revolution', Gu Mu asked his young friend Zhang Guoliang to engrave his beloved stone with the three characters '抗潮流' *kang chao liu* (countercurrent)

On 6 July 1976, in the hope of bringing some stability to the productive economy and controlling the deteriorating condition of the economy, a national planning work meeting was convened in Beijing, in line with Gu Mu's recommendation. During the meeting, Wang Hongwen cooked up a plot with Huang Tao, who headed the Shanghai municipal industry and transport directorship, and the deputy chief of Liaoning provincial revolutionary committee, Yang Chunpu. 'Huang of the south and Yang of the north' burst forth to attack Gu Mu, claiming that his words were only a superficial document; the core business at hand, they claimed, was not to strengthen the leadership of economic work, but rather to sweep out the 'rightist reversal of verdicts' wherever it was found. They said: "The rightist reversal of verdicts originated in last summer's state council brainstorming sessions."

Gu Mu stolidly refrained from discussing the words of Huang and Yang in any briefings. Three days later, Huang and Yang ran amok. Gu Mu stuck to his guns. Ji Dengkui said: "Failing to include in a briefing what someone said out loud is undemocratic. If you do not faithfully report in writing what was said in the meeting, you will regret the consequences." Gu Mu was determined to avoid associating with the henchmen of the 'Gang of Four', so he simply joined with Ji Dengkui in asking Hua Guofeng for a ruling. Hua Guofeng sided with Gu Mu, but he indicated that he wanted to discuss the matter with Zhang Chunqiao while they shared the vigil at the bedside of Mao Zedong, who was grievously ill.

The next morning, Hua Guofeng phoned Gu Mu and told him that the matter of the summary report on the previous day's meeting would be handled as Gu Mu proposed. Gu Mu's stubborn resistance gradually gained the upper hand.

On 24 July, the politburo heard a presentation on economic planning work. Yao Wenyuan continued to focus on 'finding the source of the evil winds', demanding to know what the state council's conference on guiding principles, held the preceding year, had been all about. Gu Mu, armed with statistics, replied: "The meeting discussed how we could advance the national economy. Li Xiannian and Hua Guofeng chaired the meeting. We got real work done. I attended the most sessions. The conference lasted from 16 June to 11 August, convening a total of 13 times. There is a written record of every session." He went through every detail of attendance at the conference: Chen Yonggui attended eight times, Li Suwen was present eight times, Wu Guixian attended eight sessions. Only Deng Xiaoping failed to attend a single one. Gu Mu fought back with the written record and hard numbers, leaving Yao Wenyuan with nothing to say. The meeting room fell silent.

Soon after that session, in yet another meeting, Zhang Chunqiao said to Gu Mu: "Economic conditions are bad. You had better do something."

Gu Mu replied: "The root problem is that the leadership system in the productive sectors has been plunged into chaos. The veteran cadres who could manage production have been attacked and subjected to 'struggle', and can only watch from the sidelines. The newcomers understand nothing and their words carry no weight. No one can manage anything. Nothing they say holds up. Inevitably, everything collapses at the lower levels."

Zhang Chunqiao responded to Gu Mu: "Your estimate of the seriousness of the problems completely lacks credibility."

Gu Mu managed to suppress his anger, and said: "In that case, there is nothing I can do under the present circumstances."

That very evening, while Hua Guofeng and Zhang Chunqiao were standing vigil at Mao's bedside, they had a chat. Zhang Chunqiao did not, in fact, agree with Wang Hongwen's supporters, 'Huang of the north and Yang of the south', in their assault on Gu Mu. This premier, specifically selected by the 'Gang of Four', simply did not know much about the present or future state of the national economy.

At 4am on 28 July, the great Tangshan earthquake happened. In Beijing, the meeting room shook violently. One veteran cadre whispered in Gu Mu's ear: "This is our opportunity to dissolve the conference." Gu Mu was just at that moment thinking about how to bring the meeting to an end, so he took advantage of the earthquake and closed the session.

On 4 August, Gu Mu went to the bedside of Chen Yun, who was also very ill. Chen Yun expressed four ideas to Gu Mu. First, the military must be kept calm. Second, Hua Guofeng must be firmly protected from political attack. Third, the elder cadres must remain active in current affairs for a while longer. And fourth, the banner of Chairman Mao has to be raised very high.

At the end of his long and eventful life, Chen Yun had become a wise mentor. In his diary, Gu Mu called Chen's four injunctions 'My guide for dealing with the world', thus providing a sign of the secret compact between the two men.

Chapter 41

Acquiring Important Information from the Den of the 'Gang of Four'

On 3 October 1976, when he was paying another visit to comrade Chen Yun, Gu Mu jotted down in his diary the main points of Chen's insightful analysis of the situation:
1. To hang together;
2. To hold high the banner of Chairman Mao;
3. To encourage newcomers;
4. To hold down daredevils (meaning to be prudent and patient for actions of the senior leadership);
5. To hold fast to the position;
6. To have two (Ye and Li) promoted ahead of the other four;
7. To be democratic;
8. To be well prepared for the big event.

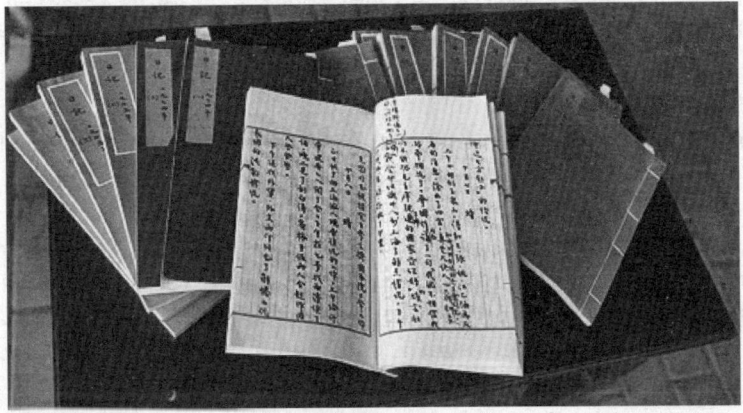

Gu Mu's diaries are of historic significance. The volume above shows the entry for 7 October 1976

Gu Mu (left) attends an art exhibition in Chairman Mao's Memorial Hall

Hearing Chen's views, and in contrast to feeling dejected at the time of the four points he referred to on 4 August, Gu Mu was now hopeful about the future. Two days later, on 6 October 1976, the 'big event' anticipated by Chen ultimately occurred: the concerted cracking down on the 'Gang of Four' by the central government.

Around the same time as the 'Gang of Four' were arrested on 7 October, Gu Mu accepted a confidential mission: Marshal Ye ordered him to explore prevailing conditions in Shanghai. Considering that city had long been under the control of the 'Gang of Four' and rife with the deep-rooted influence of cliques, Gu called in Lin Hujia, Yuan Baohua and others for an immediate discussion and set up a working group to accelerate the revolution and promote production. It was decided that the group, composed of people selected from central commissions and departments, would be headed by Xu Liang and would immediately head for Shanghai.

When assigning tasks to the working group, Gu told Cao Dacheng that he was responsible for intelligence gathering and asked him to privately invite Wang Yiping, his comrade-in-arms, to assist him. Cao suggested that Gu write a personal letter so that he would be in a better position to win the trust of Wang.

Gu said with a sigh: "Yes. It is important and I will need to give him something in return." Taking up a painting by Huang Zhou and rolling it up, he continued: "Wang loves it. Just give it to him. Tell him it is a gift from me and that I need his help with something important. He will see my point."

At 10pm on 8 October, in darkness, Cao went to the home of Wang. As expected, on seeing the painting and having heard the news about the hunting down of the 'Gang of Four', Wang immediately called together Yang Xiguang, Li Yanwu, Li Yongfu and other old comrades. They agreed to meet at the home of Cheng Shifa, a friend of Cao's father-in-law and a great master of Shanghai-style arts, under the pretext of discussing calligraphy and painting.

Gu Mu (left) and Wang Zhen (right) pay a visit to Marshal Ye Jianying

Gu Mu at a ribbon-cutting ceremony of Shanghai-based Baoshan Iron and Steel on 23 December 1978

Gu Mu at a reconstruction site in Tangshan in 1978

Chapter 42

Heading a Chinese Government Delegation to Western Europe

China's reform and opening-up process took off towards the end of 1978 when the third plenary session of the 11th central committee of the CPC was convened. However, it would take the launch of an extended process of investigation, discussion and preparation before the campaign was established as a basic policy of the state.

In 1977, the remnants of the 'Gang of Four' were mostly eliminated and, at the start of 1978, economic work was put towards the top of the agenda. The central party committee and the state council, with a view to drawing on foreign practices and pressing ahead with socialist modernisation, decided that Gu Mu would head a delegation to study the economy of western Europe.

The development of large state-owned enterprises was always a concern for Li Xiannian and other state leaders. Here, Gu Mu, Li Xiannian (third from the left), Chen Pixian (fourth from left) and others visit China's First Automobile Works in early 1978

Deng Xiaoping and Gu Mu

The delegation, which was the first high-ranking economic inspection group sent overseas by the Chinese government, included six leaders above vice-ministerial (provincial) level: Qian Zhengying, minister of the department of water and power; Peng Min, deputy director of the national construction committee; Zhang Gensheng, vice-minister of the department of agriculture and forestry; Ye Lin, deputy head of Beijing revolutionary committee; Wang Quanguo, deputy head of Guangdong revolutionary committee; and Yang Bo, deputy head of Shandong revolutionary committee. Additional delegates included Li Hao, Hu Guangbao and four other cadres of bureau and sub-department levels.

Before their departure, Gu was invited by Deng Xiaoping for a private talk. They decided that the delegation should be extensively engaged with the host countries so that the questions they brought with them could be addressed thoroughly through detailed investigation and profound study. After that, Gu Mu and the other delegates set out on their visit, burdened with the expectations of the party and the leader and with the great trust of the Chinese people looking to embark on their road to prosperity.

From 2 May to 6 June 1978, the Chinese government economic delegation headed by Gu Mu visited France, West Germany, Switzerland, Denmark and Belgium. Their focus was the industrial, agricultural, scientific and technological modernisation in developed countries, the reasons for their rapid economic progress during the 1950s and 1960s, and their means of organising and managing socialised mass production. During what was his first visit abroad, Gu was surprised at the gap that existed between China and western countries, and was convinced that great courage and wisdom would be needed for China to catch up with them. In his memoirs, he summarised his experience in three main areas.

Members of the Chinese government economic delegation

Gu Mu reviews a guard of honour in the company of Raymond Barre, prime minister of France, upon the arrival of the Chinese delegation in Paris on 2 May 1978

Gu Mu is received by the French president, Valery Giscard d'Estaing, on 11 May 1978

First, it was undeniably true that the capitalist countries in western Europe had achieved remarkable economic growth after World War II. The progress in science and technology and increase in labour productivity helped improve the wages and welfare of workers. In these countries, great changes were taking place with regard to the economy, government regulations and the handling of social conflicts. Their record of economic development had exceeded what had been predicted by the German-Russian economist Wassily Leontief in his *Journal of Political Economy*.

Second, some western European countries had a keen interest in forging economic relations with China. In accordance with diplomatic protocol, Gu Mu should have been received by vice-prime ministers. However, in all the countries he visited, he was warmly received by the president or prime minister. In his conversation with Valery Giscard d'Estaing, the French president came straight to the point by saying that he was fascinated with economics and that they could discuss all sorts of mutually interesting topics in this area, such as what manufactured goods China needed and what cooperation the two countries could further develop. The only topic that was not discussed was politics. During his visit to Bavaria in West Germany, the state governor said at a banquet that they were ready to lend US$5bn to help China out of financial difficulties, adding that no negotiations were necessary and that a handshake would suffice instead. All these countries that were rich in capital resources were eager to open relationships and do business with China in their efforts to find markets for their quality products and advanced technologies.

Gu Mu and other delegates visit the Zurich-based MAAG Gear Wheel Co on 17 May 1978

Third, he was well informed of the many internationally accepted economic models and terms, such as supplier credit (deferred payment), buyer credit (payment by means of credit with deferred loan repayment) and compensation trade (using equipment and technology supplied by foreign parties in return for finished products). All models that involved purchase prior to payment could not only help relieve China's difficulties in making foreign currency payments, but also benefit the absorption of foreign capital or the establishment of Sino-foreign joint ventures.

During the tour, much of the time was spent on visiting factories, farms, urban construction sites, ports, markets, schools, research institutes and residential quarters. For more than one month, they were so busy and overloaded with information that they had to ask the wives of the Chinese ambassadors to help them wash and iron clothes. Normally hale and hearty, Peng Min, deputy director of the national construction committee, would doze off as soon as he got into a car. Gu Mu was always keen to learn and constantly stressed that they should see as much as they could since they were travelling at the expense of the state.

Gu Mu and delegates visit a shipyard in Copenhagen, 26 May 1978

Gu Mu and delegates visit an open-cast mine in West Germany, 5 May 1978

Heading a Chinese Government Delegation to Western Europe

Gu Mu and delegates talk with foreign friends during their visit to Europe

Vice-Premier Gu Mu is received by Switzerland's federal councillor and foreign minister, Jean-Pierre Aubert, during his friendly visit to the country, 12 May 1978

Chapter 43

Study Tour Emancipates the Minds of Central Leaders

In his recently published *Deng Xiaoping and the Transformation of China*, the American scholar Ezra F Vogel observed: "Of all the study tours in 1978, the one that had by far the greatest impact on Chinese development was the one led by Gu Mu to western Europe from 2 May to 6 June. It ranks with the November 1978 central party work conference and the December 1978 third plenum as one of the three major turning points in China's reform and opening up." This assessment of the importance of the study tour is given particular weight because of the author's status as a sober-minded foreign spectator whose sharp observations had been gathered over the previous three decades. He continues in the following chapter: "What these highly respected officials saw and learned in Europe, and how they articulated the new possibilities for China at the state forum that followed the visit, made their observations extraordinarily influential."

Hua Guofeng, Li Xiannian and Gu Mu, 1980

Study Tour Emancipates the Minds of Central Leaders

On 22 June 1978, shortly after his return from abroad, Gu Mu presented to the party central committee and the state council an inspection tour report. The report faithfully revealed the real impressions of those expert Chinese leaders brought up in a planned economy on developed countries and modern-day capitalist society in Europe. Later on, many of his ideas and suggestions were followed and refined before they came to constitute the policies and laws for China's reform and opening up.

Hu Yaobang, Gu Mu and Nie Rongzhen

In late June 1978, the Gu Mu delegation was invited to present a detailed report of the trip to a meeting of the party central committee and the state council chaired by Hua Guofeng, China's president and premier. The main leaders present at the meeting, including Ye Jianying, Nie Rongzhen, Li Xiannian, Ulanhu and Wang Zhen, all praised Gu Mu for his objectivity and for the clarity of his presentation. The meeting lasted from 3pm to 11pm.

Each and every participating central leader addressed the meeting or gave their ready response. Marshal Ye emphasised from the perspective of strategy: "Since we have not been engaged in any war with western Europe over the past decades, they will hope to see China growing into a major force for global stability. They know that we are in need of their well-developed technologies, while they are rich in capital resources and have to look for a market for them. It is therefore my belief that importance should be given to the importation of technologies from western Europe."

Firm and determined, he continued: "We used to be somewhat biased and hypocritical in our propaganda against the west and, as a result, had ourselves been constrained by it. On his study tour, Gu Mu has seen all and made a relatively comprehensive investigation. Now it is high time for us to move immediately to make sure we import the right products from the right places. In short, we do not have to discuss it any further!"

In early July 1978, the state council convened a forum on principles to guide the four modernisations; the responsible cadres of all central ministries and commissions were in attendance. The forum continued for more than 20 days. At the opening session, Gu Mu presented a lengthy report of what they had learned from the trip and added some personal impressions. "We have to be honest in acknowledging that we are lagging behind the west," he said. "We have to be clear that the gap between China and developed countries is increasingly wide. How can we catch up with them? In what way can modernisation be achieved? And how can we pick up the pace? As far as I can see, one of the most important tasks involves importing advanced technology in a vigorous way. And we shall have to jump at the chance provided by the global situation to develop ourselves by taking advantage of what has been achieved in science and technology in the capitalist world."

He said with emphasis that all senior officials would have to emancipate their minds in forging economic ties with other countries. They had to come up with more ideas and expand their ways of thinking; self-seclusion could only spoil opportunities and invite ultimate failure.

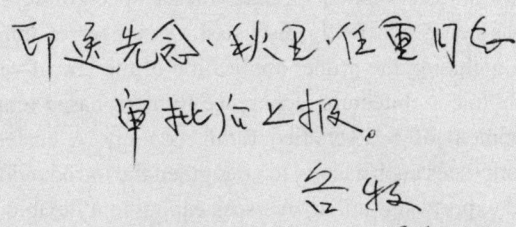

The first draft of *A Notice of the CPC Central Committee and the State Council about Establishing the Import-export Leading Group of the State Council* to be presented to the central leadership bears the signature of Gu Mu

The forum took place at a time when there was an all-absorbing national debate on the proposition that practice is the sole criterion for testing truth; all ministers made speeches on the speed of development, an issue that was being constantly discussed. A number of important ideas were raised, including the proper application of the law of value, the reshaping of economic architecture, adherence to merit-based remuneration and the development of a diversified rural economy. A heated discussion took place on issues such as how to strengthen the introduction of technologies, expand exports and utilise overseas capital in a flexible way. Before long, the results of the discussion would be incorporated into the great strategic decisions mapped out at the third plenary session of the 11th central committee of the CPC.

On 22 October 1978, while he was touring a Nissan factory during a trip to Japan, Deng Xiaoping learned that the plant produced 94 cars per worker per year. He was more than shocked because that was 93 cars a year more than China's most efficient manufacturer, the First Automobile Works in Changchun. "Now I understand what modernisation is," he declared.

At that time, decision-makers of the party and the state had already reached a consensus on learning from developed countries, although there were understandable differences in the depth of understanding. When the business of imports and exports assumed greater importance than the more pragmatic issue of foreign exchange earnings, the national strategy of opening up to the outside world began to take shape.

In February 1979, the import-export leading group was set up by the central committee. It was led by Yu Qiuli, with Fang Yi, Wang Zhen, Chen Muhua, Wang Renzhong, Gu Mu and Kang Shi'en as its deputy chiefs. The group was responsible for collective reviews of major policies, guidelines and planning, while Gu Mu was in full charge of its daily business. The priority given to the development of foreign trade was evident in the creation of a group composed of seven vice-premiers, which was more akin to a high-level cabinet.

In June 1979, when the central committee believed that it was not strong enough as an operating mechanism, the leading group was dissolved and ceded to the import and export regulatory commission and the overseas investment regulatory commission, which were under the regulation of one

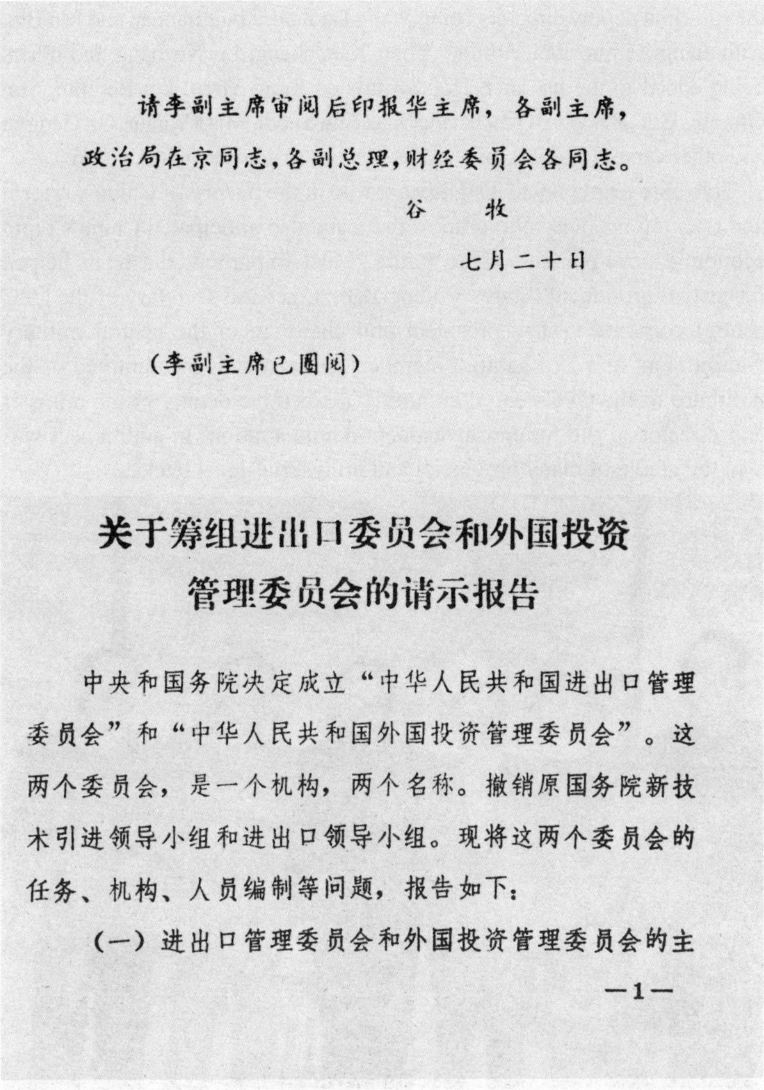

Study Tour Emancipates the Minds of Central Leaders

请李副主席审阅后印报华主席，各副主席，
政治局在京同志，各副总理，财经委员会各同志。

谷　牧
七月二十日

（李副主席已圈阅）

关于筹组进出口委员会和外国投资管理委员会的请示报告

中央和国务院决定成立"中华人民共和国进出口管理委员会"和"中华人民共和国外国投资管理委员会"。这两个委员会，是一个机构，两个名称。撤销原国务院新技术引进领导小组和进出口领导小组。现将这两个委员会的任务、机构、人员编制等问题，报告如下：

（一）进出口管理委员会和外国投资管理委员会的主

—1—

Report on Establishing the Import and Export Regulatory Commission and the Overseas Investment Regulatory Commission presented to the central committee by Gu Mu

administration led by Gu Mu. Meticulously, he put together a leading group, the full-time deputy directors being Wang Daohan, Zhou Jiannan and Ma Bin, with Jiang Zemin, Wei Yuming, Zhou Xuancheng, Lu Xuzhang and others being added to the list later. He also invited Rong Yiren, Lei Renmin, Sun Qimeng, Sun Xiaocun, Qian Changzhao, Sun Yueqi, Miao Yuntai, Gu Gengyu and other venerable economic figures to work as advisers to the group.

This elite team played a significant role in the history of China's reform and opening up. The setting up of the team also anticipated China's rapid economic development in the future. Most important, the team helped foster two prominent figures – Jiang Zemin, general secretary of the CPC central committee, state president and chairman of the central military commission, and Li Lanqing, member of the standing committee of the politburo of the CPC central committee, executive deputy prime minister and director of the foreign investment administration. In addition, it was also the cradle of many provincial and ministerial-level leaders.

Some leaders of the import and export regulatory commission and the overseas investment regulatory commission, 31 May 1985. From right to left: Li Lanqing, Zhou Jiannan, Jiang Zemin, Gu Mu, Wei Yuming and Li Hao

Chapter 44

State Leadership Borrows Foreign Brains to Promote Opening Up

Because of the continued economic blockade, combined with a decade of turmoil and self-seclusion, China became quite ignorant of developments across the globe, especially in terms of international economics. As a result, the pressing concern of the central collective leadership was focused on how to keep pace with developments in world politics and the economy, and draw on the economic experience and expertise in foreign countries.

Deng Xiaoping took Gu Mu's advice to employ some of the world's elite as advisers so that they would avoid making mistakes. With the approval of the central committee, China employed Armin Gutowski from West Germany and Okita Saburo and Masao Sakisaka from Japan. Later, it invited Lee Kuan Yew, Goh Keng Swee and others from Singapore to work as advisers on economic development.

Inscriptions by Gu Mu and Okita Saburo, former Japanese foreign minister and joint founder of the Institute of Sino-Japanese Economic Expertise, 31 July 1986

In January 1979, when the Chinese were celebrating the spring festival, Gu Mu hosted a forum at Diaoyutai state guesthouse in Beijing. Those present included officials from some major departments under the state council as well as Okita Saburo, Masao Sakisaka and their assistant Kobayashi Minoru. After introducing the modes of economic development along with their merits and demerits, the experts from Japan described in detail their experience in raising funds for energy and infrastructure construction. This was the first time that Chinese leaders of economic sectors had attended a lecture given by senior overseas figures on basic economic issues.

Gu Mu and his wife Mu Feng with Okita Saburo and his wife Hisako Saburo at the Diaoyutai state guesthouse, 28 July 1986

In autumn 1979, Okita Saburo was appointed foreign minister in the cabinet of Prime Minister Ohira Masayoshi. In line with Japanese practice, cabinet officials were not allowed to work as economic advisers to another country. After negotiations based on flexibility, the Institute of Sino-Japanese Economic Expertise was established in 1981 for the purpose of exchanging knowledge and information as well as policy consultation. The members comprised officials, experts and scholars from both countries. Okita Saburo was appointed adviser and Masao Sakisaka his deputy; those designers and think-tank members who had made outstanding contributions to the rapid growth of the Japanese economy were participating members. On the Chinese side, Gu Mu was elected adviser and Ma Hong, president of the CASS, was appointed representative; participating members included

State Leadership Borrows Foreign Brains to Promote Opening Up

Xue Muqiao (honorary director of the development research centre of the state council), Fang Weizhong (executive deputy director of the state development planning commission), Zhu Rongji (deputy director of the state economic commission), Li Hao (deputy secretary general of the state council), Shen Jueren (deputy director of the ministry of foreign trade), Gao Shangquan and Liao Jili (deputy directors of the state commission for restructuring), Li Jingzhao (deputy director of the ministry of construction), Liu Hongru (vice-president of the People's Bank of China), Sun Shangqing (director of the development research centre of the state council) and Pu Shan (director of the institute of world economics and politics at the CASS). It was agreed that an annual closed-door meeting on China's economic development would be held, alternately, in China and Japan. By 2008, as many as 29 sessions had been held.

Gu Mu was well known to be on good terms with those reputed entrepreneurs from overseas. This was exemplified in the idea to employ foreign advisers that was proposed when he was holding talks with Inayama Yoshihiro, chairman of New Japan Steel, when the Baoshan project took off in Shanghai in 1978.

Gu Mu (far left) and Masao Sakisaka, seen here riding a donkey in Turpan

Making use of foreign knowhow was of symbolic significance and had a profound influence at home and abroad. All friends from overseas agreed that China's decision to employ politicians and economists such as Okita Saburo as advisers revealed that the country was indeed opening up and integrating itself into world economic development.

In the second half of 1979, Armin Gutowski from West Germany was invited to visit. One of the five leading German advisers, he lectured at a large-scale seminar sponsored by the state council on the successful practices and experience of West Germany in its development of a market economy after World War II and answered questions raised by leaders of the ministries and commissions under the state council. This was followed by a series of specialised lectures attended by those from China's economic and academic sectors.

Gu Mu indicated that the importation of knowledge was more often than not misunderstood as bringing in general knowledge of science, technology and economic management as well as ordinary talented personnel. For the leadership of a state, it was actually a larger-scale initiative that could help a nation avoid the inevitable twists and turns. As we can see it now, Gu's warning was indeed honest and valuable.

Gu Mu, Xue Muqiao (third from left) and Professor Armin Gutowski (fourth from left)

Chapter 45

Focusing on Absorbing Funds Without Fear of Debt

In June 1978, in his report to the politburo about his study tour to western Europe, Gu Mu discussed the problems concerning the importation of technology and terms of payment. Importance was attached to the question of how to make best use of the foreign currency deposits held by the Bank of China. He proposed that various ways could be deployed that conformed to international practices. Shortly after that, Deng Xiaoping nodded his agreement, saying that importation would proceed by every means and what was important was to lose no time. "We may as well borrow some money and pay interest on it," he said. "Don't mind that. We can start to earn the money back earlier. We must believe that we are able to pay off all debts." Subsequently, at a forum held by the state council in July, a consensus was eventually reached on making use of loans from western countries and attracting foreign investment.

For a considerable time, Gu Mu applied himself to how to absorb loans from foreign countries and overseas businesses. As the reform and opening up was just under way, negotiations with Japan were of particular importance.

In August 1978, China, upon receiving information from a Japanese man called Kazumi Kimura, who was a good friend to the Chinese people, applied for a long-term loan from the Japanese overseas economic cooperation fund on favourable terms. In September 1979, Gu Mu headed a delegation to Japan and accepted the first tranche of loans (50bn yen, equivalent to about US$230m at the time) provided by the Japanese government in support of China's modernisation drive. This first long-term and low-interest loan secured by China from a foreign government after the reform and opening up would be invested in constructing Shijiusuo port, the Beijing-Qinhuangdao railway, the Yanzhou-Shijiusuo railway, the second phase of Qinhuangdao port, Dayaoshan tunnel on the Hengyang-Guangzhou railway and Wuqiangxi hydropower station. The Chinese government more or less took into account the requests of the Japanese in choosing these key projects, a case in point being the large-scale port at Shijiusuo from where coal would be exported to Japan.

Gu Mu was invited to address a forum involving Chinese and Japanese government officials that was held in Japan in November 1982. Delegates from China included Gu Mu, vice-premier and director of the foreign investment commission under the state council, Huang Hua, vice-premier and minister of the ministry of foreign affairs, Yuan Baohua, director of the national economic committee, Han Guang, director of the state commission of infrastructure. Zheng Tuobin, minister of foreign trade, Lin Jiahu, minister of agriculture, Wang Binggan, minister of finance, Ren Duanyun, deputy director of the state planning commission, Gan Ziyu, deputy director of the state import and export regulatory commission, and Fu Hao, ambassador to Japan. Delegates from Japan included foreign minister Yoshio Sakurauchi, finance minister Michio Watanabe, Kichirō Tazawa, minister of agriculture, forestry and fisheries, Shintaro Abe, minister of trade and industry, Kosaka Tokusaburo, minister of transport, Kawamoto Toshio, director of economic planning, and Katori Yasue, ambassador to mainland China

Focusing on Absorbing Funds Without Fear of Debt

Gu Mu meets the Japanese prime minister, Ohira Masayoshi

Gu Mu and Yoshio Sakurauchi sign the minutes of talks, 16 December 1979

Gu Mu presents a gift to the former Japanese prime minister, Kakuei Tanaka (left)

In 1980, Gu Mu, as the chief delegate from China attending the meeting of Chinese and Japanese ministers, received a loan of 56bn yen (equivalent to about US$260m at the time) through negotiation.

From 1979 to 1983, the Japanese government loaned China 339bn yen in total, and from 1984 to 1989, the loan amount rose to 470bn yen. As a consequence, Japan became China's largest creditor among foreign governments. The sources of loans accessible to China were constantly expanding. In 1980, it succeeded in securing from the Kuwait Fund a negotiated loan of 43.6m dinars in additional to a loan of 900m Belgian francs from Belgium.

In 1979, a steering group was established when China was determined to win back its seats in the World Bank and the International Monetary Fund (IMF) with a view to securing loans from the former. Gu Mu was appointed head of the group and was asked to guide the overseas investment regulatory commission to coordinate work in this area.

Gu said in his memoirs that he proposed after negotiation with the department concerned under the overseas investment regulatory

Gu Mu makes the cover of the May 1980 issue of Japan's *International Development*

commission that if the World Bank could provide a loan, it would be first used to develop China's education, which was falling far behind others. In April 1981, a government delegation formed jointly by the overseas investment regulatory commission, the ministry of finance, the ministry of education and the Bank of China travelled to the World Bank in the US for talks. The first loan agreement of more than US$200m from the bank was concluded, which would help 200 colleges and universities improve their environment for teaching and scientific research. It would also herald the start of a process that would bring about a remarkable change in China's higher education, which was lacking in equipment.

The World Bank also helped China foster and train talent. The overseas investment regulatory commission not only organised relevant personnel to attend training programmes offered by the institute for international economics under the World Bank, but also formed inspection tours to Pakistan, the Philippines and Thailand for a field study about how to win a loan from the World Bank and how to bring it into full play, under the arrangement of the bank. A multitude of cadres skilled in the business of international credit were brought in to play a significant role in not only winning World Bank loan projects, but in expertly handling loan transactions between China and other countries or international organisations.

Chapter 46

Encouraging Foreign Investment

Since the state council forum in July 1978, the work of attracting overseas investment started. The most popular aspects of cooperation at that time were for both sides to jointly invest capital, jointly operate, jointly enjoy rights and interest (or exercise authority), and jointly share risk. This arrangement did not lead to an increase in debt and, compared with borrowing from abroad, did more good than harm.

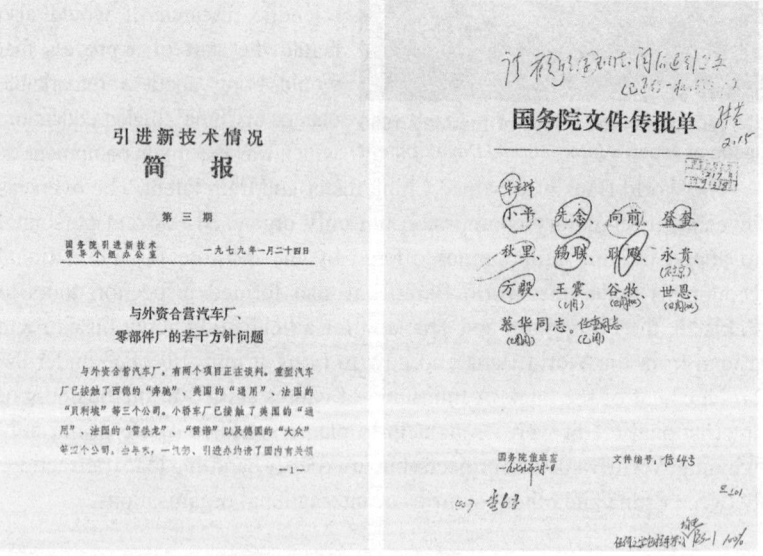

A copy of a brief report submitted to the steering group on introducing new technologies under the state council by Li Lanqing, head of the preparatory office of the heavy-duty truck company, in January 1979, as well as a photocopy of approvals by leaders in the central committee of CPC

Gu Mu hurried to draft *The Law of the PRC on Equity Joint Ventures*. This law aimed to address two problems in contractual joint ventures and cooperative enterprises. The first problem was corporate income tax. After much research, the tax was levied at 30% plus a local income tax of 3%. In total, a corporate income tax rate of 33% was slightly lower than that in most countries and regions in southeast Asia. Another problem concerned the investment proportion of foreign businesses. At first, the authorities drew from India's practice and planned to impose a 49% cap on foreign investment. But Rong Yiren later stressed that China's goal was to attract more foreign investment. So, instead, they imposed a minimum foreign investment proportion of 25%.

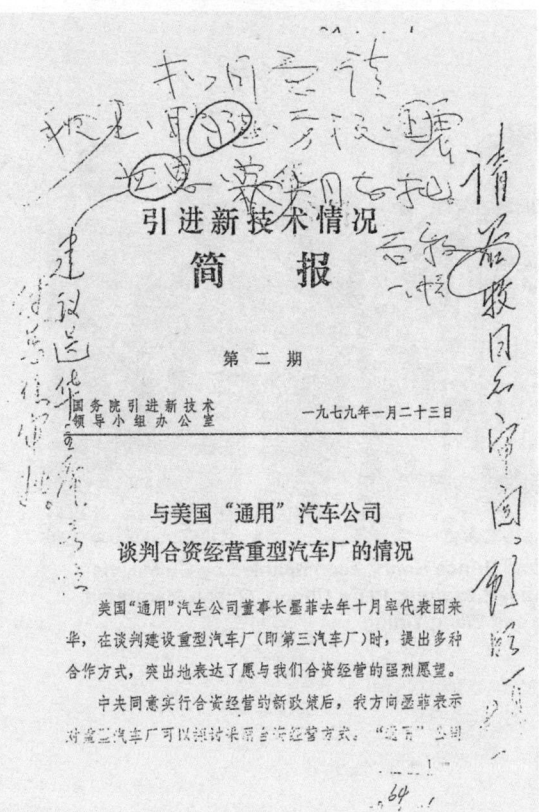

Gu Mu reviewed the article *Negotiation with General Motors on Establishing a Heavy-duty Truck Factory in the Form of a Joint Venture* published in *A Brief Report on Introducing New Technologies* (1979, Issue No. 2) compiled by the steering group on introducing new technologies under the state council. Gu commented: "Agreed. Please send it to comrades Qiuli, Geng Biao, Fangyi, Wang Zhen, Shi'en and Muhua for approval"

On 1 July 1979, in the second meeting of the fifth NPC, the *Law of the PRC on Equity Joint Ventures* was passed and it was introduced on 8 July. This law encouraged foreign businessmen, overseas Chinese businessmen and compatriots from Hong Kong and Macau to establish businesses in mainland China. In the second half of that year, only six joint ventures were authorised and just US$8.1m of foreign investment was introduced. But this was only the first step. In 1979, other types of foreign investment made remarkable progress. For example, more than 140 small and medium-sized compensation trade projects were recorded, and 2,000 projects involving the processing of imported materials were signed. As for wholly foreign-owned enterprises, they did not start to appear until 1981.

Denmark's Queen Margrethe II and Prince Henry, accompanied by Gu Mu, visit the Huangpu river in 1979. From left to right: Peng Chong, Queen Margrethe, Prince Henry, Gu Mu, Mou Feng and Wang Yiping

Chapter 47

Carrying Out Major Reform of the Foreign Trade System

In the 30 years before the initiation of reform and opening up, China modelled its foreign trade on the Soviet Union's experience. All foreign trade was conducted by the ministry of foreign trade and its specialised import-export companies. For three years, from 1979 to 1981, Gu Mu chaired the national import-export commission (which was originally known as the import-export small group), in charge of dealing with long-standing problems and carrying out far-reaching structural reform of the country's foreign trade system. The commission took four important steps.
1. The old system was monopolised by the state, with all activities set annually in an economic plan and with two annual sessions of the Guangzhou fair. The reforms built a new system that gave import-export authority over various commercial products to a number of regions and government agencies, thereby opening up a host of new foreign trade channels. In the three municipalities directly subordinate to the national government – Beijing, Tianjin and Shanghai – as well as the provinces of Guangdong, Fujian and Liaoning, the new system created locally run import-export firms. The new arrangements also gave direct import-export trading authority to ministry-level agencies in metallurgy, machine-building, armaments, aviation and maritime transportation. At the same time, the reforms reorganised seaports to perform specialised functions, so that cargoes produced in the vicinity of the ports could more efficiently move from point of production to export markets.
2. In the existing system of production and distribution, the state handled everything; producer and distributor had no direct contact, and industry and commerce enjoyed no direct linkages.

In succeeding years, the reforms introduced a wide variety of new forms of industry-trade links. For example, in Shanghai, beginning with the toy and pharmaceutical sectors, new forms of industry-trade management were introduced, responsible for the coordinated management of production and sales.

3. For those state enterprises that did not lend themselves to mobilisation and active reinvention, the reforms initiated the practice of multi-channelled management and established certain management-realignment methods. In only two years, 1980 and 1981, 15 new regulations were adopted, including the *Measures Regarding Loans for the Support of Production of Goods for Export, Temporary Regulations for Export Licensing, Measures for the Management of Customers, Regulations on the Division of Labour Between Specialised Foreign Trade Companies and Foreign Trade Companies at the Provincial, Municipal and Autonomous Region Levels, Measures Regarding the Management of Plants Dedicated to Production for Export*, and *Measures Regarding the Management of Production Bases for Agricultural Sideline Products Destined for Export*.

4. The inherited system of complete state control of profits and losses was reformed, including the so-called 'big rice bowl' system in which profits were shared around. Thenceforth, localities were allowed to retain more of the foreign exchange they earned from exporting. Ordinary provinces and municipalities were permitted to retain 10% of their exchange earnings, while Guangdong and Fujian could keep 25%. Minority nationality autonomous regions were permitted to retain half of such earnings.

Reform after 1978 quickly stimulated exports. From a level of US$9.75bn in 1978, China's exports more than doubled to US$22bn in 1981.

Once the system of multi-channelled foreign trade management was put into practice, and authority began to devolve downward while restrictions were relaxed, competition emerged among different locations, with competitors cutting prices to promote sales. This gave Gu Mu a very uneasy feeling. Party central authorities and the state council supported him, with the clear instruction: solve problems through negotiation, but don't play petty or manipulative games.

Carrying Out Major Reform of the Foreign Trade System

On the morning of 15 July 1981, when Deng Xiaoping gathered Wan Li, Yao Yilin and Gu Mu together to discuss how to utilise foreign investment capital to fund important medium- and long-term economic projects, Deng said to Gu Mu: "We need to speed up the progress of foreign trade reform, while unifying authority over foreign trade at the highest level in 'that commission of yours' [the national import and export commission]." With that, Gu Mu put together, in the name of that commission, a *Report on Basic Guidelines*, summing up developments in foreign trade since 1979 and proposing a series of recommendations on the next steps to be taken.

On 23 July, the central party secretariat met to discuss work in the foreign economic and trade sector. Hu Yaobang and many members of the secretariat took part; senior figures with responsible posts in the state planning commission, the import and export commission and the ministry of foreign trade joined the meeting. When Gu Mu had finished his presentation, drawn from the recently prepared *Report on Basic Guidelines*, he went on to stress two points.

First, since a vast increase in exports was needed, it would be essential to focus at the beginning on matters of mentality or spirit – thinking had to be freed up, throughout the system, from resource bases to production sites to operational management, to larger systemic reforms and to whole matrixes of interrelated policies. It would not do to sit and wait for things to happen; it was necessary to stride forth and conduct some business!

Gu's second point was that the active utilisation of foreign capital was to be the key breakthrough in the development of the national economy. On this, Gu noted, views within the party were far from unanimous. It was essential to reach a unified understanding on this key point. Medium-sized and smaller projects could be given greater freedom in this respect.

The party central leaders all expressed their approval of Gu Mu's report as well as his other opinions. A spirited discussion followed. Gu Mu summed it all up by making five points.

1. We shall understand that international economics and trade is elevated to the level of great strategic importance… We must master two sets of skills, improving the domestic economy and developing greater economic interaction globally, so that we may go out into the world. With regard to what we need to bring into China, we must be prepared to pay the costs of educating ourselves. This may be

expensive in the short run. We must save time wherever we can, and move as speedily as we are able.
2. We must liberate our thinking as we deal with international economics and foreign trade. From now on, the Chinese economy's construction can no longer travel the path of isolation and self-sufficiency. This is a basic policy, and it must be supported at all levels.
3. The active utilisation of foreign capital will entail certain interest expenses, but it serves to buy us time. We must not agonise about this. Joint ventures and Sino-foreign managed projects should be the direction we pursue.
4. Actively expand our exports. Foster and promote exports. The rate of export growth should exceed the rate of overall GNP growth.
5. Adopt two forms of activism. Stimulate those cadres who are able to build new realities, but criticise those personnel who merely look on from the sidelines or who drag their feet. If we don't do that, we will have no hope of bringing order out of chaos, and our great undertaking will be hopeless as well.

Gu Mu, vice-premier of China, paid a visit to Spain from 6 to 10 April 1981. He held talks with Leopoldo Calvo-Sotelo, prime minister of Spain, on 6 April

Chapter 48

Hong Kong China Merchants Group Starts to Build an Industrial Zone

The creation of special economic zones (SEZs) was one of the most important features of China's process of reform and opening up. It involved the comprehensive reform of systems and mechanisms. The process was tortuous and complex. After the third plenary session of the 11th central committee of the CPC, an awakened China raised its head to look overseas. The country's desire to change its destiny was stimulated. It was anxious to accelerate the modernisation drive.

At that time, more than 80 countries and regions in the world had set up more than 500 export processing zones, free trade zones and free ports to efficiently develop foreign trade and technical exchange. This gave Chinese people an example, inspiring them to strengthen international economic communication and promote the construction of the domestic economy.

In China's corporate history stretching back more than 100 years, China Merchants Group is one of the greatest enterprises. It was established by Li Hongzhang in 1872. On 9 October 1978, Yuan Geng, the 29th chairman of the group, on behalf of the ministry of transportation, drafted *Request Instructions to Make Full Use of Hong Kong China Merchants Group* and submitted it to the party central authorities. He boldly proposed an ideology of "making use of the advantages of Hong Kong and Macau, backed by the mainland, for an overseas orientation and a diversified economy".

On 12 October 1978, this request was approved by the party central authorities and the state council. Li Xiannian, vice-president of the central committee of the CPC and vice-premier of the state council, wrote: "We need to strengthen the leadership and push forward internal reorganisation. We should be bolder and more far sighted. In this way, we will accomplish a lot more than what is outlined in the report."

Leaders of the ministry of transportation were encouraged. They actively communicated with China Merchants Group. After much investigation and study, they decided to establish an industrial zone in Bao'an county, adjacent to Hong Kong. This idea was supported by leaders of Guangdong province such as Liu Tianfu, Wang Quanguo and Zeng Dingshi. They wrote the *Report on Hong Kong China Merchants Group Establishing an Industrial Zone in Bao'an, Guangdong*. The report was signed and sent to the party central authorities by Guangdong's provincial revolutionary committee on 6 January 1979.

From 10am to 11.45am on 31 January 1979, Li Xiannian and Gu Mu met Peng Deqing, deputy minister of transportation, and Yuan Geng. Li and Gu listened to their report on Hong Kong China Merchants Group establishing Guangdong Bao'an industrial zone. Li drew a circle on the map and asked China Merchants Group to exploit the Shenzhen Nantou peninsula, which covered 30 square kilometres. Yuan Geng was shocked by the size of the area and said: "How dare we accept such a large place?" In the end, they only asked for the Shekou area of Nantou peninsula, which covered some 300 mu (200,000 square metres).

Gu Mu listens to a report on the process of establishing Shenzhen Shekou industrial zone presented by Hong Kong China Merchants Group's long-standing vice-president, Yuan Geng, April 1984

Hong Kong China Merchants Group Starts to Build an Industrial Zone

Li Xiannian asked Gu Mu what he thought of China Merchants Group's *Report*. Gu Mu said: "You sign 'inclined to agree' and I'll ask relevant departments' opinions."

Li Xiannian answered immediately: "Sure, I'll sign it." Then he wrote on the *Report* the comment "Inclined to agree – Comrade Gu Mu will discuss it with relevant comrades and then carry it out as the *Report* stated."

On 2 February 1979, Gu Mu gathered leaders of relevant departments and committees in the ninth court of the state council to implement China Merchants Group's proposal of establishing an industrial zone in Guangdong. Gu Mu made it clear from the very beginning: "Factories built here will surely get special treatment. Apart from that, the local administration should be based on the national system, there should be some economic privileges, including the freedom to import and export, like in Hong Kong".

Yuan Geng gave a brief introduction to his report to Li Xiannian and Gu Mu. He said: "We should make full use of the advantage of adjoining Hong Kong and of our own abundant land and labour force resources. We should use investment, technology, patents and equipment supplied by Hong Kong and foreign countries. We should combine the advantages of Hong Kong and the mainland. We can exclude the shortcomings of opening factories in Hong Kong. Factories will be managed in the Hong Kong way, which means they will be managed by China Merchants Group. Products will be exported from Hong Kong to repay foreign loans and foreign investment. The establishment of this industrial zone will not need any money from the ministry of finance or the banks. All that is required is that the MOF waives taxes for 10 to 15 years and at a later date everything will revert to the state." Yuan Geng's speech generated a heated discussion.

Then Gu Mu decisively brought the discussion to an end by saying: "No more discussion. The principle has been decided. All of us will support it. It's only an area of 300 mu. The ministry of transportation will take the first step. Let's give it a try, and start to carry it out as the *Report* stated (and as instructed by Comrade Xiannian)."

Chapter 49

Guangdong Committee Proposes Setting up Provincewide EPZs

In the enlarged meeting of CPC Guangdong provincial committee from 8-25 January 1979, Xi Zhongxun, first secretary of the committee, brought up the idea of "using foreign investment, introducing advanced technology and equipment, developing compensation trade, processing and assembling businesses, and developing joint management". Wang Quanguo, secretary of the provincial committee, proposed to write a report to the central party committee, suggesting: "Before China's systems problems are solved across the whole country, more privileges should be given to Guangdong. We need more authority."

On 21 February 1979, Wu Nansheng, vice-secretary of Guangdong provincial party committee, was appointed by the committee to publicise the main ideas of the third plenary session of the 11th central committee of the CPC in his hometown, Shantou. He came up with the idea of establishing export processing zones (EPZs) like those in Taiwan, and reported it to the provincial party committee. The idea was supported by Xi Zhongxun, secretary of Guangdong provincial party committee. Xi said: "If we do it, we do it across the whole province. The central party committee will hold work meetings in April. Get prepared to report it to the central party committee."

In the work meeting to discuss economic construction that the central committee held in April 1979, Xi Zhongxun made a speech on behalf of the south-central group of this committee. He said: "Power is currently too centralised in the central party committee. It's hard for local governments to get things done due to their limited authority." He added: "Guangdong adjoins Hong Kong and Macau and contains many overseas Chinese. We should make good use of this advantage to actively develop foreign economic and technical exchanges. In this aspect, we hope the central party committee can give Guangdong more authority to go faster and bolder."

Leaders of the central party committee, including Deng Xiaoping, all supported this proposal. So they appointed Gu Mu to help provincial party committees and governments of Guangdong and Fujian to carry out investigations, and submit a concrete implementation proposal to the central party committee.

The breakthrough of reform and opening up happened first in Guangdong. There were historical reasons. Gu Mu said: "The four special economic zones are located close to the ports of the maritime silk road in ancient times — Quanzhou, Fujian province, in the Yuan dynasty and Guangzhou in the Ming and Qing dynasties. There are profound maritime cultural traditions and many overseas Chinese. These factors connected China with abroad."

In the 1950s, Marshal Ye Jianying headed the administration of Guangdong province. He thought that the overseas Chinese should play a role in breaking the imperialist blockade of China. Guangdong carried out some special policies to protect the capital of overseas Chinese and to use Hong Kong as a free port. For example, comrade Fang Fang gave a large sum of money to Zhuang Shiping, a patriotic overseas Chinese, to establish Nanyang Commercial Bank in Hong Kong.

Practices in the 1950s had a profound influence on Guangdong. Wu Nansheng used to take charge of the communication work between Guangdong and Hong Kong and Macau before the 'Cultural Revolution'. He had many friends in Hong Kong, such as Zhuang Shiping, the chairman of Nanyang Commercial Bank and Fei Yimin, chief editor of *Ta Kung Pao*. His friends knew Hong Kong and Macau, especially their legal system and foreign trade situation. Wu Nansheng used to gather information from them and was enlightened by them.

Chapter 50

Deng Xiaoping Says 'Special Zone' Sounds Better

In late April 1979, during the central party committee's work meeting on economic issues, Xi Zhongxun, first secretary of Guangdong provincial party committee, presented a report to Deng Xiaoping and other comrades. He proposed: "I hope the central party committee can give Guangdong more authority, more autonomy and flexibility, allowing it to build export processing zones in Shenzhen and Zhuhai, which adjoin Hong Kong, and also in Shantou, the famous hometown of overseas Chinese. As for what they should be called, they were variously known by comrades as 'export

Outside the Guangzhou Xiaodao hotel, 26 May 1979. From left to right: Gan Ziyu, Mou Feng, Xie Ming, Duan Yun, Liu Tianfu, Gu Mu, Xi Zhongxun, Wang Quanguo and Jia Shi

processing zones', 'free trade zones' and 'investment promotion zones'. We are still discussing it." Comrade Deng Xiaoping agreed with this proposal. He added, "Special zone' sounds like a better name. Shaan-Gan-Ning [Shaanxi-Gansu-Ningxia] area used to be called a special zone! The central government does not have money to give you. But we can give you special policies to let you fight your own way out." Deng Xiaoping suggested that the central party committee should approve Guangdong's proposal. Then the committee and the state council took Deng's suggestion and instructed leaders of Guangdong and Fujian to organise further demonstrations, come up with a concrete plan, then work with Gu Mu to accomplish this mission as soon as possible.

On 31 May 1979, the vice-premier of the state council, Gu Mu, led a group visit to Gushan in Fuzhou. Front row from left to right: Cai Liangcheng (first secretary of Fuzhou municipal party committee), Liao Zhigao (first secretary of Fujian provincial party committee) Gu Mu, Duan Yun (deputy director of the national planning commission), Ma Xingyuan (provincial governor of Fujian province), Mou Feng, Zheng Ying (wife of Liao Zhigao), Zheng Huilan (wife of Ma Xingyuan). Back row: second left is Hu Guangbao (Gu Mu's secretary), third left is Bi Jiohang (vice governor of Fujian), fourth left is Guo Chao (vice-governor of Fujian), fifth left is Xiao Yuan (Gu Mu's guard), seventh left is Wang Zhiqiang (Duan Yun's secretary)

From 11 May to 5 June 1979, Gu Mu led a state council work group to inspect Guangdong and Fujian. He opened a symposium in Guangdong to meet with Xi Zhongxun, Yang Shangkun, Liu Tianfu, Wu Nansheng, Wang Quanguo, Zeng Dingshi, Liang Xiang and other comrades. He also met Wang Kuang, secretary of Hong Kong working committee, before leaving for Fujian to meet Liao Zhigao. He also visited Marshal Ye Jianying who was in Guangdong at the time.

After much study, Gu Mu and the provincial party committee of Guangdong and Fujian worked out a plan for the two provinces to exploit their potential economic advantages. The priority was economic system reform. The planned economy was over-centralised. Local enthusiasm had to be mobilised. According to this thought, Gu Mu prepared several important measures and helped comrades from both provinces to draft reports asking for instructions from the central party committee.

On 15 July, the central party committee and the state council approved the request and decided to implement 'special policies and flexible measures' in Guangdong and Fujian. They also authorised the establishment of four special economic zones (SEZs) in Shenzhen, Zhuhai, Shantou and Xiamen.

The implementation of this important policy helped people get a better understanding of the opening-up policy. The fact that it was now policy meant that the process of opening up could begin. From then on, 'special zone' became the most popular phrase in the process of reform and opening up.

A group photo in the Seven Star Cave complex in Zhaoqing, March 1980. From left to right: Liu Tianfu, Xu Shijie, Gu Mu, Duan Yun and Gan Ziyu

Chapter 51

Gu Mu Decides to Change 'Special Export Zone' to 'Special Economic Zone'

The process of opening up coastal areas that Gu Mu led can be summarised as 'cautiously pushing forward, consolidating at every step'. Every step was tough but solid. Every step was summarised in a central file or a legal document from the NPC.

On 15 July 1979, the central party committee sent central files to approve the proposal of implementing special policies and flexible measures in Guangdong and Fujian's foreign economic activities. The central party committee decided to give both provinces more autonomy to exploit their potential advantages and develop faster when the international situation was favourable. The central party committee wanted Guangdong and Fujian to develop their economies as fast as possible. The central file contained many detailed provisions, such as delegating authority over state-run enterprises and public institutions to the two provinces, granting them independence in financial policy, expanding the rights of foreign trade in the two provinces, allowing individuals to accept investment from foreigners and overseas Chinese, allowing goods and materials and commerce to be governed by the market mechanism, enlarging the two provinces' authority to manage labour rates and prices, and establishing special zones in the two provinces.

At that time, China was still practising a planned economy, which made it very difficult for the central party committee to carry out these special policies in Guangdong and Fujian. The process was complicated. The committee had to convince all relevant departments to support the decision. In the second half of 1979, Gu Mu worked in Beijing as well as in Guangdong and Fujian. He was frequently travelling from one place to another. It was his accumulative efforts that gradually pushed this work forward.

现在是觉醒的时候了*

（一九七九年五月十六日）

谷　牧

今天下午在中山故居听了孙中山五十四年前的一段讲话录音，今晚又听了你们的汇报，很有感触。澳门五平方公里这么小的地方，有三十五万人口，加上香港共五百万人口，而广东有着五千多万人口。澳门原来也很落后，有的是赌场，现在发展起来了。对比之下，我们落后了。不要说我们全国九百六十万平方公里土地，就拿广东来说，我今天经过顺德、中山，看到这么好的土地，这么好的资源，这么富的广东，也完全可以利用这个有利条件，多赚外汇，发展我们的经济。在这方面我们显得落后。孙中山的话很有启发，对我们有鞭策。如果还在"睡觉"，就看不见问题；如果"醒"了，就看到问题了。看了你们这里的形势，更加觉得中央下决心解决广东的体制问题十分必要。如果现在再不下决心，就象孙中山所说的，我们确实是在"睡觉"了。我们不能再"睡觉"了，要"醒"过来，来一个大转变。先从小范围搞起，这没有多大危险性。

---

* 这是谷牧同志在珠海市视察时同省、市负责同志的谈话要点。

On 16 May 1979, Gu Mu paid a visit to Sun Yet-sen's former residence. He expressed his feelings to comrades in provincial and municipal departments. His words were recorded and summarised in an article entitled *Now it's Time for the Party to Wake up*

Gu Mu Decides to Change 'Special Export Zone' to 'Special Economic Zone'

On 20 September 1979, Gu Mu returned to Guangdong province. Two days later, he talked to provincial party committee members in charge of establishing special economic zones. When Xi Zhongxun asked about the scale of this plan, Gu Mu said: "The central party committee wanted Guangdong to move faster, to travel full steam ahead. If you take a step like women with bound feet, you will not be able to take the lead. Guangdong has to run at top speed, to run faster than the whole country." He added: "Guangdong will be synonymous with the establishment of special economic zones. You have to act like Sun Wukong [the Monkey King], who is brave enough to make havoc in heaven. And you should not be tied down by rules and regulations."

Gu Mu was appointed by the central party committee to chair a work meeting of Guangdong and Fujian in Guangzhou from 24-30 March 1980. The meeting examined and summarised the implementation process of the central government's No. 50 document. Before the meeting, Jiang Zemin, vice director of national import and export commission, led an advance team to visit Guangdong. The meeting confirmed the progress achieved, directly faced the shortcomings and encouraged free speech. In the words of Gu Mu, the meeting "put every problem on the table and discussed it. After two weeks of discussions, we agreed on many things. We also made clear the relationship between relevant departments of the central party committee and departments of local governments. We decided to give more authority to the two provinces to help them realise 'special', 'flexible' and 'faster'."

The meeting also discussed the term 'special export zone'. All participants agreed that it did not encapsulate the anticipated functions of these areas. Gu Mu instantly decided to change 'special export zone' to 'special economic zone', which conveyed more meaning.

In Gu Mu's book *Memoirs*, he wrote: "Establishing special economic zones in a socialistic country cannot be found in any classic Marxist or Leninist text. It was an unprecedented, pioneering experiment of social economy. Therefore, in the meeting, we studied the principles of establishing special economic zones in great detail." The minutes of the meeting were endorsed by the central party committee and publicised to all big cities in the country on 16 May.

On 27 July 1980, a rainstorm caused the flooding of Luohu district in Shenzhen and submerged the lower bodies of Wu Nansheng, secretary of the provincial party committee, and other specialists who were there to participate in Shenzhen's city planning. However, to bring the Luohu flood under permanent control would need an enormous investment. Wu Nansheng believed the provision of suitable resources was essential, arguing that "one cannot make bricks without straw", so he went to Gu Mu and told him: "One cannot make bread without yeast." Then he asked Gu Mu whether the government could provide some state loans as 'yeast'.

Gu Mu agreed immediately and asked about the usage and payment method of the loan. Then he helped loan Rmb30m to Wu Nansheng. Wu was so excited and said to Gu Mu: "With this 'yeast', the establishment of Shenzhen SEZ will not need government investment. After Shenzhen SEZ is established, we can take an area of 400,000 square metres as commercial land. The investment cost is Rmb90 per square metre, and the income will be HK$5,000 per square metre. The total income will be about Rmb2bn."

This is the origin of the saying that Shenzhen SEZ was started by a Rmb30m loan.

Chapter 52

The NPC Approves 'Provisions for Guangdong SEZs'

As early as 1979, Gu Mu had set to work with the relevant leadership figures in Guangdong and Fujian to start drafting a document in the form of statutory regulations. He ordered each province to make a first draft. In late July 1980, during the final phase of the drafting, Qin Wenjun of Guangdong and Cai Changjin of Fujian each brought his province's *Draft Rules on Special Zones* to the state import and export commission, whose vice-chairman at that time was Jiang Zemin, for discussion.

Gu Mu chairs a working session with representatives from Guangdong and Fujian, March 1980

At these meetings, the Fujian draft was discarded, and a revised version of the Guangdong draft was made the principal working document; it underwent a total of 13 revisions. For example, the terms "land price" and "land rent" were not compatible with the nation's post-land reform circumstances, and were altered to read "fixed term of usage" and "land-use fee", respectively. Two months of work finally produced a legal document comprising six sections and 26 articles, pending final submission, debate and approval.

Gu Mu with comrade Jiang Zemin

On 21 August 1980, at the 15th session of the fifth NPC standing committee, chaired by Ye Jianying and with Vice-Premier Gu Mu in attendance, Jiang Zemin, in his capacity as vice-chairman of the state import and export commission, was given the task of explaining the *Provisions for the Guangdong Special Economic Zones (SEZs)*. He explained: "Since we are lacking in experience with such economic zones, the words in this document should not be taken as provisions for economic zones in general. Thus, we have drafted a single document called *Provisions for Guangdong SEZs* and request its approval."

On 26 August, the *Guangdong SEZs Provisions* were passed at a meeting chaired by Ye Jianying. Thus was formally announced, in legal form, at the moment of opening up to the outside world and reform of the economic system, the birth of China's SEZs.

Chapter 53

Four Economic Zones Emerge from their Cocoons

Once the *Guangdong SEZ Provisions* were approved, the state council quickly approved the location and special functions of SEZs in Shenzhen, Zhuhai, Shantou and Xiamen. By 1993, Shenzhen SEZ was authorised to occupy 327.5 square kilometres; Zhuhai's SEZ covered 121.3 square kilometres; Shantou SEZ occupied 234 square kilometres, and the area of Xiamen SEZ reached 131 square kilometres.

At the time, thanks to Shenzhen SEZ's proximity to Hong Kong and its importance as a conduit for the land transportation of foreign trade goods, its conditions for building foreign trade contacts were exceptionally strong, and the possibilities of its rapid development were superior. Thus, the land area authorised for Shenzhen SEZ was the largest among the four zones. Through its China Merchants unit in Hong Kong, the ministry of communications invested in an industrial zone in Shekou and this, too, was included within Shenzhen SEZ. Construction of Shekou industrial zone had broken ground in May 1979, with first-stage development confined to a single square kilometre. But once the work was underway and advanced international managerial experience was brought to bear, Shekou became the birthplace of the slogan that would soon become synonymous with reform itself: "Time is money, efficiency is life."

The high-speed, high-efficiency results soon came to be known as the 'Shekou Model'. Luohu area, at the spot where Shenzhen's Luohu customs port connected to Hong Kong, became the fastest-developing area in the entire Shenzhen SEZ. At its formal inauguration in August 1979, a combination of levelling of hills and filling in of low-lying areas created the so-called 'seven connections and one plain'. In addition to making use of some locally generated funds, most of the financing came from banks. Managing debt, expanding development in a 'snowballing' fashion, introducing competitive forms and carrying out engineering, design and work programmes through processes of tendering and contracting, produced results both at high speed and of superior quality.

Gu Mu and the Zhuhai 'openers of the wilderness'

At Zhuhai SEZ, initial plans set up three segments, totalling 6.81 square kilometres. At first, development focused on travel and tourism. In January 1980, work began on the first Sino-foreign joint venture, the Zhuhai Shijingshan travel centre. The centre opened for business that August. Drawing on the management experience of the international Hilton Hotels chain, the centre quickly acquired a reputation for its smiling and courteous service to its guests, and became the model of gracious service for all hotels and guest houses after the inauguration of 'reform and opening up'.

In Shantou, construction was initially approved for the Longhu segment measuring 1.6 square kilometres, with the manufacture of products for export as its main function. In keeping with instructions from party central authorities that SEZ development proceed in an orderly manner, work began formally in the second half of 1982.

Four Economic Zones Emerge from their Cocoons

Gu Mu enjoys a friendly conversation with a worker during his December 1980 investigation visit to Shenzhen

As for Xiamen's zone, the state council in October 1980 approved the establishment of an SEZ in the area of Huli village on Xiamen island, with a planned area of 2.5 square kilometres, the first segment of which was to encompass a single square kilometre. Much time was spent debating exactly what lands would constitute the special zone under Fujian provincial management, and progress was slowed. The initial elements in the Xiamen SEZ programme were mainly the building of Gaoqi airport and the expansion of deepwater berthing facilities at the port of Dongdu. The actual development work on the Huli village segment did not start until groundbreaking in early 1982.

In order to strengthen the leadership and management of the SEZ programme, the state import and export commission in September and October 1980 sent a team headed by its vice-chairman, Jiang Zemin, on an overseas investigation tour. The team visited Sri Lanka, Malaysia, Singapore, the Philippines, Mexico and Ireland, taking in a total of nine export processing zones, free trade zones and industrial parks in six countries. They held talks with more than 10 specialists invited by the United Nations. From their observations of these international special zones, the investigation team brought back five key points: 1) a well-developed legal framework was essential for strong operational functioning; 2) development work required a broad overall plan, but had to move up progressively from smaller- to larger-scale projects; 3) management systems required flexibility, with both local authorities and enterprises enjoying very substantial autonomy; 4) much attention had to be paid to human resource development, and to the raising of the quality of the workforce; and 5) broad, preferential policies would be needed to attract businesses to the zones. Returning to China, the investigation team presented their results to party central and the state council.

Chapter 54

Ten Guiding Opinions on the Development of Special Zones

From 27 May to 14 June 1981, Gu Mu convened a work session with participants from Guangdong and Fujian. In addition to provincial leaders Ren Zhongyi and Xiang Nan, he invited a number of economics scholars to take part. The meeting provided the guiding thinking for this new national enterprise – the development of special economic zones – and offered a careful and detailed review of broad strategic plans and key policies.

The meeting produced a systematic set of 10 opinions, and wrote them up as a summary. This summary was sent out throughout the party system, at the instruction of party central authorities on 19 July 1981, and provided a set of concrete norms for SEZs to follow during the process of reform and opening up.

The core findings of the '10 opinions' were:

1. Planning and developing special zones must take place in accord with local conditions, and each must have its particular emphases, whose implementation must be given priority;
2. Preferential customs duties must be applied to goods and commercial products imported for the use of the special zones themselves;
3. The movement of foreign business people into and out of special zones must be simplified and made more convenient;
4. The system of labour wages in the zones must be reformed, and labour should be arranged on the basis of contracts;
5. Permissions granted by the relevant province, municipality or autonomous region should be the basis for managing foreign trade activities within the zones;

A group of central leaders in the early 1980s. From left to right; Xi Zhongxun, Fang Yi, Gu Mu, Yang Dezhi, Hu Yaobang, Wan Li, Yao Yilin, Yu Qiuli and Wang Renzhong

6. The renminbi shall be the principal currency used in the zones, with any usage of foreign currencies confined within limited designated spheres;
7. Capital for the development of zones can be raised from multiple sources, mainly from international investors. Income arising from the development of land in the zones is to be held for the benefit of the entire zone;
8. Foreign investment is permitted in infrastructural development projects within the zones;
9. Management systems within the zones and in areas not within the zones must be separate;
10. Upon receiving the necessary authority, zones may implement rules and regulations specific to themselves (the full NPC approved a resolution in November 1981, bestowing that authority on Guangdong and Fujian).

Ten Guiding Opinions on the Development of Special Zones

Gu Mu at the fifth plenum of the 11th CPC central committee in 1980

Chapter 55

Special Zones Face the Biggest Ideological Upheaval

At the start of the reform and opening-up process, an immediate and pressing problem was the lack of commercial goods inside the nation. At the end of the 1970s, neither televisions, nor tape recorders, nor computers, nor high-quality textiles could meet the needs of the market. Moreover, the price structure of the domestic market was divorced from that of international markets. With measures to cope with those problems inadequate to the task, it was not long before a massive wave of smuggling erupted. Central authorities realised that only decisive actions in response would suffice.

From 15 to 23 December 1981, party central brought together the first party secretaries from every province, autonomous region and centrally controlled municipality for a sit-down meeting. After that meeting wound up, the Guangdong and Fujian representatives were recalled for more discussions on how to develop means of attacking the problems of economic crimes that they had encountered, such as smuggling and trafficking in smuggled goods. The central leaders stated their points strongly: the seriousness and harmfulness of economic crimes had to be fully recognised. These crimes had to be clearly defined and cleaned up, as part of the larger struggle against the corrosive ways of thinking that characterised capitalism.

Gu Mu was ordered to establish an anti-corruption leading small group under the state council, and headed the new organisation. Working with the general administration of customs, he established administrative officers, adopted a set of effective measures, and strengthened both interceptions on the water and inspections on land. He stiffened the administrative control of the fishing industry, straightened out the lowest-level units of both party and government authority, prosecuted the biggest criminals and snuffed out the wild gale of smuggling.

Because the deluge of smuggling and trafficking in smuggled goods mostly occurred in the newly opened areas, some people were inclined to cast doubt on the entire reform and opening-up programme, particularly the creation of SEZs. It was said that SEZs gave foreign capitalists new enclaves of capitalism on Chinese soil. Others said that, except for the five-starred national flag, absolutely everything had been upset. Some veteran cadres observed the circulation of foreign currencies within the SEZs with dismay and anger, arguing that pushing aside China's national currency, the renminbi, was impermissible. In addition, some comrades who had worked for long years in Hong Kong or Macau raised their doubts; they were sometimes considered to have higher, broader vision.

One of the most influential documents to be circulated was called *Origins of the Foreign Concessions in the Old China*. It did not assert that the corrupt government of the Qing dynasty was powerless to prevent the establishment of the foreign concessions in the period of imperialist invasion of China; instead, it argued that the humiliation of the nation and the loss of sovereignty lay in the errors committed by the chief imperial official of the time in Shanghai, the Daotai Wu. It went on to imply that the current reform and opening-up programme was reminiscent of the tragic misconduct that led to the establishment of the concessions, since granting land-use rights to foreign businesses in the SEZs simply turned the zones into old-style foreign concessions.

Though he was walking on thin ice, Gu Mu maintained an attitude of calm in the face of these raucous voices. His principle was: carrying out reform and opening up had already been settled on as a crucial element in implementing the entire panoply of measures for socialist modernisation. It had been written into the key document, *Resolution on Certain Questions in the History of Our Party*. Everyone knew that creating the SEZs was supported by comrade Deng Xiaoping and decided by the central party authorities. The standing committee of the NPC had established the programme in law. Organs under the state council were carrying out this major programme. While opinions might vary here and there, it was imperative that forward progress on the SEZ programme be supported.

In early 1982, with the reform of organs belonging to the state council, the former state import and export commission merged with the ministry of foreign trade and the foreign trade and economy commission. Gu Mu chose He Chunlin and seven others to form a small team responsible for handling SEZ matters within the merged ministry. He put a great deal of effort into conceptualising and putting into operation the office of special zones, in the face of opposition from some officials who felt that such a title was too grandiose. Later, the group's title was changed to 'special zones working group', and was formally placed under the direct control of the general office of the state council.

Some of the people under consideration for service with this special organisation were asked: "If you board this SEZ boat, aren't you afraid the craft will capsize?" At the first meeting of the small group, Gu Mu put all his cards on the table: "Anyone feeling queasy is free to leave. But whatever problems arise, the lash will not fall on you. I alone am responsible. I am one of those who is prepared to burn down the house of Zhao."[1]

These eight comrades stood firm, and cheerfully stood up to their new responsibilities. Their work produced excellent results.

Chapter 56

Helping to Promulgate 'New Document No. 50'

In March and April 1982, Gu Mu led a small group on an observation mission to Guangdong. He invited the head of the institute of international trade research, Shu Ziqing, and figures from the research office of the state council's general office to join the mission.

Gu Mu visits the Australia-invested Wushigu work site in Shenzhen

Gu Mu convenes a discussion meeting during a visit to a factory in Shenzhen

In his book *Breaking Out of Encirclement: The First Years of Opening Our Doors*, Li Lanqing described Gu Mu's basic attitude during those times. In the book, Gu Mu was quoted as saying: "Thus far, the SEZs have done nothing to sacrifice our sovereignty nor bring dishonour to our country, and have neither done a lot of damage or imposed huge costs. They have not resulted in any problems that could lead us to alter our strategy. Thus, we can't really harbour any serious doubts about the path that we have chosen. Fearing that the SEZs will be unmanageable does not match with reality." At the same time, he brought up the matter of drawing general conclusions from experience: "The purpose of that is to continue our forward progress; there is no other meaning to it."

In July 1982, following on the investigations in Guangdong in March and April of that year, Gu Mu asked the leaders of all four SEZs to come to Beijing to make situation reports and conduct further research. The 12th party congress had just closed. Gu Mu then took the SEZ group to Fujian for additional investigations. The main thrust of those investigations had four main components: first, the nature and functions of our nation's SEZs;

second, evaluation of the initial stages of establishing and developing the SEZs; third, the autonomy of SEZ management; and fourth, infrastructure construction in the SEZs.

Gu Mu's investigative inquiries in Fujian were exhaustive. From months of thinking, he assembled his opinions into a report summary. In early 1982, Chen Yun had put forth an instruction: "In carrying out the SEZ policies in Guangdong and Fujian, the primary task before us is to sum up our experiences with the greatest seriousness." On 30 October, Chen issued another instruction: "The crucial job to be accomplished in the SEZs is to reach overall conclusions based on actual experiences." In reviewing his own thinking, and after making his on-site investigations, Gu Mu was following through on these two instructions.

As it happened, Hu Yaobang was also in Fujian at that time.

Gu Mu and Hu Yaobang traded ideas and reached the shared view that the central party secretariat should call a special meeting to debate the ongoing work in the SEZs.

That meeting convened on 15 November 1982. General Secretary

Gu Mu accompanies Hu Yaobang on an inspection visit to Fujian in 1982

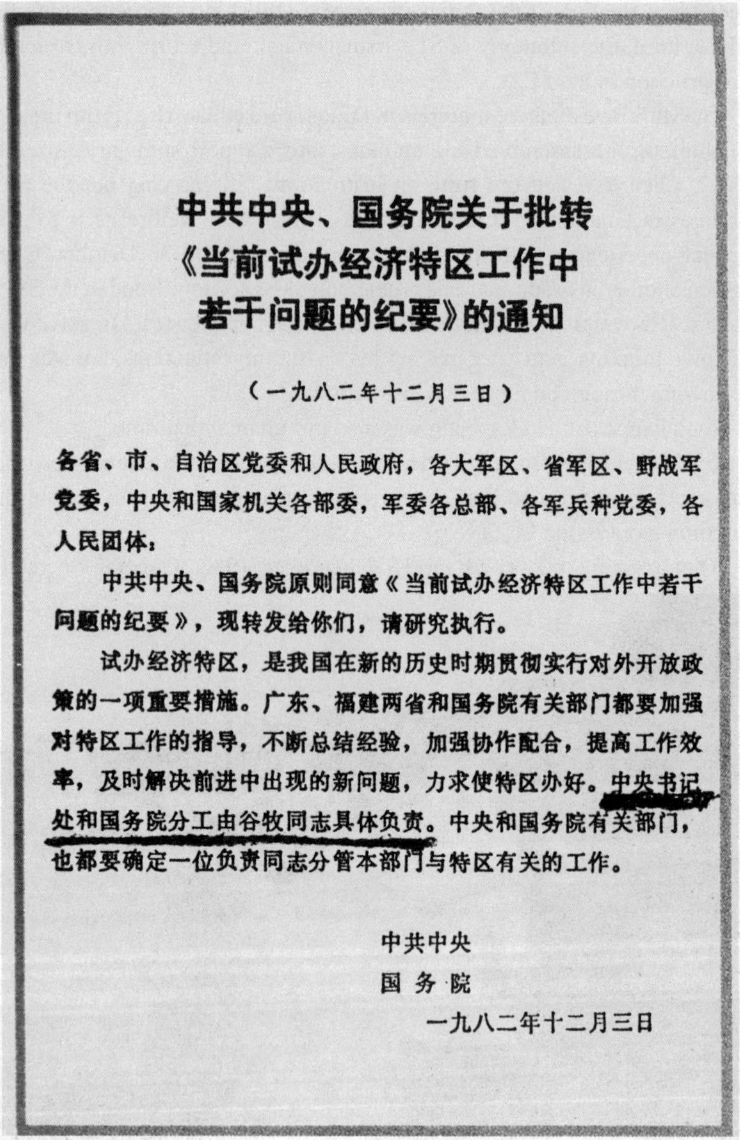

中共中央、国务院关于批转
《当前试办经济特区工作中
若干问题的纪要》的通知

（一九八二年十二月三日）

各省、市、自治区党委和人民政府，各大军区、省军区、野战军党委，中央和国家机关各部委，军委各总部、各军兵种党委，各人民团体：

中共中央、国务院原则同意《当前试办经济特区工作中若干问题的纪要》，现转发给你们，请研究执行。

试办经济特区，是我国在新的历史时期贯彻实行对外开放政策的一项重要措施。广东、福建两省和国务院有关部门都要加强对特区工作的指导，不断总结经验，加强协作配合，提高工作效率，及时解决前进中出现的新问题，力求使特区办好。中央书记处和国务院分工由谷牧同志具体负责。中央和国务院有关部门，也都要确定一位负责同志分管本部门与特区有关的工作。

中共中央
国务院
一九八二年十二月三日

The announcement by party central and the state council approving the circulation of *Summary of Various Questions Encountered in the Experimental Operation of Special Economic Zones*

Gu Mu reports to Chairman Ye Jianying on the work of creating SEZs

Hu Yaobang and other members of the party secretariat attended. After consideration, all participants indicated their agreement with the *General Outline of A Situation Report* that Gu Mu had prepared. The 'summary' of the meeting's conclusions appeared on 20 November, and was made public as a central party document on 3 December.

This was the fourth central party document dealing with SEZ work. It was the only central document on the SEZs that emerged from the period of Gu Mu's personal responsibility for implementing the 'opening' side of the 'reform and opening up' strategy. Because the first central party document on the SEZs had been known as *Document 50*, this new document became known as the *New Document 50*. In approving the new document, party central wrote: "In this new era of our nation's history, in which we are fully implementing the policy of opening to the outside world, establishing special economic zones is a vital measure. The party secretariat and the state council have each assigned concrete responsibilities for this to comrade Gu Mu."

Armed with this assignment, Gu Mu created a joint administrative conference, made up of Gan Ziyu from the state planning commission, Wang Lei from the state economic commission (later succeeded by Ma Yi), Wei Yuming from the ministry of economics and trade, Xie Ming (later Tian Yinong) from the ministry of finance, Jiang Xi from the ministry of commerce, Liu Hongru from the PBOC, Ding Chaozong from the BOC, Gao Zuo from the general administration of customs, and the deputy secretary-general of the state council, Wu Qingtong.

When *New Document 50* was made public, cadres in the SEZs and the general public were greatly heartened. In Shenzhen, some people celebrated by letting off strings of firecrackers.

Gu Mu (squatting, front row second from left) and Wu Nansheng (fourth from left, standing) carry out an on-the-ground investigation of planning and development of infrastructure in Shantou SEZ, 1983

Gu Mu and Guangdong Party Secretary Wu Nansheng (right) listen to the Hong Kong businessman Gordon Wu (Hu Yingxiang) of Hopewell Holdings introduce plans for the construction of the Guangzhou-Zhuhai-Shenzhen expressway

Chapter 57

Setting up SEZs Calls not for Tightening, but for Loosening

From 22 January to 16 February 1984, Deng Xiaoping went to Guangzhou, Shenzhen, Zhuhai, Xiamen and Shanghai to see things for himself. He got back to Beijing on 17 February and, one week later, called in a group of leading party figures for a chat. He made his point very clear: "In creating the SEZs and carrying out reform and opening up, there must be a clear guiding pattern of thinking. In brief, it means, 'Do not tighten down, loosen up'." The whole party and the entire nation were stimulated. Later, those in the cultural world sang of *A Tale of Springtime*.

Gu Mu writing in his own hand: 'Reform And Opening Up: Bravely Move Forward'

From his conversations with Deng, Gu understood that Deng had a number of things on his mind with respect to the overall direction in which SEZ development needed to travel.

First of all, Deng forcefully confirmed the achievements gained in developing the zones. "Shenzhen's development is proceeding rapidly... Development in the Shekou industrial area is moving even more quickly... Zhuhai's development has a good future."

Second, Deng spoke of the function the SEZs were playing in the building of socialist modernisation. "The zones are a window for technology, a window for management, a window for knowledge and a window for our external policies."

Third, Xiamen SEZ was to be expanded. "We won't call the Xiamen one a 'free port', but it can adopt a number of free port policies."

Fourth, port cities needed to be opened to the outside world. "We should look at opening a number of additional port cities, such as Dalian and Qingdao. We don't have to call these places special zones, but they should implement a variety of special zone policies."

Fifth, Hainan island needed to be vigorously opened up.

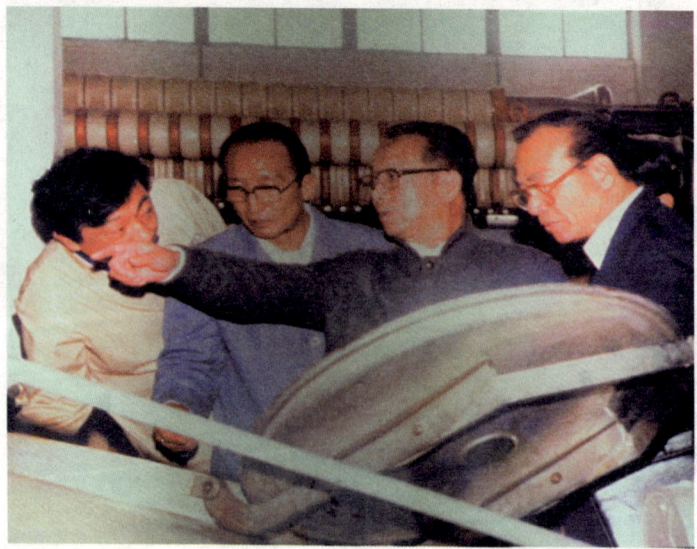

Gu Mu inspects the Pearl River Brewery

On his inspection tour of the south in the spring of 1984, Deng Xiaoping wrote an inscription while visiting Shenzhen SEZ: 'Shenzhen's development and experiences prove: our policy of establishing SEZs is correct'

The central party secretariat and the state council turned to Gu Mu to carry out the necessary research and to execute these tasks, and asked Gu Mu to deploy the necessary personnel.

Between 3 and 6 March and then 10 and 18 March, Gu Mu travelled to the two major port cities preparing to be opened, Tianjin and Dalian. His observations there led him to four conclusions.

First of all, opening major port cities had to be undertaken in close coordination with the technological upgrading of the long-established enterprises there.

Second, in the centres of these older cities, where infrastructure was inadequate, a 'microclimate' had to be generated to ensure the recruitment of overseas investment. This concept later materialised with the creation of economic and technology open zones in each of those cities.

Third, as conditions in each of the several port cities slated for opening differed, a 'one size fits all' approach was not appropriate; each case had to be treated on its own merits.

Fourth, the first task was human resource development; cadres had to be trained, and outmoded outlooks had to be refreshed.

Chapter 58

'Opening to the Outside World' Requires People Who Get the Picture

On 26 March 1984, the central party secretariat and the state council convened a session in the Huairen Hall of Zhongnanhai to discuss a number of coastal cities. The area covered was broad, and many administrative units participated. Senior cadres from more than 40 agencies within party central, the state council and the central military commission took part. Gu Mu and Hu Qili put the meeting together. This was the largest meeting on the work of the 'opening to the outside world' that Gu Mu had organised.

Gu Mu with General Secretary Hu Yaobang (third from right) on an inspection visit to Shenzhen in May 1984. Far right is Guangdong Provincial Governor Liang Lingguang. Second from right is Shenzhen Deputy Party Secretary and Executive Vice-Mayor Zhou Xiwu. Second from the left is Liang Xiang, vice governor of Guangdong province and secretary of the Shenzhen party committee. Third from left is Zou Erkang, secretary general of the Shenzhen municipal party committee (photo by Zhang Guoying)

'Opening to the Outside World' Requires People Who Get The Picture

Gu Mu and Ren Zhongyi (second from left) scan the broad view of Shenzhen in 1984

Gu Mu made very clear that the nation's work of 'opening to the outside world' had only just begun. He argued strongly for the increased utilisation of foreign investment and introduction of technologies from abroad. He advocated a temporary hold on the development of new SEZs. He argued that, while investment capital should be sought through multiple channels, it would not be possible to look to the state for heavy investment increases.

Gu Mu asserted further that 'opening up' had to proceed in accord with actual conditions, one step at a time, with feet firmly planted on the ground; doing everything at the same time would not work.

"The SEZs must respond to comrade Deng Xiaoping's demands," Gu said, "pressing ahead with their own energy, and leading the way forward."

Gu stressed the importance of human resource development and training. And he called for the simultaneous, urgent pursuit of ideological work and the development of 'spiritual civilisation'.

One minister, who had been worrying about the challenge of maintaining overall balance while working on 'opening to the outside world', observed: "Now that comrade Gu Mu has brought forth these concrete measures, we can all rest more easily." While discussing the question of names for the new development zones, the meeting first prepared to call them 'economic development zones'. Then Li Lanqing, who was in charge of the tasks in Tianjin, observed that development zones were not simply 'mini-environments' for the purposes of drawing in foreign investment and speeding up economic development; they also needed to bring in advanced technology. Li recommended calling the zones 'economic and technological development zones (ETDZs)'. This recommendation garnered everyone's support, and was adopted by the meeting.

The meeting lasted 10 days. At its conclusion, Deng Xiaoping, Li Xiannian and other comrades joined together for group photos. Deng Xiaoping coined the impromptu phrase 'Opening to the outside world requires people who get the picture', to the delight of all present. Later on, people often used an adaptation of that phrase – 'The man who gets the picture' – to describe Gu Mu.

Gu Mu observes the selection of the location of Qinhuangdao ETDZ during a visit to Hebei

'Opening to the Outside World' Requires People Who Get The Picture

Gu Mu and his wife Mou Feng climb Shanhaiguan, where the Great Wall meets the sea

On 24 February, before Gu Mu's March conference, Deng Xiaoping and the central party leadership decided that the coastal cities to be opened would include Shanghai, Tianjin, Dalian, Qingdao, Yantai, Ningbo, Wenzhou and Beihai. Nantong and Lianyungang, in Jiangsu province, were added later. At the request of the provinces of Guangdong and Fujian, each of which had been opened in its entirety, the cities of Guangzhou, Zhanjiang and Fuzhou were added, and during the drafting period Qinhuangdao was added to the list as well. In this way, the number of open coastal cities rose to 14, reflecting clearly the overall trend in the nation's reform and opening up.

On 23 April 1984, Gu Mu went to Hangzhou to report to Chen Yun on the recent conference on coastal cities. Chen fully approved the opening of the port cities, but emphasised the importance of continually reviewing accumulated experiences. Once that meeting was finished, the party politburo formally debated the *Summary of the Conference on Certain Coastal Cities*. On 4 May, the summary was made known to the entire nation as a central party document.

The central party authorities attached comments to the summary when it was made public. In opening the port cities and running the SEZs, it noted, the central authorities would not be able to provide heavy funding; what it would provide was policy guidance. First, special treatment was to be offered to foreign business people making early investments or bringing advanced technology. Second, the autonomy of the coastal port cities was to be broadened, so as to ignite their energies in support of their activities in opening to the outside. In fact, this instruction entailed a number of major reforms to the economic management system then in place.

The various agencies and areas in question, party centre continued, must carry out concrete programmes in accordance with the summary document, strengthening the qualifications of the leadership teams and building the ranks of cadres involved in the effort. Overall direction, and the investigative functions, were to be strengthened as well, in order to guarantee the thorough implementation of these key policies from party centre. The central party authorities and the state council placed Gu Mu in charge of overall supervision, authorising him to scrutinise the implementation of these orders and to arbitrate or mediate in any conflicts that might arise along the way. To this end, the party ordered that the leading SEZ body under the state council (still known, during the recent conference, as the state council SEZ group) was to be further beefed up.

Gu Mu with Chen Yun

'Opening to the Outside World' Requires People Who Get The Picture

Without question, Gu Mu personally bore even heavier responsibilities after that. From April until the year's end, Gu Mu entered his busiest and most labour-intensive period of work since the beginning of the opening up and reform programme. He took on 10 principal tasks:

- Establishment of a broad inter-agency committee on the open coastal cities and special zones, comprised of responsible figures from 15 agencies operating under the state council. Those assisting Gu Mu in this work included Gan Ziyu, vice-chairman of the state planning commission; Ma Yi, vice-chair of the state economic commission; Vice-Minister Wei Yuming of the ministry of economics and foreign trade; Liao Jili, advisor to the commission on economic system restructuring; and Wu Qingtong, deputy secretary general of the state council.
- In August, the state council general office SEZ group was formally elevated to become the state council office of special zone management, headed by He Chunlin, with Hu Guangbao and Zhang Ge as deputy chiefs.
- After study and consultation, foreign currency quotas were allotted to each of the 14 open coastal cities expressly for use in promoting technological transformation.
- The finance ministry was assigned the task of consulting with all relevant agencies and gaining state council approval of a lowering of income taxes for foreign-invested enterprises engaging in production activities in the open cities to 24%.
- The ministry of posts and telecommunications was assigned the job of establishing basic changes in the telecommunications system, with investment funds from the state planning commission, and with specific arrangements carried out locally in each of the cities.
- At the request of Shandong, open city policies were established for the city of Weihai, which at that time was under the direct administration of Yantai municipality. The port of Longkou was confirmed as an open port.
- In keeping with the request of Liaoning province, the port city of Yingkou was ordered to apply certain policies already implemented in other coastal open cities.

- Shenzhen was to create a development zone research programme, for the purpose of training cadres for work in the zones.
- All 14 open cities, plus the four SEZs and Hainan island, were to participate in a giant investment and trade conference in Hong Kong.
- To ensure state council approval of the measures relating to the 14 coastal port cities, Gu Mu conducted on-the-ground studies. In May, he travelled to Ningbo, Wenzhou and Nantong (receiving a report from Lianyungang while he was in Nantong). In June, he went to Guangzhou and Beihai. He visited Dalian in July, Qinhuangdao in August, Yantai and Qingdao in September, Tianjin in October, and Fuzhou in December. Returning to Beijing, he met with all the many agencies involved. It was February of the following year before he wrapped up his work.

Gu Mu with a group of workers

Gu Mu hears at first hand about plans for the development of the Beihai economic development area

Chapter 59

Linking Key Points to Build a Continuous Belt of Opening To the Outside World

Starting in 1984, Gu Mu began to inspect the situation in Guangdong and Fujian as they implemented special policies and adopted specially flexible measures. The two provinces had been at the forefront in putting 'opening to the outside world' into practice since 1980. Especially in 1982, they had faced very heavy pressures from public opinion. Gu Mu decided that the fundamental strategy was not eligible for further debate or reinterpretation, and he immersed himself in his work.

In 1984, while observing a construction project in Shenzhen, Gu Mu converses with the construction team. The four walls of this workers' shed were built of reed mats, an indication of the hard conditions facing the pioneers of that time

Gu Mu holds a meeting in Guangzhou

After Deng Xiaoping's inspections and the opening of the 14 coastal cities in 1984, no one again publicly raised the phrase 'The special zones will be unmanageable' or called for a revision of the special policies and measures adopted by Guangdong and Fujian. The two provinces used international investment and advanced technology to take their first giant steps. By the end of 1984, they had drawn in actual useable capital totalling USS$1.7bn, which amounted to 40% of the national total. Nationally, 1,856 foreign-invested projects had been approved, exceeding the cumulative total of the preceding five years.

From 3 to 7 December 1984, Gu Mu convened a conference in Fuzhou involving representatives from Guangdong and Fujian, plus figures from the various government agencies under the state council that were directly involved, for the purpose of carrying forward the reform and opening programmes and economic construction work in the two provinces. The meeting generated a number of recommendations.

First, investment limits on approved projects were to rise. The two provinces could raise up to Rmb100m in domestic investment funds, and up to US$10m in external investments per project.

Linking Key Points to Build a Continuous Belt of Opening To the Outside World

Second, the two provinces could experiment with locally organised financial bodies and could call them banks. (Under this provision, after careful preparations, Shenzhen Development Bank was opened for business in 1987, and Guangdong Development Bank and Fujian Enterprise Development Bank did so in 1988.) With state council approval, such banks would be allowed to issue debt both domestically and internationally.

Third, the proportion of foreign exchange generated by exports that could be retained within the zones and open cities was to be increased from 25% to 30%.

Fourth, powers of foreign trade management within the zones and open cities were to be broadened.

On the question of whether the customs authorities should collect industrial and commercial taxes on imports, the views of the two provinces,

Gu Mu on an investigation visit to Quanzhou

on the one hand, and the finance ministry, on the other, diverged, and a stalemate ensued. Gu Mu took the problem back to Beijing, where he organised a special meeting. In order to mediate the conflict, he employed a series of methods to raise the proportion of commercial and industrial tax revenue collected by the customs authorities to be turned over to the central treasury. The state council subsequently sent out a document limiting the duration of these special provisions for the two provinces to five years.

While the meeting with the two provinces was underway, another idea emerged among the highest leaders of the party: once the Pearl and Yangtze river deltas were opened, further openings should be arranged for the Liaodong and Jiaodong peninsulas to open as well, so as to create a continuous open coastal belt from Dalian Bay in the north to the city of Beihai in the south.

Gu Mu also recommended that three cities located midway between the Yangtze and Pearl river deltas – Xiamen, Zhangzhou and Quanzhou in southeastern Fujian – be turned into 'breakthrough points', to be called the 'Minnan (South Fujian) triangle'. This notion quickly brought approval from all concerned.

Gu Mu on an investigation visit to Xiamen

Linking Key Points to Build a Continuous Belt of Opening To the Outside World

Gu Mu chats with fishermen at Baihutan (White Tiger Beach) in Beihai city, Guangxi Zhuang autonomous region, July 1984

After another period of study, on 22 January 1985, Gu Mu convened a joint conference on work on the coastal open cities and special zones. At the meeting, he proposed that the Pearl river delta, the Yangtze delta and the Minnan triangle move ahead according to the following basic steps:

- From the small to the large;
- From the smaller triangles to the larger ones;
- Focus on the key locations. For the Yangtze delta, that meant Suzhou, Wuxi, Changzhou, Jiaxing and Huzhou. For the Minnan triangle, that meant Quanzhou and Zhangzhou. For the Pearl river delta, that mean Foshan and Jiangmen. This would create a linked network of 59 key cities and counties.

The conference also raised the idea of a trade-industry-agriculture strategy for economic development. Production was to be geared to newly generated export demand, technology importation was to be managed well, a series of 'industrial satellites' were to be created, and agricultural experimental stations were to be placed in specially reserved areas.

Between 25 and 31 January 1985, Gu Mu then convened a discussion session with the Yangtze and Pearl river deltas and the Minnan triangle of Xiamen, Zhangzhou and Quanzhou. After discussion, the meeting produced a summary of its proceedings. That summary was distributed nationally as a formal document after approval by party central authorities and the state council.

Deng Xiaoping remarked that he only accomplished two things in 1984. One was opening 14 coastal cities, and the other was proposing the 'one country, two systems' formula for resolving the Taiwan and Hong Kong situations. He demanded that trade with Taiwan be developed on the basis of 'economics promoting politics, animating the unification of the motherland'.

In early 1985, Deng called Gu Mu in for a chat. He was altogether satisfied with progress on the 'opening' front, and said: "It seems to me that this has great prospects." He also emphasised two important questions.

Gu Mu reports to Deng Xiaoping on Ningbo's development, 1 August 1984. Deng said: 'Let the people from Ningbo all over the world join forces to build Ningbo'

Gu Mu (far left) with a group of state council advisors on the economy of coastal cities, engage in lively discussion with the former deputy premier of Singapore, Goh Keng Swee (far right)

The first was how to solve the human resources problem. He recommended that Gu Mu consider bringing in various international experts for consultations, and that he set up a system of short-course training programmes specially aimed at the particular skills required by the 'opening' process.

The second concern Deng raised related to strategies for the renovation of outdated technologies in old enterprises. He wanted Gu Mu to assist Lu Xuzhang with a passport problem that prevented him from moving easily back and forth between Hong Kong and mainland China. He left it to Gu Mu to build close relationships with prominent Ningbo natives residing abroad. Gu noted: "At Deng Xiaoping's instruction, in May 1985 I engaged the former vice-premier of Singapore, Dr Goh Keng Swee, as economic advisor on coastal development, and later made him also advisor on the tourism industry. From that year on, the state council special zones office commissioned Nankai University and the Foreign Trade University to run

In 1984, the state council established the Ningbo economic readjustment small group. This was the first high-level working group of its kind in a single city, and it brought dynamism to the economic construction of Ningbo. This photo shows the founding members of the Ningbo small group, including Gu Mu (front row, fourth from right), YK Pao (fifth from right) and Lu Xuzhang (sixth from right)

an ongoing series of training classes for cadres working in the 'opening to the outside world' programme. By the end of 1992, 35 sessions had trained more than 1,200 people."

As for Deng Xiaoping's commission to Gu Mu regarding Ningbo, this writer made use of the words of Bao Peiqing in the book, *YK Pao, My Father*: "China gave birth to the first small group responsible for coordinating the development of a medium-sized city. Vice-Premier Gu Mu served as group leader, and Vice-Chairman Chen Xian was deputy leader of the group [Chen Xian was also a Ningbo man]. Gu also asked Lu Xuzhang and YK Pao to serve as advisors. These were the four most important people. Other members of the small group included seven or eight figures of vice-ministerial rank, detailed to the small group from their ministries and commissions under the state council, and leading figures from the Zhejiang provincial and Ningbo municipal governments. The purpose was to make arrangements in a unified fashion to handle major problems arising in Ningbo during the city's economic development and the larger reform and opening up programme. This was a formidable lineup. Subsequently, both Premier Zhu Rongji and Vice-Premier Zeng Peiyan took part in meetings of the Ningbo small group.

"Setting up such a body to provide leadership and coordination for a single medium-sized city, as the state council did, was a path-breaking act by the Chinese government. It established firm grounds for the faster economic development of Ningbo and for further progress in reform and

In May 1989, while in Shantou SEZ, Gu Mu inscribed a poem by the great Song dynasty reform official, Wang Anshi. His calligraphy was carved into a stone wall in the shape of a sail from a traditional craft. On returning to Shantou, Gu Mu posed for a photo in front of this stone wall

opening up. Establishing the coordinating small group was Deng Xiaoping's way of advancing reform and opening up among China's municipalities. Realising his call to 'Let the people from Ningbo all over the world join forces to build Ningbo' was a major strategic measure.

"Vice-Premier Gu Mu was a longstanding leader on the front lines in China's industrial and economic development, rich in experience. Guided by Deng Xiaoping's thinking on the subject of reform and opening up, his trajectory was firm, his pattern of thought clear. Because Gu Mu vigorously advocated reform and opening up, and did so with enormous experience in economic affairs, he was a man of great strength. The Ningbo coordinating small group met six times, and not a single person failed to attend any of the meetings."

Chapter 60

Timely Discovery Leads to Solving New Problems with the SEZs

Once the national effort to 'open to the outside world' got fully underway, Gu Mu turned to resolving new problems in the SEZ programme as they popped up. He quickly turned his attention to weaknesses and deficiencies in the development of the zones. In his memoirs, he named several of those:

- Progress on the basic construction front was too long and drawn out, and involved too many disparate programmes;
- Too many projects were not production programmes, and the growth of export production was too slow;
- Many goods produced in the SEZs were marketed domestically, with profiteers using the disparity between internal and external prices to buy cheaply and sell at high prices. Cases of illegal profiteering were appearing, giving rise to resentment in other parts of the country.

These practices were not in keeping with directives to the zones issued by the central authorities: "Put primary emphasis on foreign capital"; "Place industrial production programmes at the core"; "Ensure that export products predominate"; and "Use our energies to import advanced technologies".

In developing the Shenzhen zone, however, a number of comrades, including some specialists and academics, held dissenting views on these issues. To their minds, conditions for industrial development in Shenzhen were primitive, and there was an inherent contradiction between the principle of producing goods for export and the main aim of foreign investors, which was to secure access to domestic markets for their products. They urged that Shenzhen develop as a centre of finance, commerce, foreign trade and tourism. These voices grew louder over time.

In late February 1985, Gu Mu called an SEZ discussion meeting in Shenzhen. He assumed the leading role, and forcefully argued that the SEZs ought not content themselves solely with putting up skyscrapers. If the SEZs were to realise Deng Xiaoping's call for the opening of the 'four windows', it was necessary, he argued, to make industrial production the core and to produce export products to earn foreign exchange. "This year, we must climb one hill and add one higher storey to our edifice," Gu Mu urged.

But Gu Mu's forthright guidance did not yield ideal results. Excessive numbers of engineering projects in Shenzhen continued to grow, surpassing planned levels for 1984 by 40%. Some voices vehemently disagreed with Gu Mu's ideas and took bitter exception to the well-intentioned criticisms offered by others in the meeting.

In March 1985, Gu Mu travelled abroad. When he returned home in April, he was suffering from a severe eye ailment, and sent another written message to Shenzhen, but again without significant result. Gu Mu took the view that, if he could not resolve these issues through local discussion, further work was going to be needed system-wide.

Thus he took three steps:
- First, he asked Zhang Gensheng and Yu Mingtao, old comrades who had worked in Shenzhen, to go to Shenzhen for an exchange of views with the officials in charge on the scene;
- Next, he threw his support behind the plan to send Liu Guoguang, vice-president of the CASS, with a so-called 'small group' of specialists, to Shenzhen, in order to carry out a month-long strategic review of Shenzhen SEZ's development and produce a systemic report of its findings. He made clear that the main goal in developing the zone was to build an internationally oriented framework;
- Third, he assigned the former deputy chairman of the state economic commission, Yuan Baohua, to perform his own investigation and analysis, bring all the relevant government agencies together for discussion, and come up with a single coherent view of the situation.

The reports of Yuan Baohua and Liu Guoguang clearly advocated that the SEZs had to move to contribute to building international orientations of the economy. Yuan Baohua even pointed out: "The SEZs are not supposed to produce only goods for immediate monetary return. They must produce their own high-quality competitive products." He recommended the creation in Shenzhen of a specialised concentration for scientific research and production of industrial components, drawing on the strengths of government agencies responsible for electronics and aeronautics. Building such a "base", he argued, would be beneficial both for the improvement in China's own electronic products and for developing China's exports, while potentially complementing Hong Kong's deficiencies in those areas.

Lastly, Gu Mu assigned Zhou Jiannan and He Chunlin to convene a meeting in Shenzhen to discuss the development of outward-facing industry in the zone. He invited representatives from administrative units which held jurisdiction over those enterprises in the zone that were both bringing in external resources (capital, technology and management improvements) and connecting to the larger domestic economy. By working with these enterprises' parent agencies, with their vertical connections to higher levels of authority in their respective fields, he sought to ensure that enterprises with heavy components of technology and solid managerial backing would play essential structural roles in the development of an outward-oriented economy.

At the same time, the top figures in the state council, acting in accord with instructions from Deng Xiaoping, determined that a shakeup of the leadership team in Shenzhen SEZ was required. One morning, Deng Xiaoping held a meeting with foreign guests, with Gu Mu in attendance. Before the foreigners arrived, Deng and Gu chatted about the tasks in Shenzhen. According to Gu Mu's memoirs: "Maybe he had heard news through other channels. He said: 'What's going on? These people are too proud for their own good. If we're going to help in this situation, at the right moment we're going to have to make some changes.' That very evening, I was strolling by the lake in Zhongnanhai, when I bumped into comrade Deng Xiaoping. He came back to the subject of re-arranging the leadership team in Shenzhen. Within a single day, Deng Xiaoping had raised the subject twice, so I assumed his remarks were not made casually. I quickly sent a report to the colleagues at the state council. The central leadership promptly decided to make Li Hao, who was then serving as deputy secretary general of the standing committee of the state council, mayor of Shenzhen, and transferred Liang Xiang to become secretary of the Shenzhen party committee."

Chapter 61

The Conference at which Gu Mu was Most Critical of the SEZs

From 25 December 1985 to 5 January 1986, entrusted by the state council, Gu Mu convened a conference in Shenzhen on the work underway in the special zones. Some 200 cadres attended, from Fujian and Guangdong, the four SEZs, and 29 government ministries and agencies under the state council. Of all the meetings and conferences that dealt with the SEZs, this was the biggest, and it lasted the longest. At this conference, Gu Mu raised more critical comments than he had at any other meeting. Most of his criticisms were aimed at Shenzhen.

As a prelude to the discussion, the meeting first circulated a document from the state council SEZ office entitled *A Research Outline on the Development Situation in the SEZs and Opinions on How to Proceed From This Point Forward*. The outline made a number of very sharp points. In the previous two years (1984 and 1985), investment in capital construction in the zones had been much too great. The structure of investments had been insufficiently rational. A comprehensive design was lacking both for the geographic distribution of production nationwide and the rational organisation of production among economic sectors and within individual sectors. Management standards, and the quality of both cadres and the workforce, failed to meet the requirements of the outward-oriented economy. Many enterprises were still weak when it came to generating hard currency through exports, and still faced difficulties in balancing their foreign exchange. Management efficiency levels were too low. Information feedback was brittle. A few units carried out illegal activities; some of the cases were relatively severe, particularly in Shenzhen.

From the lessons he had distilled out of his lengthy experience dealing with capital construction, Gu Mu knew that, when it came to reining in excessive capital construction activity, one had to maintain a spirit of 'heroes breaking arms'. To the assembled conferees, he said: "Perhaps these words sound too strong. I have thought long and hard about whether to say these things publicly to you all, and have finally decided to do so. If I didn't come out with them, I would fail in my duty."

On 7 February 1986, the standing committee of the state council, in accord with the *Summary of Proceedings of the Recent Conference on SEZ Work*, published the summary as an official state council document and distributed it nationwide.

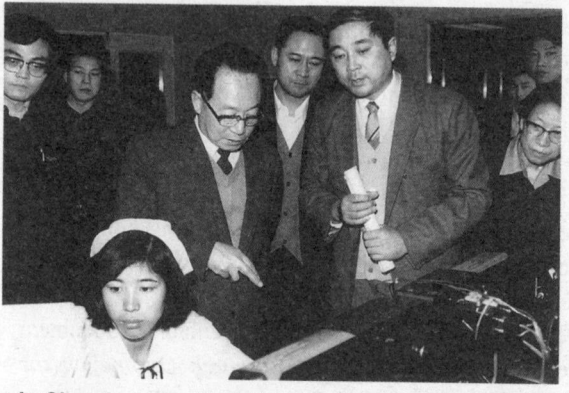

In Shenzhen, Gu Mu (third from right) leads members of the conference on SEZ work on a visit to Tianma Microelectronics, a unit of CAAC Shenzhen Technology Corporation, 30 December 1985. The general manager of Tianma, Wang Bin (far right) accompanies Gu Mu. They observe the process of cutting liquid crystal glass. Second from right is Hu Guangbao, deputy director of the state council SEZ office. Gu Mu's secretary, Li Qiang, is on the left

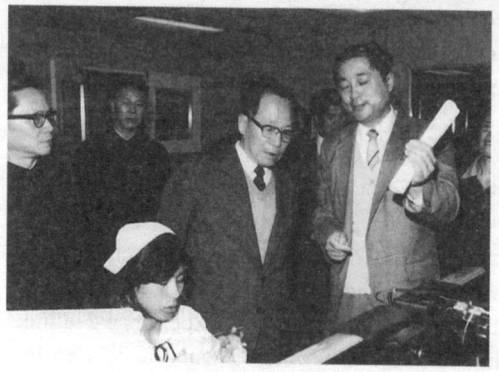

Following the visit, Gu Mu observed: 'The SEZs possess all the conditions necessary for running export businesses to earn hard currency, and for making use of our nation's labour force and our talents. Tianma Microelectronics offers a model for 'marching forward on the pathway to producing precision-made, high-quality light industrial goods' in the SEZs'

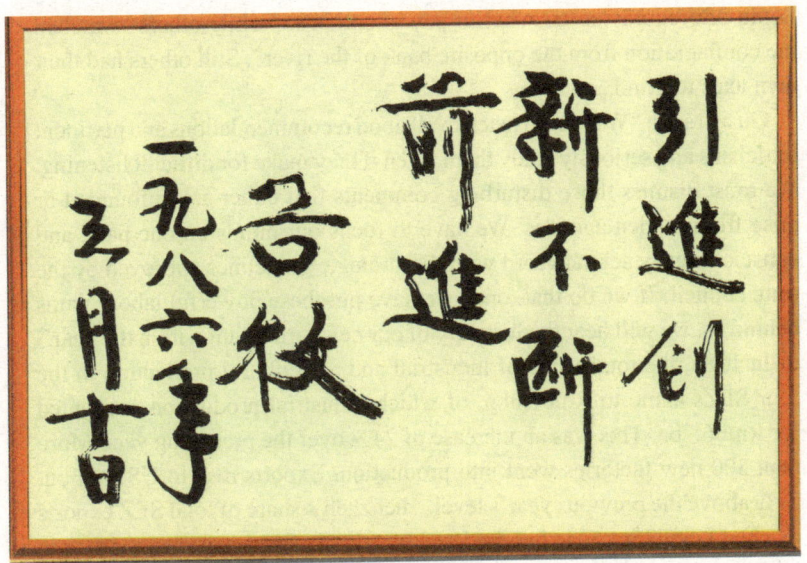

Gu Mu's inscription for Xiamen SEZ, March 1986

The SEZ conference in Shenzhen was a new beginning in setting the zones back on the right track. Each zone developed a strategic plan according to the linked notions of 'compressing' and 'preserving' in order to shrink the capital construction front, put greater emphasis on industrial production, improve the quality of its products, work hard to open new overseas markets, increase exports, and upgrade the quality of its companies while overcoming confusion and disorder in selling their products.

In 1986, capital construction in Shenzhen dropped by 30% year-on-year. Several hundred sub-par firms were dissolved or merged, with considerable pain. In the first half of the year, as capital construction was reined in and social programme costs were curtailed, market conditions in the SEZs were very weak; hotel and guesthouse occupancy fell sharply, and business in the food and beverage sector stagnated. Some media voices abroad took the opportunity to add fuel to the fire, with such mocking lines as "To build an advanced industry in Shenzhen is more difficult than climbing to the heavens" (a parody of a famous poem by the Tang dynasty poet, Li Bai), and "With business in the zones depressed, their future is uncertain", and "Gu Mu's view of Shenzhen's development prospects is too optimistic".

Some offered advice on what to pay attention to, while others "watched the conflagration from the opposite bank of the river". Still others had their own axes to grind.

Gu Mu said: "We should listen to all good recommendations and pertinent criticisms and seriously study them, even if they make for difficult listening. We must dismiss those disturbing comments that either are unfounded or arise from hidden agendas. We have to focus our minds on one path, and conscientiously act in accord with the strategic guidelines approved by the state council. If we do that, once we have put these powerful labour pains behind us, we will hear the lusty cry of our newborn infant within the year."

In 1986, the total value of industrial and agricultural production in the four SEZs came to Rmb7.6bn, of which industrial production accounted for Rmb6.7bn. This was an increase of 24% over the preceding year. More than 300 new factories went into production. Exports rose to US$1.03bn, 27% above the previous year's level. Shenzhen's share of total SEZ exports reached US$725m. One hundred and twenty-six firms exported more than US$1m each, and 22 companies exported more than US$5m apiece.

Chapter 62

SEZ Development Embarks on a New Course

From 6 to 10 February 1987, Gu Mu convened another conference on SEZ work in Shenzhen. This was his sixth such conference during his stewardship of the work of opening to the outside world and building SEZs, and the last of the series. The meeting reviewed the results arising from the 1986 conference's focus on the building of an externally-oriented economy, and moved another step forward in establishing a common consensus. The state council circulated the conference summary as an official document on 11 April 1987.

The session at which the state council approved the conference summary saw the first discussion of the separation of land ownership and land usage rights. Debate on the issues of fixed terms for land usage rights, compensation for such rights, and transfer of those rights to others constituted the first step in the reform of the entire nation's land-use system.

Gu Mu borrowed from a poem by the Song dynasty reformer, Wang Anshi, the lines, "Find greatness in the ordinary, conquer hardships as though they were easy", to describe the processes of creating and operating the SEZs. In his memoirs, he wrote: "On the matter of our country's establishment of the SEZs, we have to admit that our shared understanding has grown progressively deeper. In the beginning, opinion was divided on the simple matter of 'Should we or shouldn't we do this?'. This was effectively resolved by 1984. Then came the uneasy question, 'Can we run the zones well enough?'. That took up most of our attention at the 1985 and 1986 SEZ conferences. From 1987, though, the zones' real achievements have increasingly put those doubts to rest. By 1992, the combined value of production in the four SEZs – Shenzhen, Zhuhai, Shantou and Xiamen

281

– reached, including US$11.5bn from exports. The zones had become a significant force in the national economy."

Gu Mu returned to five essential points in reviewing the functions of the SEZs: "First of all, the zones have contributed precious knowledge, and helped us to forge and train vital human resources, as they have dealt with key issues: how to utilise the superior elements of improved production that we brought in from abroad to build the national economy; how to perfect our own management systems by drawing on the experiences of other countries in organising their societies for mass industrial production; how to hold on to our correct political orientations amid burgeoning economic engagements with other countries; and how to build a socialist spiritual civilisation.

"Second, the zones were our country's 'advance troops' in the battle for opening to the outside world; their policies, and their experiences, were then summed up and put to good use everywhere.

"Third, the zones became new bases for concentrated foreign trade development. They made it possible for our southern coastal belt to add additional cities as economic centres and new foreign trade ports, in support of the nation's vital advances in the foreign trade sector.

"Fourth, the zones were proving grounds for reform… They supported the strategy of market regulation as it evolved under the guidance of national macroeconomic policy, and they provided beneficial lessons for the establishment of a socialist market economy nationwide.

"And fifth, the zones are living examples of our country's ongoing economic policies. Their positive influence affected the smooth return and continued prosperity of Hong Kong and Macau. They had a very positive impact on the promotion of cross-Strait contacts and the step-by-step realisation of the great task of national unification under the theme 'One country, two systems'."

Chapter 63

Twenty-two Detailed Regulations to Improve the Investment Environment

Throughout the process of reform and opening up, Gu Mu put much energy into the establishment of a healthy legal and regulatory structure for the introduction of foreign investment, in order to make improvements in the 'soft' dimensions of the investment environment.

Gu Mu (third from left) with Bo Yibo (fourth from left) and Rong Yiren (far left) take part in a reception following a discussion session on the Chinese economy, jointly sponsored by China International Trust and Investment Company and *Economic Daily*, 9 September 1984

In the first four or five years of the nation's introduction of foreign investment (from publication of the *Joint Venture Law* in July 1979 until the end of 1983), progress was slow, and the scale of investments remained small.

After the broadening of the whole 'opening up' process in 1984, even though the development momentum picked up, a number of problems both 'hard' and 'soft' arose with the massive expansion of foreign investment.

At the beginning of 1982, the state council's foreign investment committee (formally known as the national import and export management commission) had been disbanded, and its duties transferred to the newly established ministry of foreign trade and economic cooperation (Moftec). But Moftec's main emphasis was on exports, and the ministry was weaker in the area of attracting foreign investment. By early 1986, international business people were complaining loudly about the country's investment environment.

At a meeting of the party's leading small group on finance and economics in April 1986, Gu Mu was once again assigned the job of managing and adjusting the ways in which China attracted and made use of foreign capital. The state council approved and established a new leading small group on foreign investment work, with Gu Mu as the group's leader and Zhou Jiannan as deputy leader. This new leading small group comprised 13 individuals from the relevant entities under the state council.

Gu Mu and He Chunlin, head of the Shenzhen SEZ office (second from right) meet reporters in Shenzhen

Gu Mu with Zhu Rongji

Once the leading small group was established, it quickly turned to the task of resolving the most pressing problems facing the production and operation of foreign-invested firms. Gu Mu made two decisions. First, the state council SEZ office, which served concurrently as the leading small group's office, would send a team to the locations that had attracted heaviest foreign investment for a careful investigation. Their views on conditions and problem-solving there would be sifted during the preparation of a document on how to respond to the urgent challenges.

Second, responsibility for managing and solving management and production problems among foreign-invested enterprises was to revert to the state economic commission and its subordinate agencies. Zhu Rongji, vice-chairman of the state economic commission, was to take direct responsibility when the need arose.

After discussion and mediation of the opinions of the various agencies, the meeting of the leading small group on management of foreign investment finalised a document that was then debated and approved by the standing committee of the state council. The document, made public on 12 July 1986, was entitled *Announcement of the State Council with Respect to Forward Steps in Improving the Operating Conditions for Foreign-invested Enterprises*. It dealt mainly with issues regarding firms that already employed foreign capital.

But because of time pressures and superficiality in the examination of these questions, the views of the various agencies involved were not fully mediated. Even though the content of the announcement seemed to be clearly printed in black and white, implementation of some of its provisions was bungled over and over again. Gu Mu therefore promptly ordered the state council SEZ office to conduct its own thorough review of the foreign investment environment, using as counter-examples two volumes of materials on techniques employed in Southeast Asia. He encouraged the investigators to reach out for a wide range of opinions on foreign investment.

On 19 August 1986, after making his report to the state council standing committee at the Beidaihe summer retreat, Gu Mu received approval from the party leadership, which ordered him to take this body of material as the foundation for a new party document that would have the status of regulations.

Thus, on 8 September 1986, the draft document that came to be known as the *Twenty-two Articles* (the full title was *Regulations Governing the Encouragement of Foreign Commercial Investments*) was approved by the leading small group on foreign investment. Five days later, the standing committee of the state council in turn approved the text. But Gu Mu, on

On a visit to a 'three imports and one compensation'-style[1] enterprise in Huizhou, Gu Mu converses with Huizhou Mayor Li Jinwei (Photo by Zhang Guoying)

the basis of his long experience, kept his hand on the controls before the document was published. Ever thorough and meticulous, he knew he had to work the document through all the regions and all the agencies that it would affect. On 20 and 21 September, he put together a two-day seminar for a group of colleagues, who made small further revisions to the text.

On 12 October 1986, *People's Daily* published the official *Regulations of the State Council Regarding Encouragement of Foreign Investment*. A *People's Daily* official editorial accompanied the text. The following day, Gu Mu and members of the foreign investment small leading group met with a group of journalists to further explain certain key questions, with excellent results.

During the drafting of the *22 Articles*, remembering past lessons of the dangers that arose when a failure to get into details allowed all the interested parties to push for their own narrow goals, Gu Mu decided that the leading small group would have to issue with one voice a set of concrete and detailed regulations, to ensure that the *22 Articles* were fully implemented.

On 18 September, Gu Mu commissioned Zhou Jiannan and He Chunlin, on behalf of the state council SEZ office, to go to the trouble of meeting with all the involved agencies and draw up a list of detailed regulations, 22 of them in all. Each of these detailed regulations had to go through four rounds of deliberation. First, the drafting unit had to produce a draft. Second, all the relevant agencies had to state their views. Third, the leading small group had to debate the draft. Finally, the draft had to be submitted to the leaders of the state council for their final approval. From October to December 1986, Gu Mu held a total of 12 sessions to discuss the *22 Articles*, averaging a session each week.

This painstaking refinement of the *22 Articles* involved a vast amount of close, meticulous work, since the impact of the articles extended widely and deeply across many sectors of the economy. The workload was enormous. The burden was possibly even heavier than coming up with the original draft of the *22 Articles* in the first place. The main document entailed minute definitions of a number of principles, and that required exhaustive and detailed discussions to produce small steps forward. Opinions from all parties had to be taken into account. By July 1987, the compilation of these detailed regulations was finally complete.

Gu Mu, after boarding a ship in the port of Shekou, waves farewell to the Shenzhen leadership, March 1995

Twenty-two Detailed Regulations to Improve the Investment Environment

Gu Mu later wrote in his memoirs: "Looking back on the years since China began absorbing foreign investment, there were two episodes in which we focused our attentions on policies and regulations. In the first, before 1981, the core documents were the *Law on Enterprises with Joint Sino-Foreign Investment* and the ensuing *Implementing Regulations*. Together, these two documents were the trailblazing steps in the work of attracting foreign investment.

"The second was the round of measures in 1986, which further perfected and systematised the body of foreign investment policies and rules. Not only at the level of general principles but also at more detailed levels, there were thus laws and regulations to abide by. This was a vital forward step in the process of attracting international investment, and had a most positive influence on our later work."

From the time that the document that came to be called the *22 Articles* first took shape to the emergence of a complete set of 22 detailed regulations, Gu Mu's firmness and grasp of detail, as well as his foresight amid all the complexities of 'reform and opening up', shine through. Thanks to his emphasis on proper preparatory work, the final measures proved effective. This work style, accumulated over long years and months, stood in stark contrast to the work habits of many others, known as the 'three slaps': 'slap your head when hoping for a brainstorm, slap your chest when making guarantees to your superiors, and slap your behind when it's time to get out.'

Gu Mu's leadership techniques during these years reached the highest boundaries of perfection. Not only did he enjoy the deep respect and affection of the cadres who worked under him directly and in the zones. His leadership was also manifested in the high management and other standards that came to be realised in the national reform and opening up effort, and in national macro-economic leadership.

Chapter 64

Intentionally Not Raising the Theme 'Hainan Can Catch Taiwan in 20 Years'

In 1987, Gu Mu took on an important project – the creation of Hainan SEZ. For Gu Mu this was the second time around.

The first attempt to develop Hainan was symbolised by a central party document issued on 1 April 1983.

At a conference on coastal city development held in March 1984, top officials from Hainan put the question directly to Gu Mu: in the spirit of the conversation that Deng Xiaoping had held with a number of senior party leaders, as detailed on 14 February, why not raise the idea of 'Hainan catching up with Taiwan in 20 years'? To them, this quotation from Deng Xiaoping was nothing less than a magic weapon. Deng had put it this way: "If we use the next 20 years to raise Hainan economically to the level of Taiwan, that would constitute a great victory."

Gu Mu did not then want to give prominence to this '20 years to catch Taiwan' phrase. He recalled how Chairman Mao, in 1958, had proposed the goal of annually producing 10.7m tons of steel, and remembered how the officials in charge simply did not have the professional spirit needed to talk about the problems they faced, with the result that the national economy suffered huge losses.

Looking back at history, Gu Mu wrote in his memoirs: "I remembered the lessons we had learned in 1958 during the Great Leap Forward. Comrade Zhou Enlai had said to us: 'Sometimes, when Chairman Mao speaks, his words are intended to stimulate debate, and we should not always take these utterances as his final decisions.' I kept Zhou Enlai's words in mind as I dealt with this particular phrase from Deng Xiaoping."

Not raising 'catch up with Taiwan' to prominence at that time symbolised Gu Mu's political maturity and his ability to keep focused on the most

Intentionally Not Raising the Theme 'Hainan Can Catch Taiwan in 20 Years'

Gu Mu on a visit to Hainan in December 1983. Third from right is Lei Yu

important questions while putting lesser matters to one side. Later, when the conversations of Deng Xiaoping were edited and published, his comments about catching up with Taiwan were not included.

But at the time, top officials in Hainan were overheated, to the point that a large-scale car-smuggling incident occurred on the island. They signed agreements to import 26 television assembly production lines, causing major and widespread, as well as more narrowly-focused, losses. Years later, this led to the removal of a number of top officials from Hainan and numerous legal cases against cadres involved in the misconduct. Some Rmb500m-600m remained uncollectible, and as much as Rmb1.1bn in imported goods were unusable. In addition, the worst typhoon in 50 years struck Hainan in 1985 with great destruction, and the island floundered in the deepest difficulties.

In the first half of 1985, the central committee on discipline inspection organised a special investigation into Hainan's 'speculation in automobiles', and took a number of very severe measures. At that time, Gu Mu was waging battles on two fronts. On the one hand, he was helping central authorities sort through the car smuggling case. But on the other, he had to re-energise those party cadres on Hainan who had descended into paralysis. Gu Mu put it strongly: "The party document of April 1983 remained unchanged. I heard absolutely nothing calling for the cancellation of that document." Gu Mu encouraged the cadres on Hainan to stay the course, and prepare themselves for forward progress in the future.

Chapter 65

First Ask Shen Nong, then Ask Edison

Gu Mu invited the former vice-premier of Singapore, Dr Goh Keng Swee, to visit Hainan and make his own recommendations as a consultant.

Gathering together all the ideas he received from various sources, Gu Mu stressed that moving forward on the development of Hainan had to begin with the genuine realities there. That meant starting with Hainan's particular resources: tropical crops, fisheries and animal husbandry. The first chapter had to be in doing right by agriculture. From this foundation, development could turn to the next stage – processing industries for the island's agricultural products and secondary products, and the development of mineral resources, all with an eye toward exporting internationally, supplying the mainland Chinese economy and making products unique to the Hainan environment. The tourism sector could be developed energetically at the same time.

Someone in the state planning commission called this: "First ask Shen Nong, the mythical founder of agriculture in Chinese civilisation, then ask Edison."

For Hainan, Gu Mu held on to the most favourable background factors. The central government's original pattern of economic assistance to Hainan, which even extended to budgets for repair and refurbishment of dilapidated primary and middle school buildings, was maintained. By 1986, conditions on Hainan had taken a turn for the better, and the dire distress of the previous year had begun to fade.

In early 1987, Gu Mu exchanged ideas with various leaders on a number of occasions, and all ultimately agreed that the faster development of this precious island depended on the resolution of three problems.

First, the system of leadership had to be smoothed out. At the time, Hainan's administrative position was as a so-called 'administrative region', half an administrative rank above ordinary 'administrative regions', under the direct control of Guangdong province. Within that administrative region was a 'level-one autonomous prefecture', itself embracing various localities and municipalities. The layers of administration were too complex, and administrative efficacy was sorely lacking.

Second, the strength of the opening programme had to be increased. And third, in order to bring sufficient skills to bear on the project, it would be necessary to transfer a body of technically qualified personnel from the mainland to the island.

Gu Mu and central leaders rejected a proposal from Hong Kong companies to "let Hong Kong companies develop Hainan, under the designation 'special administrative zone', utilising a free port on the island", because the idea came perilously close to re-creating a 'foreign concession' similar to those in the pre-liberation treaty ports. Instead, they proposed a two-pronged forward strategy that would raise Hainan to the status of an independent province and simultaneously develop a Hainan SEZ.

To this, Deng Xiaoping gave his approval, appointing Gu Mu to take charge of bringing it to fruition.

Gu Mu then brought together a group of agencies to ferment their thoughts, and invited a number of leading members of the party's Hong Kong-Macau working committee to carry information from the meeting back to the relevant figures in Hong Kong.

That July, Gu Mu made a special trip to Guangzhou to discuss a number of questions relating to Hainan with Guangdong Party Secretary Lin Ruo and the provincial governor, Ye Xuanping. He held a number of meetings with the state council SEZ office, which prepared the *Preliminary Opinions Regarding the Establishment of an SEZ on Hainan.*

In September 1987, a preparatory group for the establishment of Hainan province was formally established, under the direction of Xu Shijie as the top party figure and Liang Xiang as the senior government participant.

By November, based on two documents jointly created by the Hainan province preparatory group and the state council SEZ office, Gu Mu was able to gather the many state council agencies involved with the process to put forth *Opinions Regarding Next Steps in Accelerating Hainan Island's Opening and Economic Development.*

In December 1987, Gu Mu flew directly to Haikou to chair a discussion of matters relating to the establishment of a Hainan SEZ. He absorbed a number of good ideas, but suppressed leading Hainan officials who were pushing for even more 'favourable treatment' and who pressed over and over again a number of 'vigorous demands'.

Upon returning to Beijing, Gu Mu reported to party central authorities and the state council. Keeping in mind the principle of 'speaking differently for domestic and foreign ears', he wrote up two papers on issues emerging from his discussions. The one entitled *A Summary of Discussion Sessions on Opening Hainan and Speeding Its Economic Development* was circulated internally. The other paper, entitled *Regulatory Decisions Regarding the Encouragement of Investment for the Purpose of Developing Hainan Island*, was issued to the public. On 17 January 1988, party central authorities and the state council formally approved both of these documents.

On 13 April, at the first session of the seventh NPC, the resolutions of the state council establishing Hainan province and Hainan SEZ were approved, turning a new page in Hainan's economic development and opening up.

Chapter 66

For Coastal China and the Linked Chain of Open Areas, a Second Step Forward

In March 1988 at its work conference on the opening of the coastal region, the state council decided to extend the range of coastal SEZs to the Shandong peninsula, the Liaodong peninsula, the Bohai Rim and various other coastal areas, while linking them with the Pearl river delta, the Minnan triangle and the Yangtze delta in a single extended chain. This represented another step in the continuous process, since 1984, of adding vital extensions to the nation's open belt. From its original list of 59 municipalities and counties, the belt of open areas now included 293 municipalities and counties, embracing 426,000 square kilometres and 220m people and basically including all cities and counties on the coast of China.

Gu Mu visits Wuzhou, in Guangxi

Gu Mu takes in the sights of Nantong city in Jiangsu

Gu Mu said in his memoirs that taking this giant step was a "decision based on scientific analysis of trends in global economic development. In the global economic development, as changes took place in the cost of labour, the structure of industrial production in the developed world was undergoing continual change, and labour-intensive industry was moving towards locations with lower labour costs. In Asia, that originally meant movement from the US to Japan, and later towards Taiwan, Hong Kong, South Korea and Singapore. Since the middle of the 1980s, new changes have been underway. This has been extremely fortuitous. In response, we exchanged views on many occasions, and reached the conclusion that our coastal regions should vigorously rise to this opportunity. Moving towards the global marketplace, in a planned and phased manner, and building an externally oriented economy has been our response to a strategic question… Meanwhile, drawing in foreign direct investment and making use of capital, technology, and sales and distribution channels, has developed our outward-facing economy. In this manner, we were able to maximise the advantages of our labour power and our processing industry technology in the coastal region, building our 'labour exports' borne by our export products, while participating in the commerce and competition of the global market. Thus, we furthered the prosperity of our coastal regions and contributed to the economic revitalisation of China's interior as well."

For Coastal China and the Linked Chain of Open Areas, a Second Step Forward

Gu Mu and Li Peng

Gu Mu and Li Ruihuan

At the end of 1987, the CPC politburo discussed and affirmed these views. Deng Xiaoping encouraged the whole party: "We must act with special boldness and confidence, accelerate our pace and not squander our opportunities."

In October 1987, as an accompaniment to the party's 13th congress, Gu Mu gave an interview to *People's Daily*, which published a feature entitled *A Responsible Comrade from the State Council Discusses the Deeper and Broader Expansion of Opening to the Outside World*. After that, a document known as *Several Supplementary Regulatory Decisions with Respect to the Development of The Outward-facing Economy in the Coastal Regions*, consisting of 13 articles, was formally issued by the state council following deliberation at a meeting on state council administration called by the acting premier, Li Peng.

After the spring festival of 1988, the state council convened another conference on external work in the coastal regions, the last such meeting on a national scale during Gu Mu's stewardship of the 'opening to the outside world' programme. In his report to the conference, Gu Mu looked back on

The leadership dais at the seventh CPPCC

the important experiences and lessons gained from nearly a decade of work on opening up. He reflected on the basic principles underlying the tasks of coastal development and building an outward-looking economy, addressing both the tasks encountered along the way and the crucial linkages that were required to deal with those challenges. By this time, the news that Gu Mu was soon to step down, with the installation of a new state council in April, had made its way to the CPPCC. Everyone present took Gu Mu's report to be his 'farewell performance'.

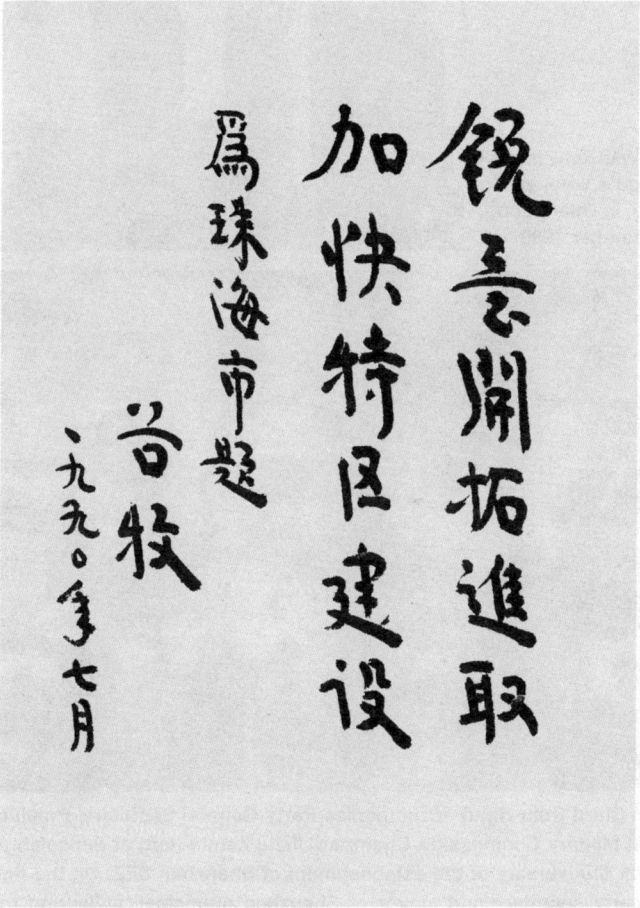

Gu Mu's calligraphy, presented to Zhuhai SEZ in July 1990

Gu Mu with Ren Zhongyi and Ren's wife, Wang Xuanfu, in Guangdong, 25 November 1990

Gu Mu (third from right) accompanies Party General Secretary, President and Central Military Commission Chairman Jiang Zemin (left) at the celebration of the 10th anniversary of the establishment of Shenzhen SEZ. On the right is Li Hao, party secretary and mayor of Shenzhen municipality. Second from the right is He Chunlin, director of the state council SEZ office

For Coastal China and the Linked Chain of Open Areas, a Second Step Forward

In the early 1990s, in his capacity as vice-chairman of the CPPCC, Gu Mu meets the chairman of the Guangdong provincial people's political consultative conference, Wu Nansheng, for a friendly conversation

Gu Mu (standing, second from right), accompanied by Guangdong Deputy Secretary General and Director of the provincial SEZ office Ding Lisong (standing third from right) and Shenzhen Municipal Government Secretary-General Li Ding (standing, fourth from right) on a visit to Shenzhen Xianke Laser Company. Third on the left is Xianke board chairman and general manager, Ye Huaming (son of General Ye Ting) (photo by Zhang Guoying)

Gu Mu during his tenure with the CPPCC, on a visit to Huizhou municipality on Daya Bay, Guangdong province (photo by Zhang Guoying)

Chapter 67

Leading the Work of the Confucius Fund

Zhou Enlai knew Gu Mu very well since Gu had been working for the premier for a long time. He appreciated that Gu Mu had achieved great accomplishments in traditional Chinese culture. So, in addition to the economic duties that were part of Gu Mu's remit, Premier Zhou also put him in charge of some important cultural projects. For example, Gu Mu oversaw the renovation of Liulichang Street, a famous district in Beijing, and the preservation and restoration of Prince Gong's mansion. After the crushing of the 'Gang of Four', Gu Mu carried out Premier Zhou's last wishes assiduously. For another project assigned by Deng Yingchao, Premier Zhou's wife, which involved leading the work of the Confucius Fund, Gu Mu devoted himself to the task in his final years.

Gu Mu visits Beijing Liulichang Culture Street in the late 1970s

In 1962, Premier Zhou Enlai and some famous professionals inspected Prince Gong's mansion and for the first time proposed that it should be preserved. In later years, it would open to the public. Ill health meant that he could not complete this task himself, so he had to pass on the responsibility to Gu Mu. Here, Gu Mu inspects the construction site of the mansion, July 1980

In June 1984 during a visit to Shandong province, Deng Yingchao, chairman of the national committee of the CPPCC, made a special trip to Confucius's hometown, Qufu. Confucius had been a respected and admired figure for more than 2,000 years and was called 'the teacher of all ages'. However, his name was traduced by rebels from the Central China Normal University during the 'Cultural Revolution'. This was a national disgrace. Though Premier Zhou tried to stop it, most cemeteries of Confucius, the Confucius family mansion and Confucius temples were ransacked. Witnessing this, Deng Yingchao became highly distressed. She sent a proposal to create the Confucius Fund to the central government on returning from her visit to Qufu. After the proposal was passed, she appointed Gu Mu as honorary chairman and Kuang Yaming as chairman. Deng made it very clear that, in the 1930s, Gu Mu was a cultural worker of the left wing. And, since he, too, came from Shandong province, he had a natural affinity with Confucius.

Leading the Work of the Confucius Fund

A statue of Confucius

Gu Mu and Li Lanqing listen to a work report on the restoration of Prince Gong's mansion.

Some leading comrades celebrate Deng Yingchao's birthday. From left to right: Tian Jiyun, Gu Mu, Yao Yilin, Yu Qiuli, Li Peng, Wan Li, Deng Yingchao, Hu Qili, Hao Jianxiu, Hu Yaobang, Qiao Shi, Xi Zhongxun and Deng Liqun

Gu Mu knew of Deng's intention to recommend him as honorary chairman. In 1973, during the middle years of the 'Cultural Revolution', when 'Lin Biao and Confucius were frequently condemned', to the later years of this period when Confucianism was criticised within the CPC and compared to 'legalism', Premier Zhou Enlai was always seen as the biggest Confucian in the party and an annoyance that needed to be eliminated. Deng Yingchao wanted Gu Mu to carry on the unfinished work of the premier. Therefore, Gu Mu shouldered a heavy responsibility and led the Confucius Fund to carry out extensive work:

- Establish and perfect the organisation. Established a council comprising more than 100 representatives, and set up professional teams;
- Develop academic research. Started the magazine *Confucius Studies*, and published papers about Confucian studies;
- Start academic communication of international Confucianism and Confucian study. In February 1986, Gu Mu visited Singapore and

agreed to cooperate in the area of Confucianism. In September 1987, the Confucius Fund jointly convened the first international forum on Confucianism in Qufu. In October 1988, the fund held the second international forum on Confucianism, in Bonn, with West Germany's Konrad Adenauer Foundation. In October 1989, the Confucius Fund and UNESCO (United Nations Educational, Scientific and Cultural Organisation) held an international academic seminar on Confucius's 2,540th birthday;
- Raise money. The Confucius Fund received money from the ministry of finance and local governments to cover organisational costs, special funds for academic study and constructing Confucius museums. It also attracted sponsorship from SEZS and overseas donors, such as YK Pao and Li Ka-shing;
- Promote Confucius study abroad. In October 1994, the Confucius Fund held an international academic seminar in Beijing marking Confucius's 2,545th birthday and established the international Confucian association. Gu Mu was the president, and was succeeded by Ye Xuanping

The honorary chairman of the Confucius Fund, Gu Mu, gives a speech at an international academic seminar celebrating Confucius's 2,545th birthday, 5 October 1994

Asked why Deng Yingchao recommended him to lead the Confucius Fund, Gu Mu said: "I did nothing extreme during the many years I worked under Premier Zhou. Maybe it's because the 'golden mean' is embodied in me to some extent." This sentence seems self-mocking, but it means more.

During Gu Mu's leadership of the Confucius Fund, the 'better left, never right' line of thought featured in several political campaigns, and was never eliminated. Studies and comments about Confucius remained sensitive for a long period after the establishment of the new China. After he took the job, Gu Mu developed a better understanding of Confucius and Confucianism.

Gu Mu believed that his first task should be to correctly understand Confucius's most fundamental contribution. Confucius started a 'charity-centred' humanitarian Confucian school; sorted and catalogued many ancient Chinese books, covering the culture of the Xia, Shang and Zhou dynasties; established a private school and broke the convention that only people in the imperial palace could study; and spread the range of knowledge across a wider area. Confucian thinking spread to Europe in the 17th century and helped promote the Enlightenment, and was incorporated into many theories and cultures around the world.

Gu Mu attends the conference on the establishment of the international Confucian association, 5 October 1994

Leading the Work of the Confucius Fund

Gu Mu with YK Pao

Gu Mu with Li Ka-shing

Gu Mu with Ye Xuanping (left) and Liu Yandong

The Qufu Confucius Research Institute, which was constructed thanks to the hard work of Gu Mu and other leading comrades

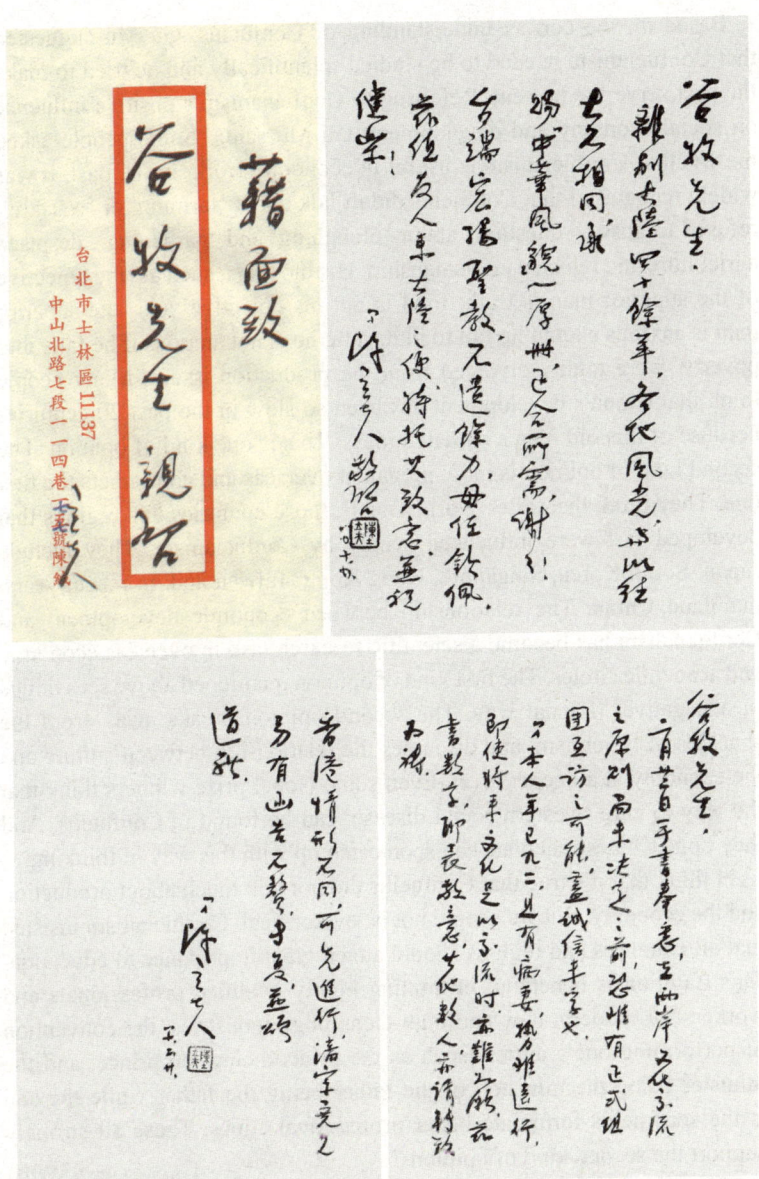

In 1991, Chen Lifu, chairman of the Taiwan Confucius and Mencius Academy, wrote two letters to Gu Mu

Based on the correct understanding of Confucius, Gu Mu suggested that Confucianism needed to be studied scientifically and he tried to make the past serve the present. Referring to Confucianism's positive influence on social economy and development, Gu Mu said: "Some people asked me whether Confucianism is useful in economic work. In the past, it was widely recognised that Confucius didn't talk about 'farming' or 'warfare', refused to answer questions about 'ploughing' and 'gardening', despised agriculture and rejected craftsmanship. His thoughts, such as 'the objective of the superior man is truth; food is not his objective' and 'the superior man is anxious should he fail to find truth; he is not anxious if he falls into poverty' were totally divorced from the production issues. Many people think that China's development has been so slow in the past 20 centuries because of this old man's outdated ideas. This is one kind of opinion. The second kind of opinion is more prevalent overseas and contradicts the first one. They think that, after World War II, those countries and regions that developed fast were influenced deeply by Confucianism. They include Japan, South Korea, Singapore, Hong Kong, Taiwan and, in recent years, mainland China. The relationship between economic development and Confucianism has become a scientific research task in overseas economic and academic circles. The first kind of opinion mentioned above sees things in a negative, rational way. The second opinion breaks away from the shackles of 'scientism' and discusses the relationship between culture and the economy at a deeper level. Even some Nobel prize winners think that the way to cure 'western social disease' can be found in Confucius. And they hope Chinese scholars can soon catch up with this way of thinking.

"I think that it's true that Confucius did not talk much about production and the economy. But we should not be overcritical. Confucianism insisted that all countries and regions should attach great importance to education. This tradition is beneficial in training highly qualified professionals and workers for modern, new and high-technology industries; the convention of performing one's duties (such as the prince being the prince, and the minister being the minister, or the father being the father while the son is the son) helps formulate better professional ethics. These all strongly support the second kind of opinion."

The third plenary session of the 11th central committee of the CPC brought an end to the wave after wave of political campaigns. Especially after heading the Confucius Fund, Gu Mu's belief in traditional culture was rejuvenated. In his last years, Gu Mu used the precious gift of a long life to become more mature in many ways. And he became more and more charming like his idol, Premier Zhou Enlai. Though most of his relatives had passed away, some of his stories were published in articles by those who cared about him and were spread across the world. For example, when Zang Kejia's daughter-in-law, Qiao Zhiying, learned of the death of Gu Mu, she published *Unforgettable Nostalgia: Lasting Friendship Forged by Gu Mu and Zang Kejia* in *Qilu Evening News*. She wrote in the article: "One day in October 2003, Gu Mu went to visit Zang Kejia, who was seriously ill in Peking Union Medical College Hospital. I was with Le Yuan at dad's bedside. Dad had many tubes in his body. He could not speak. All he could do was look at Gu Mu with tears in his eyes. Gu Mu sat by dad, holding his swollen hands. Tears were also in his eyes. He did not say a word to comfort my dad. Instead, he sat there quietly and looked at my dad for a while. Then he began to recite lines from dad's poem *Life* from his famous collection of poems, *Leaving a Lasting Impression*: 'Thousands of arrows are raining down around you, waiting for your one tiny indiscretion while you are otherwise being constantly watchful.' Our tears flowed as the poem went on."

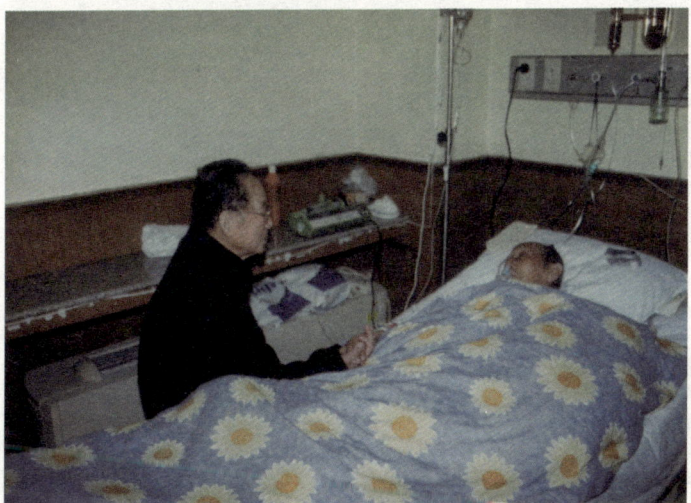

Gu Mu recites Zang Kejia's poem *Life* from his famous collection of poems, *Leaving a Lasting Impression* while visiting Zang Kejia in Peking Union Medical College Hospital

克家同志：

在您八秩寿诞之时，特向您表示衷心的祝贺。

您的一生是和诗连在一起的，从学诗、写诗，到研究诗歌理论，培育诗坛新人，可以说，您的一生都献给了诗的王国。在旧中国漫漫长夜里，您运用诗的武器，抨击黑暗，揭露丑恶，传播正义，讴歌光明，为新中国的诞生呐喊，留下了许多脍炙人口的名篇佳句，同时也为新诗的发展和繁荣作出了贡献；新中国成立后，您主编《诗刊》，扶掖新人，在诗歌理论研究上也颇有建树。祝您宝刀不老，写出更多更好的作品，为我们伟大祖国这个举世公认的"诗的王国"进一步增光添彩，为我国诗歌的进一步振兴贡献更多的力量。祝您

健康长寿

谷牧

1985年十月十一日

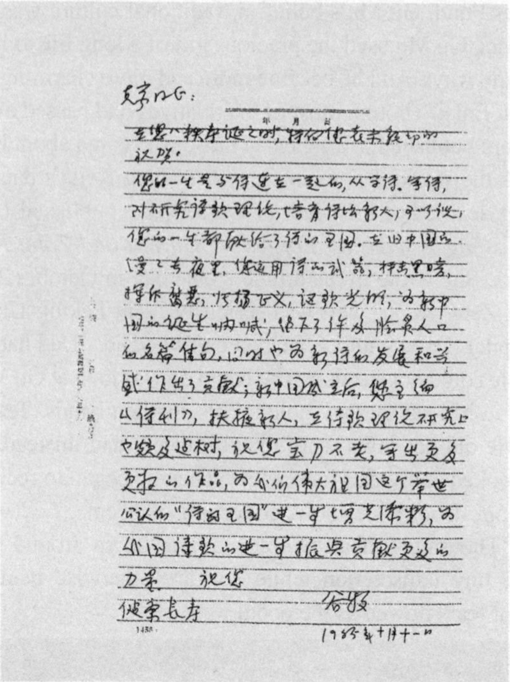

The Zang Kejia seminar was held in Jinan on 11 October 1985. Gu Mu wrote an ebullient congratulatory letter to Zang Kejia:

Comrade Kejia,

Congratulations on your 80th birthday. Your whole life is associated with poems. From studying poetry, writing poems, researching poetic theory and encouraging new generations of poets, you devoted yourself to the world of poetry. In the endless dark night of former times, you used poetry as a weapon to fight darkness, sweep away corruption, publicise justice, eulogise light and scream for the birth of a new China. You left us with so many famous poems and lines. You also contributed much to the development and vibrancy of a new style of poetry. After the new China was founded, you edited *Shikan*, helped new poets and made contributions to research into poetry. May you be like a good sword that never blunts, write many more masterpieces to add glory to our country which is already known as the kingdom of poetry, and make more contributions to further develop our nation's poetry.

Wishing you good health and a long life,

Gu Mu

11 October 1985

This letter moved the old poet very much. He copied it and sent it to his son and daughter-in-law in Changsha

Since his childhood, Gu Mu read books of the sages, studied the traditional way, received the new-style education and was influenced by the May Fourth new culture movement. At one time, he was critical, or even sceptical about Confucianism. After the great age of revolution, after much experience in the construction of socialism and leading the reform and opening-up process, the grey-haired Gu Mu was appointed as honorary chairman of the Confucius Fund and president of the international Confucian association. He started to believe again in traditional culture. Gu Mu had accomplished the mission assigned to him by Deng Yingchao. After experiencing the revolutionary war, the construction of socialism, the 'Cultural Revolution' and the commercial tide of reform and opening up, on a spirally rising ideological level, Gu Mu reached a higher level of 'righting wrongs'.

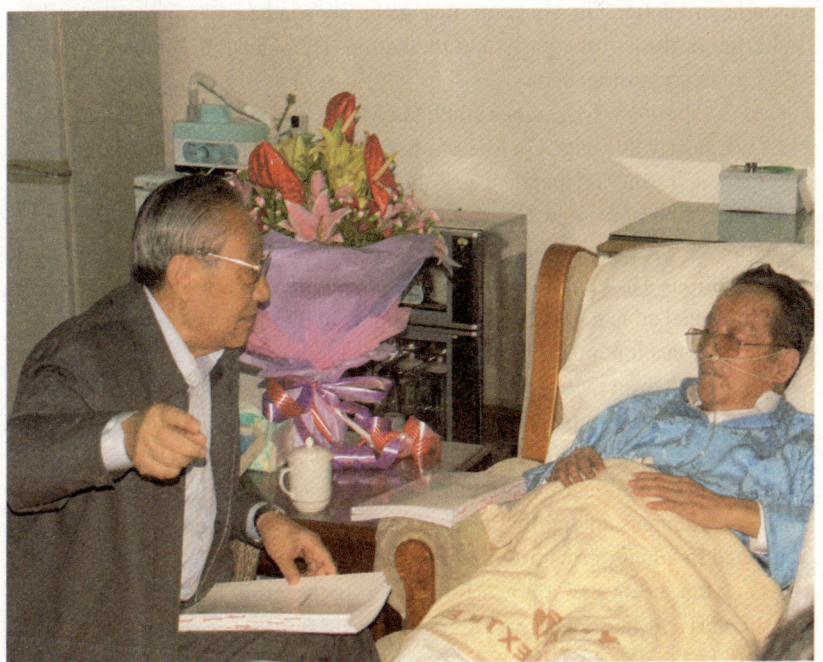

In the early summer 2008, Li Lanqing visited Gu Mu in the PLA's No. 305 Hospital. He talked about the draft of his new book *Break the Siege – The Early Years of Reform and Opening Up*. He also tried to persuade Gu Mu to publish his memoirs on the 30th anniversary of reform and opening up

Epilogue

In early 2009, Gu Mu, gravely ill, was transferred from the Number 305 Hospital to Beijing Hospital. That June, comrade Xi Jinping came to visit him in hospital, and in July, Li Keqiang did likewise. In the waning months of his life, Gu Mu continued, as he always had, to concern himself with the destiny of the party and the nation. He placed high hopes on the new generation of leaders.

At 2.55pm on 6 November 2009, Gu Mu passed away, at the age of 96.

Over nearly 80 years, Gu Mu was boundlessly loyal – to the party and to the people, to the independence of the Chinese people, to their liberation, to the creation of the new China, to the building of socialism, to reform and opening up. He gave his best throughout his lifetime, and made outstanding contributions. He was unwavering in helping both revolutionaries and those of traditional educated backgrounds to conduct their lives with dignity, in a principled fashion, pursuing truth, understanding the larger circumstances, seeking truth from facts, acting with thoroughness and judiciousness, caring for the nurturing of human talents. He strictly disciplined himself and was strict in his expectations of his offspring and those who worked beside him. He respected learning and culture, consistently expressed his respect for key elements of traditional civilisation, and conceived of himself as engaged in a long-term struggle against 'leftist' thinking.

Gu Mu's death had a powerful impact, both within China and abroad. Particularly in the open coastal areas, people will never forget: from the end of 1978 to early 1988, Gu Mu was the path-breaker for the policies of opening up. He animated those policies; in the halls of central party authority, he was their commanding general on the front line. On the ground, in the places where the open policies were carried out, Gu Mu was

Epilogue

the final arbiter of Beijing's decisions. In erecting and administering the SEZs and economic and technological open areas, as well as the opening of coastal municipalities themselves, and in attracting foreign capital and reforming China's entire system of foreign trade, Gu Mu did enormous work. People salute him for his gigantic contributions in pressing forward China's policies of reform and opening up, in realising China's 'four modernisations'.

Gu Mu with Deng Xiaoping

Jiang Zemin pays a visit to Gu Mu's home during the spring festival in 2002

Hu Jintao engages Gu Mu in friendly conversation at a Chinese new year celebration

Epilogue

At the fifth plenum of the 12th CPC central committee, on 24 September 1985, the request of Xi Zhongxun, Gu Mu and Yao Yilin to step down from the party secretariat was accepted. This photo, taken in the spring of 1999, shows Xi and Gu, two elderly figures no longer in the party secretariat, together once more

Gu Mu with Wen Jiabao

Jia Qinglin pays a visit to Gu Mu at Beidaihe

Zeng Qinghong visits Gu Mu on Gu's 88th birthday

Epilogue

Gu Mu with Li Changchun

Gu Mu with Zeng Peiyan

Gu Mu with Wu Yi

Notes

Chapter 1

1. Zhu Xi, born in 1130, a famous Song dynasty rationalist, thinker, philosopher, educator, poet and Confucian master
2. The 'Sao' style is a classic literary genre dating back to the 'Warring States' period, as represented by the poem *Lament* (*Li Sao*) by the great poet Qu Yuan from the state of Chu, from which it gets its name

Chapter 14

1. The Wanxian society (a society of 10,000 immortals) was a reactionary, superstitious and secret sect

Chapter 18

1. Li Binghong was head of the Zhejiang academy of oil painting department and, since the founding of the new China, also its associate professor and dean

Chapter 28

1. The recollections refer to recollecting 'national hardship' and 'hard times experienced in the past', while the 'three investigations' refer to investigating 'standpoint', the 'will to fight' and 'work'. This was an army purification movement to raise morale following the defection of tens of thousands of KMT troops to the PLA. Many of these defectors were less committed to the CPC's cause than the CPC fighters, which created morale problems

Chapter 55

1. 'Burning down the house of Zhao' refers to an event during the May Fourth movement of 1919 in Beijing. Angered by the actions at the Versailles peace conference of the Chinese warlord government's representatives, who had joined in signing an agreement transferring the former German concessions on China's Shandong peninsula to Japan, a group of patriotic students in Beijing set fire to the official residence of Cao Rulin, the deputy foreign minister. The term 'House of Zhao' refers to the street address of Cao's residence

Chapter 63

1. Enterprises that process imported raw materials, manufacture products according to imported samples, assemble imported parts and repay loans for imported equipment and technology with products

Chronology of Gu Mu's Life Events

1914

28 September: Born to a middle-class family in Dongdun village, Ningjin town, Rongcheng city, Shandong province

1922

Autumn: Went to his grandfather Wang Dongtang's private school in Wangjiazhuang, Moye island, Rongcheng

1931

Autumn: Joined the Communist Youth League in Rongcheng No. 1 higher primary school

1932

July: Appointed full member of the Communist Party

August: Admitted to Wendeng normal school in Shandong. Appointed school's branch secretary of the CPC. Edited the literary publication *In the Line of Fire*. Set up organisations such as the New Literature Study Group and New Science Study Group

1934

Spring: Transferred to Jiamagou primary school in Haiyang county due to a betrayal. Changed his name to Liu Mansheng. During that time, held the post of Jiaodong special secretary and set up a secret liaison station

Early August: Identity found out. Then moved to Beijing

1935

Autumn: Joined underground CPC in Beijing. Appointed to restore the league of left-wing writers in Beijing with Gu Jingsheng and other comrades. Co-established magazine *Bubble*

November: Appointed committee member of Beijing leftists' alliance

1936

30 April: Arrested with Wang Yiping. Identity not revealed

Mid May: Bailed

Early August: Appointed to join Northeast Army

1937

June: Went to conduct activist work among soldiers in the 67th Army's 107th division in Xinyang, Henan province

October: Fought in battle of Shanghai with the 107th division

1938

January: Went to liaison office of the Eighth Route Army in Wuhan to report to Li Tao and was granted an audience with Zhou Enlai

February: Appointed by Changjiangju of CPC central committee to develop Northeast Army's 112th division, 334th brigade, 667th regiment with Zhang Wenhai. Evaluated and trained the regimental commander Wan Yi to be a communist

March: Appointed member of the work committee of Northeast Army's 112th division

1939

6 September: Appointed secretary of the work committee of Northeast Army's 112th division

1940

September: Left work committee of Northeast Army's 112th division and went to Shandong branch of CPC central committee. Appointed chief secretary of the branch and director of united front work department

1941

November: Organised Daqingshan breakthrough. Got seriously injured

1942

April-July: Appointed to receive Liu Shaoqi, member of the political bureau of the central committee of the CPC who went to Shandong anti-Japanese base area to oversee the work

1943

March: Took rectification movement courses for more than six months

Appointed director of the united front work department of the political bureau of Shandong military district and director of the department's Eighth Route Army's 115th division

1944

October: Appointed second secretary of coastal area of the CPC and political commissar of second division. Encouraged people to fight against traitors and report the difficulties and sufferings in their lives, cut rents and interest rates, strived to promote production, made regional economy flourish, improved farmers' lives

1946

April: Appointed chief secretary of the east China bureau of the CPC central committee

July: Appointed secretary of coastal area of the CPC and political commissar of coastal area military division

1947

February: Fought with the second column of Northeast Field Army against the rebel forces of Hao Pengju

1948

Early November: Appointed to lead Coastal Area Army to enter and garrison Xinhailian area (Xinpu, Haizhou and Lianyungang). Fought with Huaihai Army of the central China liberated areas to liberate all areas of Xinhailian

9 November: Appointed director of the PLA's Xinhailian military management committee and took charge of Xinhailian area

December: Appointed secretary of the Xinhailian special committee of the CPC, political commissar of Xinhailian garrison and director of the elimination of traitors committee. While there, wrote four reports to both Shandong branch and east China bureau of CPC central committee. Systematically summarised the experience of taking charge of a city

1949

February: In charge of taking over KMT's Huang'anjian Uprising troops

April: In charge of the third regiment of KMT's Paratroop Uprising Army

June: Appointed deputy party secretary and deputy political commissar of central south area of Shandong province

18 November: Appointed CPC's municipal party secretary of Jinan and garrison political commissar

1950

February: Appointed mayor of Jinan and chairman of consultative conference committee

5 April: Drafted report on Jinan municipal party committee's suppression of reactionary forces work, and sent it to party committee and CPC central committee. On 13 April, Mao Zedong strongly supported the report and asked for it to be passed to all the big cities around the country

Early June: In charge of formulating an urbanisation plan for Jinan. Introduced the idea of building a new Jinan that is 'a centre of light manufacturing, transportation and a beautiful city'

1951

27 December: Drafted report on Jinan municipal party committee's anti-corruption, anti-waste and anti-bureaucratism work. Sent it to Shandong branch, east China bureau and CPC central committee

1952

6 January: Mao Zedong, on behalf of the CPC central committee, commented on the Jinan report and asked for it to be passed on to all big cities. Mao also designated Jinan as the party central committee's point of contact to guide the anti-corruption, anti-waste and anti-bureaucratism work. Later, on a visit to south China, Mao met with Gu Mu in Jinan. Gu Mu then travelled with Mao to Xuzhou

5 February: Wrote a report on 'five againsts' work experience and sent it to Shandong branch. On 10 February, Mao Zedong said the experience of Jinan's comrades must be studied

March 1952-March 1953: Appointed director of publicity department of CPC Shanghai municipal committee. Led Shanghai's 'three againsts' and 'five againsts' work

December 1953-October 1954: Appointed second deputy director of CPC Shanghai municipal committee

1953

July-November 1954: Appointed secretary of industrial production working committee of CPC Shanghai municipal committee. Paid special attention to state industry and actively promoted the private industry sector

September-January 1954: Appointed secretary of the ministry of industry of the east China bureau of CPC central committee

October-December: Appointed deputy secretary of CPC Shanghai municipal committee

November: Reported work to Zhou Enlai who went on an inspection visit to Shanghai

24 December: On behalf of Shanghai municipal committee, wrote the report *Problems of CPC Shanghai Municipal Committee's Socialistic Transformation of Shanghai's Private Businesses*

1954

November-December: Appointed member of Shanghai bureau of CPC central committee

November-August 1956: Appointed deputy director of national construction commission and member of the CPC leading group (since 1955)

1955

April-1959: Appointed deputy director of the third office of the state council. During the first 'five-year plan', involved in compiling heavy industry production technology development plan. Made contribution to smooth development of new China's economy and construction of socialistic economy

Appointed by Chen Yun to take charge of the relocation of some Shanghai business enterprises

1956

April: Joined the system reform study and management group led by Chen Yun

May: Followed Chen Yun to investigate the northeast and central south areas. Drafted *Rules on Reforming System of Industrial Management*

July-March 1965: Appointed deputy director of national economic commission, member of party committee (since May 1959) and deputy secretary of party committee (since October 1960)

1959

17-29 April: First meeting of the third CPPCC. Appointed committee member of the third CPPCC

1961

January: At the ninth plenary session of the eighth CPC central committee, decided to implement 'adjust, consolidate, enrich, boost' policy on development of national economy and to establish 'Group of 10 people' to work on industrial problems. After the conference, in order to solve the serious hardship caused by the Great Leap Forward, Gu Mu actively implemented the party's 'eight-character policy', led the Group of 10 to carry out work of developing the economy and industrial transportation, and took charge of scheduling and dispatching for production and construction in the whole country

2 February-9 June: Chaired and held 31 meetings of the Group of 10

25 April: Sent CPC central committee the report *Opinions of Quickly Solving the Problem of Workers Leaving Without Permission and Consolidating the Workers' Team*. The committee endorsed it on 30 April. Later, the state council endorsed the document *Several Regulations on Providing More Jobs to Workers in Coal Production Directly Under the Central Government*, which was researched and drafted by the NEC under the direction of Gu Mu

1962

11 January-7 February: Attended enlarged working conference of the central committee of the CPC held in Beijing (also called 'The seven thousand conference')

1964

Early: Appointed director of the political department of the CPC industrial transportation front. Organised a group to draft, on behalf of the central committee, *Decision on Setting up Political Departments in the Country's Industrial Transportation System*

16 March-3 April: Chaired national industrial transportation political working conference in Beijing

Fourth quarter: Worked with Song Yangchu, deputy director of the SEC, on 'design revolution' of industrial buildings

1965

15 March-3 April: National design working conference convened in Beijing. Gu Mu compiled the *Report on Design Revolution Movement*. The central government endorsed the report on 14 June. The state council issued *50 Rules of Design Work* that was discussed and revised in the conference for trial implementation

April-February 1968: Appointed director and secretary of the CPC organisation of state capital construction commission. During that time, Gu Mu actively implemented the party's policy of accelerating 'third line construction' and improving industrial distribution. He inspected the 'third line' area in depth, planned new distribution for the area, made great contributions to transportation infrastructure in the area, along with the construction of the national defence and electronics industries

21 August-4 September: Chaired national relocation working conference in Beijing

20 October: Chaired national capital construction conference in Beijing

Mid November: Followed Deng Xiaoping and Li Fuchun to inspect the 'large third line'

1966

Late July: Followed Liu Shaoqi to Beijing construction institute to carry out on-site research

September: Appointed by the party central committee to assist Zhou Enlai at the state council in developing the economy. In the 'Cultural Revolution', Gu Mu was always criticised during the daytime and worked at night. During those tough days, he did not forget the country's construction. He tried to minimise the losses caused by the 'Cultural Revolution'. He conducted himself with high moral integrity

16 November: Chaired industrial transportation symposium, where he fought against clauses such as 'allow workers to establish organisations' in a draft of *12 Instructions on the Cultural Revolution in Factories*. Then drafted *Several Regulations of* the *Cultural Revolution in Industrial Transportation Enterprises* (also known as *15 Rules of Industrial Transportation*)

4-6 December: Reported results of the industrial transportation symposium to an enlarged meeting of the political bureau of the central committee

Mid-December: Went to the 'large third line' in the southwest to inspect the construction process

1967

30 January: Kidnapped upon arrival at Beijing airport after a flight from Chengdu

Early February: Arranged to stay in Zhongnanhai Rockery Courtyard guesthouse with Yu Qiuli and assisted Zhou Enlai, Li Fuchun and Li Xiannian with economic work

14 and 16 February: Attended meeting of central committee members in Huairen Hall in Zhongnanhai. During the meeting, Tan Zhenlin, Chen Yi, Ye Jianying, Li Fuchun, Li Xiannian, Xu Xiangqian, Nie Rongzhen and others strongly criticised the seriously wrong behaviour of the 'Cultural Revolution'. This resistance, falsely labelled as the 'February Countercurrent', was suppressed. Gu Mu was also classified as Little Companion of the February Countercurrent

1968

April: After national construction committee was put under military control, it was arranged for Gu Mu to leave Zhongnanhai to accept the criticism of the masses at the committee site

1969

Year end-June 1970: Sent down to a construction site in Jiangyou county under the command of first battalion of the basic construction engineering forces and later another site in Guan county under the 61st battalion

1970

11 July: Appointed by Zhou Enlai to conduct on-site research in Hanjiang oil field in Qianjiang county, Hubei province

Year end: Informed by the state council to go back to Beijing to attend criticism meeting of Chen Boda

1971

From fourth quarter: Attended party committee caucus of state construction commission as a non-voting delegate, and remained in this type of auxiliary role for more than a year

1973

March: Resumed leading role. Appointed director of revolutionary commission and team leader of the party's core group of state capital construction commission, also deputy director of revolutionary commission and deputy team leader of the party's core group of state planning commission

March: Along with Su Yu, headed up the state council port construction group

April: Inspected major coastal ports from north to south China

Late August: Elected member of the central committee during 10th national congress of the CPC

27 September: Chaired first national port construction conference. Later, following Su Yu's departure due to illness, Gu Mu took sole charge of port construction work. Under the care and support of Zhou Enlai, remarkable achievements were made, providing valuable experience for the construction of larger ports during reform and opening up

1975

January: Appointed deputy premier of the state council, director of the revolutionary commission and secretary of the CPC organisation of the state capital construction commission. Following the instruction of Deng Xiaoping, co-organised and carried out the overall rectification of the national economic strategy

25 February-8 March: National meeting of party secretaries in charge of industrial work held in Beijing. During the meeting, according to Deng Xiaoping's instruction, Gu Mu led the discussion and revision of *Decision on Improvement of Railway Work*. On 5 March, CPC central committee and state council approved and issued the document. Railway transportation then became a means to improve the efficiency of other sectors. This document promoted the improvement of railway transportation, and then facilitated the development of the coal and electric power industries

Late April: Reported steel production problems to executive meeting of the state council

8-29 May: Attended iron and steel industry symposium in Beijing and revised *Instructions of Working Hard to Accomplish This Year's Steel*

Production Target that he drafted on behalf of the central government. This document was sent to the central committee of the CPC and state council and was later endorsed

End May: In accordance with Deng Xiaoping's speech, Gu Mu sent the CPC central committee and the state council a plan to make five significant improvements in the iron and steel industry and organised relevant department to explore for iron ore and prepared to set up large integrated steel complexes

Early June: Appointed head of the state council leading group for iron and steel

18 June-11 August: Attended state council planning work theory discussion meeting and led state development planning commission to draft *Several Problems of Accelerating National Industrial Development*. Then, Gu Mu revised it according to Deng Xiaoping's instructions and produced *20 Rules of Industry*

Mid October: Invited to attend national coal conference held by the coal department. Made a speech and communicated the experience of reorganising the iron and steel sector

1976

End May: Suggested to the CPC central committee political bureau that a national work planning symposium be convened to discuss how to stabilise the economy and prevent continuing deterioration. The symposium was held on 6 July in Beijing

9 September: Mao Zedong passed away. Gu Mu appointed by the central committee of the CPC to take charge of ordering a glass coffin for condolences. Later, appointed as member and office chief of the leading team to preserve Mao Zedong's body and build a memorial hall

7 October: Gang of Four crushed. Under the orders of Ye Jianying, Gu Mu organised 30 people and hurried to Shanghai to control the supporters of the Gang of Four and reported to Hua Guofeng, Ye Jianying and Li Xiannian. This work lasted until 20 October

1977

12-18 August: 11th national congress of the CPC held. On 19 August, Gu Mu was elected to be member of the central committee

1978

26 February-5 March: First meeting of the fifth NPC held. Gu Mu appointed deputy director of the state council and director of state infrastructure commission

2 May-6 June: Appointed by CPC central committee to lead Chinese delegation to visit France, West Germany, Switzerland, Denmark and Belgium. Afterwards, on 22 June, Gu Mu wrote *Report on Visiting Five European Countries* and sent it to main leaders of CPC central committee and the state council

30 June: Reported on results of visit to five European countries to the political bureau of the central committee of the CPC at the Great Hall of the People

July: Reported on results of visit to five European countries at a China modernisation theory discussion meeting held by the state council

1979

March-November 1983: Appointed to additional post of political commissar of Infrastructure Engineer Army, temporary party committee of Infrastructure Engineer Army and first secretary of party committee of Infrastructure Engineer Army

March-March 1981: Appointed as member of party committee of the state council's finance and economics committee

11 May-6 June: In order to implement Deng Xiaoping's instruction to establish SEZs, Gu Mu appointed by the central committee of the CPC and the state council to lead the working group to inspect Guangdong and Fujian, and meet leaders of both provinces to work out an implementation plan

15 July: CPC central committee and the state council endorse the report *Exploiting Guangdong's Favourable Conditions, Expanding Foreign Trade, Accelerating Economic Growth* written by Guangdong provincial party committee and *Report on the Request to Use Overseas Chinese Capital and Foreign Investment, Develop Foreign Trade, Accelerate Fujian's Socialisation Construction*

August: Appointed director of state import and export regulatory commission, secretary of the party committee and director of foreign investment management commission. Gu Mu put in charge of Sino-foreign joint venture enterprise laws. He advocated attracting foreign investment, introducing foreign loans, earning support from the World Bank on training talent in China, and promoting reform of the foreign investment system. He made a great contribution to the initiation and development of opening up in the new era

September: In order to secure loans from the Japan Overseas Economic Co-operation Fund, Gu Mu led a delegation to Japan. After negotiations with Japan's Prime Minister Masayoshi Ohira and Foreign Minister Sunao Sonoda, they agreed to a 30-year loan of Yen50bn (about US$230m) with an annual interest of 3%. This was the first low-interest long-term loan from a foreign government in the reform and opening-up period

End of year: First national import and export meeting convened. In the meeting, Gu Mu circulated the report *Actively Develop International Economic Cooperation, Expand Foreign Trade, Accelerate Modernisation Construction*

1980

Early: Arranged for national bureau of cultural relics and state infrastructure commission to co-draft report entitled *Request to Strengthen Protection and Preservation of Ancient Buildings and Cultural Relics*. Secretariat of the central committee and the state council endorsed the report. Then, Gu Mu took charge of the recovery work of Prince Gong's palace for a long period of time, and made great contributions to protect national cultural heritage

Early: Appointed China's chief delegate of Sino-Japan government members meeting. After negotiating with Japan, both sides agreed to the second loan of Yen56bn (about US$260m). Later, Gu Mu and Japan's Ookita Sabulou set up the Sino-Japan economic knowledge exchange, creating an unofficial way for senior figures on both sides to communicate

23-29 February: Elected secretary of the secretariat of the CPC central committee in the fifth plenary session of the 11th central committee of the CPC

Late March: Appointed by the central government to chair Guangdong-Fujian working meeting in Guangzhou. On 16 May, central committee of the CPC and the state council endorsed the meeting summary

1981

27 May-14 June: Chaired Guangdong-Fujian working meeting in Beijing, thoroughly discussed guiding ideology and basic concepts and some important policy ideas, finally formed '10 Opinions'

19 July: Central committee of the CPC and the state council endorsed the meeting summary that was written according to '10 Opinions'. On 23 July, in a meeting of the secretariat of the central committee about foreign trade affairs, Gu Mu reported in detail on the process of opening up and strategic thoughts and relevant policies to the central committee

End December: Gathered leaders of Guangdong and Fujian to the central committee to discuss cracking down on illegal economic activities. In the meeting, Gu Mu was appointed to organise the crackdown against smuggling. Later, appointed as the leader of the state council's crackdown on smuggling group

1982

Early: Organised SEZ working group affiliated to the general office of the state council

13 February: Listened to report on process of recovering Prince Gong's Palace and renovating the Liulichang Cultural Street that was undertaken by members of the national government offices administration, the ministry of culture, ministry of public security, state infrastructure committee integration directorate, Beijing government and construction committee

March-October 1988: According to Chen Yun's instruction, Gu Mu led a group to investigate how to establish SEZs in Guangdong and Fujian and summarised the findings

May- April 1988: Appointed state councillor while remaining in charge of opening up and SEZs in secretariat of the central committee and the state council

1-11 September: 12th national congress of the CPC opened. From 12-13 September, the first plenary session of the 12th CPC was held, in which Gu Mu was elected secretary of the secretariat of the central committee

Early November: Presented a document to the central committee and the state council entitled *Outline on Organising the Work of the SEZs* and gave opinions about the process and shortcomings of establishing SEZS along with the nature of such zones and how they are managed. On 15 November, the secretariat of the central committee discussed the report outline

3 December: Central Committee of the CPC endorsed *Summary of Several Problems of Establishing Pilot SEZs* that Gu Mu and the relevant department of the state council jointly wrote according to the discussion results of secretariat of the central committee

December: Appointed by the central committee of the CPC and the state council to organise the research and study of opening up and developing Hainan island

1983

February: After returning from Africa, Gu Mu went straight to Hainan to inspect the opening up and development of the island

March: Held SEZ work joint administrative meeting. Through discussion and study, a draft version of *Meeting Summary of Accelerating Hainan Island's Opening and Construction* was written

1 April: Central committee of CPC and the state council endorsed *Meeting Summary of Accelerating Hainan Island's Opening and Construction*

December: Went to Guangdong and Fujian to examine both provinces' implementation of using flexible measures on special occasions and the opening-up work of Shenzhen and Xiamen SEZs and Hainan, which the central committee of the CPC later endorsed

1984

February: Deng Xiaoping suggested: 'Apart from the current SEZs, we could consider opening up several other port cities'. Then Gu Mu, according to the instruction of the central committee of the CPC and the state council, took charge of opening up port cities

March: Went to inspect the opening-up process in Tianjin and Dalian

26 March-6 April: Organised a part of the coastal cities symposium held by secretariat of the central committee and the state council. In the meeting, Gu Mu led the drafting of *Summary of a Part of the Coastal Cities Symposium*

4 May: Central committee of the CPC and the state council endorsed *Summary of a Part of the Coastal Cities Symposium* and decided to further open 14 coastal cities such as Dalian and Qinhuangdao and introduced the idea of gradually establishing ETDZs

August: Chaired national tourism administration working conference to study system reform

September: Secretariat of the central committee decided to establish the Confucius Fund, a public academic and educational research body supported by the state. Gu Mu was appointed chairman of the fund to promote the study, inheritance and development of Confucianism. He devoted all his energy to develop a patriotic united front and international communication

1985

25-31 January: Chaired relevant provinces, cities and departments symposium in Beijing and drafted *Summary of the Yangtze and Pearl River Deltas, and Southern Fujian-Xiamen-Zhangzhou-Quanzhou Delta Symposium*. On 18 February, the central committee of CPC and the state council endorsed this summary (China [1985] 3), and decided to develop the Yangtze and Pearl river deltas, and southern Fujian-Xiamen-Zhangzhou-Quanzhou as coastal economic development zones

26 February: Chaired SEZ symposium in Shenzhen and gave a speech

24 September: Attended fifth plenary session of 12th central committee of the CPC. The session allowed Xi Zhongxun, Gu Mu and Yao Yilin to be granted their wish to resign as secretaries of the secretariat of the central committee, and five people were elected to replace them, including Qiao Shi

30 November: Inspected Hainan island and gave a speech

25 December-5 January: Chaired SEZ symposium in Shenzhen and wrote meeting summary that was endorsed and sent to the whole country by the state council on 7 February 1986

1986

March: Appointed leader of the national tourism administration coordination group

April: Appointed leader of state council foreign investment work leading group. Later, organised and drafted *Notice of State Council Further Improving Production Conditions of FIEs*

Late August-early September: Appointed by the state council to draft *State Council's Regulations on Encouraging Foreign Investment* (also known as *22 Rules*)

1987

Early: Appointed by central committee of the CPC and the state council to work on the establishment of Hainan SEZ

6-10 February: Chaired SEZ working conference in Shenzhen. The resulting summary document endorsed as a state council document on 11 April 1987

March: Convened meeting of the heads of national tourism administration and introduced principle to 'adjust measures to local conditions, actively give guidance, develop steadily'

12 May: Sent *Preliminary Ideas of Further Opening up Hainan Island* to central committee of the CPC. Central committee of the state council endorsed it and requested Gu Mu to start establishing Hainan SEZ

8-10 December: Chaired preparatory meeting on establishment of Hainan province and Hainan SEZ and wrote *Summary on Establishment of Hainan Province and Hainan SEZ Preparatory Meeting* and *Regulations on Encouraging Investment on Developing Hainan Island*

Late: Guided the state council SEZ office to write *Additional Regulations of Developing Export-oriented Economy in Coastal Areas* on behalf of the state council

1988

4 March: Reported on state council conference on opening up coastal areas

April: Elected deputy director of the CPPCC's seventh national committee, and appointed director of the national political and economic committee. Also made party member of the CPPCC's seventh national committee

September: Organised economic affairs committee of the CPPCC to open agriculture symposium and drafted *Opinions and Suggestions on Developing Agriculture*

1991

Early: Suggested focusing on improving economic performance, carrying out comprehensive administration, and setting up economic performance comprehensive appraisal system

1992

Early: Organised CPPCC committee for economic affairs to investigate the circulation situation in rural market and wrote *The Suggestion of Restoring National Supply and Marketing Cooperative General Agency*. The central committee of the CPC and the state council later endorsed it

1993

14-27 March: Attended first meeting of the eighth CPPCC

6-14 April: Led delegation to Japan, attended 13th Sino-Japan economic knowledge exchange and gave a speech

3 July: Accompanied Jiang Zemin to meet former prime minister of Australia Bob Hawke and Thailand's prime minister Suchinda Kraprayoon in Yingtai, Zhongnanhai

23 November: Met Singapore Senior Minister Lee Kuan Yew in Ningbo

1994

11 May: Met Oosata Sabulou, attended 14th Sino-Japan Economic Knowledge Exchange and gave a speech

5 October: Attended international academic seminar of Confucius's 2,545th birthday and international Confucius academy seminar and gave a speech. Gu Mu established International Confucian Association and appointed as director

7 October: Accompanied Jiang Zemin to meet Chinese and foreign participants of Confucius Academy seminar. On 14 October, Gu Mu wrote the tablet inscription 'Loyal soldiers were buried here, but their spirit lasts forever' for Daqing mountain in Shandong province

1996

22 and 26 March: Talked about the importance of Deng Xiaoping in the new era of reform and opening up in an interview with party literature research centre of CPC central committee

1997

15 May: Interviewed for a documentary on Zhou Enlai by CCTV

1998

3 September: Interviewed by CCTV about the process and experience of establishing SEZs

9 November: Attended Liu Shaoqi's economic thought seminar in the Great

Hall of the People and gave a speech entitled 'Liu Shaoqi's Economic Construction Thought is the Party's Precious Treasure'

14 December: Attended the CPPCC to commemorate the 20th anniversary of the third session of the 11th central committee of the CPC symposium in the CPPCC Hall

1999

12 February: Interviewed by CCTV about the detail of establishing SEZs

7 October: Attended international academic seminar marking Confucius's 2,550th birthday and International Confucius Academy seminar and gave a speech in the Great Hall of the People

2001

16 November: Gu Mu's wife Mou Feng passed away in Beijing after failed medical treatment

2003

5 November: Inspected the removal and reparation of Prince Gong's mansion and its rear garden

2004

19 March: Interviewed by Nanjing military region art studio about Sir YK Pao and the development of Ningbo

30 June: Interviewed by Hong Kong's ATV about visiting five western European countries, his opinions on reform and opening up, and life after retiring from senior positions

12 July: Interviewed for CCTV's *The Sun of the East* about the visit to five western European countries, the origin of SEZs and China's reform and opening-up policy

2006

18 April: Awarded lifetime achievement award by World Packaging Organisation

30 May: Interviewed by party literature research centre of the CPC central committee about the history of reform and opening up and the state import and export administration commission

2008

30 June: Awarded Order of the Rising Sun by Japanese government in

recognition of his remarkable contribution to developing China-Japan friendship and promoting bilateral communication and cooperation over a long period of time

7 August: *Gu Mu Memoirs* finalised, signed off and sent to Central Party Literature Press for publication

2009

2.55pm, 6 November: Gu Mu passed away

16 November: Gu Mu's memorial service held in Babaoshan revolutionary cemetery